GENERAL SMUTS'
CAMPAIGN
IN EAST AFRICA

LIEUT.-GENERAL THE RIGHT HON. J. C. SMUTS, K.C., P.C.

GENERAL SMUTS' CAMPAIGN IN EAST AFRICA

by

BRIG.-GENERAL J. H. V. CROWE, C.B.

WITH AN INTRODUCTION BY
LIEUT.GENERAL THE RT. HON. J. C. SMUTS, K.C., P.C.

The Naval & Military Press Ltd

published in association with

FIREPOWER
The Royal Artillery Museum
Woolwich

Published by
The Naval & Military Press Ltd
Unit 10 Ridgewood Industrial Park,
Uckfield, East Sussex,
TN22 5QE England
Tel: +44 (0) 1825 749494
Fax: +44 (0) 1825 765701
www.naval-military-press.com

in association with

FIREPOWER
The Royal Artillery Museum, Woolwich
www.firepower.org.uk

*In reprinting in facsimile from the original, any imperfections are inevitably reproduced
and the quality may fall short of modern type and cartographic standards.*

INTRODUCTION

By Lieut.-Gen. the Rt. Hon. J. C. Smuts, K.C., P.C.

General Crowe has asked me to write some introductory words to the following interesting and valuable account of the East African campaign, and I gladly consent to do so. He has brought to his task unusual qualifications, as he was in command of the Royal Artillery in East Africa during the period covered by his book and in that capacity accompanied me in the field throughout the campaign. He was thus able to acquire ample first-hand knowledge of the operations he describes and of the very exceptional conditions under which they were carried on.

Several of the minor side-shows of the world-war are not only replete with incident, adventure, and interest to the general reader, but deserve the careful attention of the military student as types of campaigns successfully conducted under very novel conditions. General Botha's South-west African campaign, for instance, will ever remain a model desert campaign in which water and transport difficulties, considered insuperable by the enemy, were successfully overcome, and brilliant and daring strategy resulted in the rapid collapse of the enemy. Our East African campaign of 1916, again, presents a striking instance of a tropical campaign in which within the space of ten months a vast territory was occupied in the face of a resolute and powerful enemy backed up by natural obstacles and climatic difficulties of the most formidable character. These matters are dealt with in considerable detail by General Crowe, but it may be permitted me here to direct attention to some of the more general features of this campaign.

During the nineteen months which had elapsed since the outbreak of the war before my arrival in East Africa, the enemy had on the whole been superior to us both in strategy and effective striking force, and it says much for the tenacity of our defence that during that period British East Africa was not overwhelmed. The enemy, while entrenching himself in our territory and successfully striking minor blows at us in many directions and unceasingly threatening our long railway communications with the coast at many points, wisely foresaw that the real struggle would come later, and devoted his attention mainly to the recruitment and training of a large native army under German officers. The word had gone forth from Berlin that East Africa, the jewel of the German Colonial Empire, was to be held at all costs, and the German commander, Colonel von Lettow Vorbeck, was the man to carry out this order to the bitter end. The initial stocks of guns, machine guns, rifles, and ammunition were from time to time very largely augmented by several blockade runners, and heavy artillery was supplied by the *Königsberg* and other warships on that coast. When, therefore, I arrived in February, 1916, with South African reinforcements to take the offensive, I found opposed to me a very large army, in effective strength not much smaller than my own, well trained and ably commanded, formidably equipped with artillery and machine-guns, immune against most tropical diseases, very mobile and able to live on the country, largely untroubled by transport difficulties, and with a *moral* in some respects higher than that of our troops, who, in inferior strength, had borne the heat and the burden of the defence for the last eighteen months.

Powerful as was the enemy's military force, the physical and climatic difficulties of the country added vastly to his power of defence. For 130 miles from the coast to the neighbourhood of the Kilimanjaro Mountain the enemy territory was protected by the high mountain ranges of the Usambara and Pare Mountains. The only practicable gap in this natural rampart was a space about four or five miles wide between the northern extremity of the Pare Mountains and the foothills of the Kilimanjaro, in which Taveta lies and in which the enemy had been entrenching and fortifying himself for the previous eighteen months. This dangerous gap, in which the main enemy force was concentrated, was the gateway—then very much closed—to German East Africa, and towards it my predecessor, Major-General M. J. Tighe, had been building a railway and laying water-pipe lines over the waterless Serengeti Plains. About eight miles in front of the Taveta gap stands like a sentinel Salaita Hill, on which our forces had made a disastrous attack the very day on which I sailed from South Africa. This gap had to be forced at whatever cost. I preferred to manœuvre the enemy out of it, and after spending a week in the most searching reconnaissance of the weak spots of the enemy's dispositions and in misleading movements and ruses, I advanced the bulk of my force by night against the enemy's left flank, took from him the foothills of Kilimanjaro by surprise and without any effort on the morning of March 8th, and within twenty-four hours compelled him to evacuate his practically impregnable Taveta positions. There followed the series of actions at Reata and Latema Hills, at Euphorbia Hill, at Rasthaus, at Massaikraal, on the Soko Nassai River, at Kahe Hill and station, and on the Ruwu River which, within the next twelve days, gave us complete possession of the entire Moschi-Aruscha area, and finally drove the enemy army after repeated defeats over the Ruwu into the Pare Mountains and down the Tanga Railway towards the Usambara Mountains. Never had I seen so sudden and complete a transformation in the spirits of opposing forces ; our men, who had retreated before the enemy in the confusion at Salaita Hill, now advanced with dauntless élan against the hidden foe in the dense bush of the mountain slopes or the Ruwu swamps. The enemy, on whom fortune had hitherto almost invariably smiled, now found himself suddenly and repeatedly manœuvred or hurled out of his carefully prepared entrenchments. And this spirit of our men was destined in the following ten months to carry them through the greatest privations and over the most appalling obstacles to the distant valleys of the Rufiji and Ulanga Rivers in the south of German East Africa. The campaign henceforth assumed more and more the character of a campaign against nature, in which climate, geography, and disease fought more effectively against us than the well-trained forces of the enemy.

The pause which followed on the occupation of the Moschi-Aruscha districts gave an opportunity for the full consideration of the strategical problems ahead of us, and the rainy season which set in with extreme violence forced us to consider how the climate and seasons were going to affect our campaign. Our object was not merely the defeat of the enemy, but the effective occupation of his huge territory in the shortest possible time. Merely to follow the enemy in his very mobile retreat might prove an endless game, with the additional danger that the enemy forces might split up into guerilla bands doubling back in all directions and rendering effective occupation of the country impossible. In view of the size of the country it was therefore necessary to invade it from various points with columns strong enough to deal with any combination that could be brought against them, and for these columns as they advanced to clear the country also laterally. General Northey was operating eastwards and north-eastwards from Lake Nyassa ; a Belgian column was launched eastwards from Lake Kivu (to the north of Lake Tanganyika) ; in April another Belgian column and a British column were set in motion in a southerly direction from the Uganda border west of Lake Victoria Nyanza ; a mounted brigade under Van Deventer was launched southwards from Aruscha to Kondoa Irangi, which is the most important strategic point on the interior plateau of the enemy territory ; and finally, towards the end of May, three columns advanced south-eastward from the Moschi area against the Pare Mountains and towards the Usambara Mountains. The combined result of all these movements, as far as possible co-ordinated for mutual assistance into groups according to the anticipated strength of the enemy in the various localities, was that by the beginning of September two-thirds of the enemy country had been effectively occupied up to and including the whole of the Central Railway from Dar-es-Salaam to Lake Tanganyika ; and to the south of this railway General Northey had occupied a large territory up to and including Iringa. The successful occupation of so much country in so short a time was largely due to the careful adoption and co-ordination of the various lines of advance, which compelled a general retreat of the enemy without the chance of any other forces remaining behind or doubling back to molest our lines of communication.

It is impossible for those unacquainted with German East Africa to realise the physical, transport, and supply difficulties of the advance over this magnificent country of unrivalled scenery and fertility, consisting of great mountain systems alternating with huge plains ; with a great rainfall and wide, unbridged rivers in the regions of the mountains, and insufficient surface water on the plains for the needs of an army ; with magnificent bush and primeval forest everywhere, pathless, trackless, except for the spoor of the elephant or the narrow footpaths of the natives ; the malaria mosquito everywhere, except on the highest plateaux ; everywhere belts infested with the deadly tsetse fly which make an end of all animal transport ; the ground almost everywhere a rich black or red cotton soil, which any transport converts into mud in the rain or dust in the drought. In the rainy seasons which occupy about half the year much of the country becomes a swamp and military movements become impracticable. And everywhere the fierce heat of equatorial Africa, accompanied by a wild luxuriance of parasitic life, breeding tropical diseases in the unacclimatised whites. These conditions make life for the white man in that country far from a pleasure trip ; if, in addition, he has to perform real hard work and make long marches on short rations the trial becomes very severe ; if, above all, huge masses of men and material have to be moved over hundreds of miles in a great military expedition against a mobile and alert foe, the strain becomes unendurable. And the chapter of accidents in this region of the unknown ! Unseasonable rains cut off expeditions for weeks from their supply bases ; animals died by the thousand after passing through an unknown fly belt ; mechanical transport got bogged in the marshes, held up by bridges washed away or mountain passes demolished by sudden floods. And the gallant boys, marching far ahead under the pitiless African sun, with the fever raging in their blood, pressed ever on after the retreating enemy, often on much reduced rations and without any of the small comforts which in this climate are real necessities. In the story of human endurance this campaign deserves a very special place, and the heroes who went through it uncomplainingly, doggedly, are entitled to all recognition and reverence. Their commander-in-chief will remain eternally proud of them.

It may be said that I expected too much of my men, and that I imposed too hard a task on them under the awful conditions of this tropical campaigning. I do not think so. I am sure it was not possible to conduct this campaign successfully in any other way. Hesitation to take risks, slower moves, closer inspection of the auspices, would only have meant the same disappearance of my men from fever and other tropical diseases, without any corresponding compensation to show in the defeat of the enemy and the occupation of his country. Timid Fabian strategy would, of all, have been the most fatal in this country and against this enemy.

Besides we had often to hurry to get out of a deadly
stretch of country or to cover a wide waterless belt,
or because great and rapid moves held the promise
of big prizes. The most important centre of Kondoa-
Irangi could only have been captured almost bloodlessly after that famous forced march of Van
Deventer's from Aruscha ; Wilhelmstad was occupied
bloodlessly after a relentless pursuit of the enemy
for 130 miles from the Ruwu River ; Dar-es-Salaam,
Morogoro, and the Central Railway were captured
without opposition after the tremendous march from
the Lukigura River north of the Nguru Mountains,
in which continuous fighting took place all the way
and every man who did not fight was occupied behind
in bridge-building, road-making, and bush-cutting.
And even when these places had been captured the
advance was continued southward without pause
for another 100 miles of continuous fighting through
the Ulugura Mountains to Kissaki and the Mgeta
River in the strong hope that this supreme effort
might end the campaign. One hundred and eighty
miles of the most difficult mountain and river country
had been covered in one month in the face of an
enemy who was fighting every inch of the ground
out of which he was not manœuvred by wide and
difficult turning movements. Simultaneously General
Van Deventer on my right was making even a longer
march from Kondoa-Irangi southwards to Kilimatinde and the Central Railway, and from there
eastwards to Kilossa, and from there again southwards to the Great Ruaha River—all in one continuous advance, with fighting most of the way, a
march in which some of his units actually covered
800 miles in that awful country and climate. It is
true that efforts like these cannot be made without

inflicting the greatest hardships on all, but it is equally true that the commander who shrinks from such efforts should stay at home. The transport and supply difficulties which arose from these great efforts were enormous and had to be dealt with mostly by improvised staffs. The way they were dealt with and finally overcome deserves the close attention of the military student.

The problems created by so big a campaign and so rapid an advance in a country which was still virgin soil, practically untouched by the hand of civilisation, without roads or bridges or any communications, except two effectively destroyed railway lines, were very great indeed. The establishment of means of communication, the creation of sea-bases as our advance rapidly progressed southward, were tasks of great magnitude involving time and prodigious labour, and requiring appliances which could not be secured in those distant parts. I found Mombasa our only sea-base in February, 1916; in the following July the occupation of Tanga and the restoration of that wrecked port and the railway from it enabled us very materially to shorten our lengthy railway communications to the interior; in September Dar-es-Salaam had to be adopted and restored as our sea-base, and as everything there had been effectively destroyed, and such appliances as had existed were never meant for an undertaking of the magnitude of our campaign, it took us several months' unremitting labour to prepare it for our purposes. In October, again, we commenced the preparation of Kilwa as a new sea-base from which big forces could operate south of the Rufiji River; there was a magnificent natural harbour, but absolutely nothing in the way of landing appliances or arrangements. Finally, before I left in January, 1917, I had begun the preparation of Lindi farther south as our final sea-base, in case the enemy forces should escape to the southern frontier of German East Africa. Only those who have had experience of improvising sea-bases for the operations of large forces can appreciate what the preparation of these four bases meant to us in labour and trouble of all kinds. The devotion of our administrative staffs and the work of our pioneer, railway, and labour units in that tropical moist heat of the African coast and low country have been above praise.

While during the months from September to December, 1916, Dar-es-Salaam was being prepared as a base, and the Central Railway from it was being restored, and the sixty or seventy wrecked bridges along it, many of very considerable dimensions, were being rebuilt ; while Kilwa harbour was being made ready for the reception of a large force which was being transferred to it, my attention was also pre-occupied with two other tasks : the evacuation of our sick from the country, and the situation which had arisen in the interior on General Northey's front. I believe between October and December we evacuated between 12,000 and 15,000 patients, mostly malaria cases, from our hospitals and ambulances along the Central Railway. Nothing could show more eloquently the deadly nature of the country into which we had now moved, and our only consolation was that the Rufiji Valley into which we had driven our enemy was more deadly still. While this evacuation was going on, General Northey was, with Van Deventer's assistance, waging a grim struggle in the direction of Iringa against the enemy forces which had broken away from the Belgian and

British columns in the Tabora area. The retreat of these German forces from the north impinged violently against Northey's lines of communications and broke them in some places, but by December the situation had cleared and Northey had given the enemy some staggering blows and reduced him to the defensive.

By the middle of December most of this work on our bases and communications had been completed, the short rainy season was passing, and I was prepared to resume what I hoped would be our final advance. By Christmas Van Deventer and Northey were on the move in the interior, and on January 1st, 1917, I moved southwards to the Rufiji; while General Hoskins, who was based on Kilwa, moved north-west in order by this converging movement either to enclose the enemy on the Rufiji or compel his retreat to the southern frontier of his colony. All our moves were successful, and the great Rufiji River was, on January 3rd, crossed by General Beves after a flank march which will remain memorable even in this campaign of fine marching. Every effort was made, after flinging the enemy across the Rufiji, to join hands with Hoskins and cut off his retreat. But once again it was proved to us that in the African bush, with its limited visibility, it is practically impossible to enclose an enemy determined to escape.

While these operations were going forward, I was, about the middle of January, ordered to relinquish my command in order that I might, at the request of the South African Government, represent South Africa on the forthcoming Imperial Conference, and on January 20th I sailed from Dar-es-Salaam, with the deepest regret that I had not been allowed the privilege of finishing my work. After I left the heavy rainy season set in almost immediately and put a stop to our further moves, and the enemy was thereby enabled to retreat to the south. The rainy season lasted till June, when the advance was vigorously resumed by General Van Deventer, with the result that by the beginning of December the bulk of the enemy's remaining forces had been captured, and the remnants still in the field had retired over the Rovuma River into Portuguese East Africa.

The enemy's stubborn defence of his last colony is not only a great tribute to the military qualities of General von Lettow, but is a proof of the supreme importance attached by the German Imperial Government to this African colony, both as an economic asset and as a strategic point of departure for the establishment of the future Central African Empire which is a cardinal feature in the Pan-Germanic dream. With German East Africa restored to the Kaiser at the end of the war, and a large Askari army recruited and trained from its 8,000,000 natives, the conquest or forced acquisition of the Congo Free State, Portuguese East and West Africa, and perhaps even the recovery of the Kameroons may be only a matter of time. In this way this immense tropical territory, with almost unlimited economic and military possibilities, and provided with excellent submarine bases on both the Atlantic and Indian seaboards, might yet become an important milestone on the road to World-Empire. The East African campaign, therefore, while apparently a minor side-show in this great world-war, may yet have important bearings on the future history of the world. And it is to be hoped that our rulers will bear these wider and obscurer issues in mind when terms of peace come to be arranged at the end of this war. I cannot end

these few introductory words without expressing
the fervent prayer that a land where so many of our
heroes lost their lives or their health, where under
the most terrible and exacting conditions human
loyalty and human service were poured out so lavishly
in a great Cause, may never be allowed to become a
menace to the future peaceful development of the
world. I am sure my gallant boys, dead or living,
would wish for no other or greater reward.

J. C. SMUTS.

February 1918.

CONTENTS

xix

CHAPTER VI

CHAPTER VII

CHAPTER VIII

CHAPTER IX

CHAPTER X

CHAPTER XI

CHAPTER XII

CHAPTER XIII

CHAPTER XIV

APPENDIX A

APPENDIX B

FRONTISPIECE

LIEUT.-GENERAL THE RIGHT HON. J. C. SMUTS, K.C., P.C.
From a photograph by J. Russell & Sons, London.

LIST OF MAPS

GENERAL SMUTS' CAMPAIGN IN EAST AFRICA

CHAPTER I

INTRODUCTORY

THE campaign in East Africa was fought under conditions which render it absolutely unique in our history. The composition of staff and troops, the armament of these troops, and the nature of the country fought over, all combined to create unprecedented difficulties which had to be faced and overcome by the General entrusted with the control of the operations.

At the time that General Smuts was called to take over the command, he held the portfolio of Defence in the Union Government.

A lawyer by profession, with a distinguished Cambridge career behind him, his previous actual experience of soldiering was gained in the South African War, to which he had added more recently in the campaign in German South-west Africa.

At the outbreak of the South African War, General Smuts, who then held the post of Attorney-General in the Transvaal, joined General Joubert's headquarters in Natal and went through most of the operations round Ladysmith and on the Tugela. After the capture of Pretoria he accompanied De la Rey to the Western Transvaal and took part in most of the fighting in that area. In July, 1901, he was sent to the Cape Colony to take command of and reorganise all the Boer forces in the colony. General Smuts still held this post at the conclusion of hostilities, when he was called to attend the conference to consider and discuss the terms of peace. He took a leading part in drawing up those terms, by which the Boer Republics eventually came under the Union Jack.

In the South-west African campaign, while General Botha conducted operations from Walfisch Bay against the main enemy forces in the north, General Smuts had directed the columns which converged on Keetmansdorp in the south from the Orange River, the Kalahari, and Lüderitz Bay. When the southern portion of the German territory had been successfully occupied, General Smuts had returned to the Union.

Little is known as yet of this campaign by the " Man in the Street " in other parts of the Empire. It was very much a side-show, and the troops taking part were all recruited in the Union. The operations, however, were characterised by peculiarly daring and successful strategy, as will be realised when the history of the campaign is written.

In addition to his actual experience in the field, General Smuts had devoted time to the study of military history, and had not failed to assimilate what was to be learned from the theoretical study of the art of war. It is doubtful if the authorities at home were aware of this. They knew that General Smuts was a man of exceptional ability and that he had had some practical experience in the field, but the factor by which they were probably influenced when they decided to ask him to take the command was, that a large proportion of the troops engaged would be South Africans, many of them Boers, and it was all-important that the commander should not only have the confidence of these troops, but that he should understand how to handle them.

The Commander-in-Chief of the British Forces in East Africa had many nationalities besides South Africans to deal with, as we shall show later.

A General in the field is concerned not only with what is in front, but still more with what is behind him. In other words, he cannot think of his advance against the enemy opposing him without at the same time thinking of his sources of supply and of the line of communications along which his supplies are to come. " An army moves on its belly," and it is always said that for every thought a General gives to the head he gives two to the tail.

It could not be anticipated that General Smuts would possess any knowledge of this branch of the art of war. An intimate knowledge of the administrative work of transport and supply in the rear of an army demands special study and training. In the South African War the Boer commandoes were not worried with lines of communication. They carried their supplies with them.

The supply and transport work with an army in the field is carried out by the administrative branch of the staff, and it is important that this branch should be manned by a well-trained and efficient personnel.

Brigadier-General R. H. Ewart, the D.A. and Q.M.G., and as such the head of the administrative branch, was an officer of the Indian Supply and Transport Corps, who had been withdrawn from one of the French bases, where he was concerned with the supply and transport work of Indian troops still serving in France, when the campaign in East Africa was decided on.

Brigadier-General W. F. S. Edwards, the Inspector-General of Communications, was a retired officer, who at the outbreak of war was Inspector-General of Police in British East Africa.

The co-ordination of the work of the staff falls to the Chief of the General Staff, and for this post General Smuts selected Brigadier-General J. S. Collyer. General Collyer's military knowledge and training had been acquired entirely in South Africa. As a young man he left England for the Cape and joined the Cape Mounted Rifles. At the time of the South African War he accepted a commission, and subsequently had served on the staff with the Union Permanent Forces. He had acted as Chief of the Staff to General Botha during the campaign in Southwest Africa.

The head of the Intelligence was an officer who at the outbreak of war was a student at the Quetta Staff College; while the Director of Signals was a young engineer officer who was in the Indian Public Works Department. These two officers had been in East Africa since operations commenced.

The remainder of the staff had accompanied Sir Horace Smith-Dorrien from England.

Of the General Staff, not an officer had ever previously filled an appointment on the General Staff with troops. The greater number of the supply and transport staff were settlers, who had never had any previous military training.

So we find that at the heads of the important branches there were officers who, however capable, had received no previous training in the duties they were to undertake, if we except General Collyer,

who had had the training gained in a similar position
in the campaign in South-west Africa, but under
very different conditions from those which he now
had to face.

As regards the troops composing the forces of which
General Smuts took command, they were indeed a
heterogeneous assortment.

Among the fighting troops there were two brigades
of infantry, one and eventually two mounted brigades
and five batteries of artillery from South Africa, one
regular British infantry regiment, Driscoll's Scouts
(Royal Fusiliers), regular native Indian regiments,
and a squadron of regular Indian cavalry; Imperial
service troops from India, from different States,
Kashmir, Jhind, Kaparthalu, Bhurtpur, Faridkot,
etc. ; the regular battalions of the King's African
Rifles of British East Africa, British corps formed
of settlers in Rhodesia and East Africa, a mounted
corps of Boer settlers in British East Africa known
as Belfield's Scouts, a detachment of Arabs from
the coast, and a corps of scouts raised in Uganda.
Then the artillery was the most wonderful assortment
conceivable : there were two batteries of mountain
artillery from India, a volunteer battery from Calcutta, a brigade and a battery of territorial artillery
from home, batteries manned by marines and by
seamen, by scouts, by men from native Indian
regiments, etc.; while their armament, excepting
the mountain batteries and the batteries from South
Africa, included nothing but out-of-date guns.

It could not be possible to bring together a greater
hotch-potch of units and mixture of races. Later
to these were added regiments from the Gold Coast,
Nigeria, a regular West Indian regiment, and a
" British West Indian Regiment."

The general policy of the home authorities was that as far as possible no troops which could be employed in the theatres of operations in Europe should be made available for East Africa. In other words, that this campaign should not be allowed to absorb any of the force which could be usefully employed at the decisive point.

To take over the command of such a force, to work them as a harmonious whole in a country offering every obstacle and difficulty to military operations and movement generally, with the aid of an improvised staff, was a task which demanded a big leader of men.

They did not know the magnitude and difficulties of the operations on which they were embarking. It was indeed a bold stroke to entrust the command of these bodies of troops and the carrying out of these operations to a man who was not a soldier, who had had practically no experience in handling any considerable force. Knowing what one does now, one can only say that the Government were wonderfully lucky, for it would have been difficult to have found a more suitable commander than General Smuts proved himself to be.

One of our politicians in the course of a speech, delivered while the operations were in progress, humorously pointed to the success of the politician General. General Smuts is a politician, but not of the " wait and see " type. He has force of character and determination to ensure that what he wants he will get.

Lest other politicians should be led to attempt a similar rôle, I would say that General Smuts was successful in spite of being a politician, and that the fact that he was a politician was a distinct handicap and not an advantage.

General Smuts possessed the great asset of personal magnetism and of the nature that inspires confidence in those with whom he is brought into contact.

It would be idle to deny that the work of the staff was in some ways rendered more difficult owing to the fact that neither the Commander-in-Chief nor the Chief of the Staff was accustomed to our methods. It was necessary for the staff to realise that they were called upon as a consequence to exercise more initiative and give more play to their imagination than they would under normal conditions be required to do. Their task was also rendered more difficult by the composition of the force.

The mixture of nationalities entailed as a consequence a variety of languages. There were English, Dutch, Hindustani, Swahili, the languages spoken by the regiments from the West Coast, in addition to the different languages spoken by the various tribes from which the fighting men and porters were drawn in Eastern Africa. This caused difficulty sometimes in finding officers and non-commissioned officers to replace casualties in certain regiments; e.g. with the mountain batteries, Indian cavalry, and infantry it was necessary that Hindustani should be spoken, while for the East African regiments a knowledge of Swahili was essential. For the latter the Settler Corps could be drawn on, but Hindustani-speaking officers were not so easy to find. In no other way did the babel of tongues cause any difficulty. The Indians and Africans were soon capable of arriving at a mutual understanding—the Indians were not slow to pick up a sufficiency of Swahili, while not a few Africans learned enough colloquial Hindustani. The different races from start to finish worked together in the most perfect harmony.

When a force takes the field it is organised in so many divisions.

A division is the smallest recognised formation comprising all arms and capable of acting alone. The proportion of the various arms is the result of long experience. One division in an army is exactly the same as another as regards units, numbers, armament, etc. There are three brigades of infantry, three brigades of field guns and one brigade of field howitzers, three field companies and a signal company of Royal Engineers, three field ambulances, divisional cavalry, etc., etc. It must not be imagined that the divisions in East Africa were formed on the same lines as divisions elsewhere. For one thing there was not a field company of engineers in East Africa, and though the force was organised in what, for want of a better name, were called divisions, a division signified the force under a certain commander, and the strength and composition of the divisions varied from time to time. One may say that the forces were reorganised for each phase of the operations, and it will be necessary to refer to the Orders of Battle (*vide* Appendix) to know what a division consisted of at any particular period.

As regards the theatre of war, misleading statements regarding the roads and communications in German East Africa have appeared in the press, and these statements are probably based to some extent on the maps which have been published, in which roads are shown running in all directions. These are imaginary. There were no roads. There were cleared tracks through the bush, but as there was no attempt at metalling anywhere, with the passage of the amount of wheeled transport which was necessary in our force, these tracks were very soon made inches deep in dust, or, after rain, deep in mud. The Germans had not used wheeled transport of any kind in peace or war with animal draught, doubtless owing to the prevalence of " fly " through-out the greater part of the country, which puts horses and oxen out of the question. The two railways were the principal avenues of all traffic, and even the well-marked roads which are shown in the maps as running parallel to them, and which were never more than tracks, had practically disappeared. The columns had to cut and make their roads as they advanced.

The absence of roads, the loose nature of the soil, the absence of water on some and the continuous succession of rivers in other areas made pioneering and engineering main features of the campaign. Roads had to be cut and made step by step as the columns advanced, bridges had to be built capable of withstanding the strain of continuous heavy motor traffic. As noted above, there was not a field com-pany of the Royal Engineers with the force. The Faridkot Company of Sappers and Miners, the East African Pioneer Company, and the 61st Pioneers did invaluable work, but they could not possibly cope with the amount of engineering and road-making there was to be done, and it was always necessary to call upon the infantry and other units.

There were periods when a whole brigade of in-fantry was employed continuously for weeks in blasting, road-making, and bridge-building.

The size of the country, the enormous distances to be traversed, combined with the deadly animal diseases, rendered mechanical transport absolutely necessary in a country which was eminently unsuit-able for such transport.

3

Without mechanical transport the campaign would have been impossible or would have occupied many years.

The difficulties as regards transport and supplies hardly existed for the enemy, or at all events in a far less degree. They had an intimate knowledge of the country, their Askari army could live to a great extent on the country, and the fact that their transport was all " porter " made them independent of roads and bridges.

The vast waterless areas were another serious difficulty which hampered operations. In East Africa the water question is the first consideration. There is either too much or too little. In the rains, movement is impossible, nothing on wheels can be dragged through the mud ; and in the dry weather, when the smaller streams have disappeared, the presence of sufficient water in rivers or in holes must be verified before committing a force to a march.

As regards the climate, the hospital returns are probably the best index to the nature of the climate in which operations were carried out.

The British forces have had to fight in every climate and in all parts of the world, but it had not previously fallen to our lot to wage war against an European enemy, or rather a force officered by a highly trained European personnel, through primæval forest under a tropical sun.

When the above facts are considered, it will be admitted that there are many points with regard to this campaign which render it unique.

The commander was not a professional soldier. He was not of British birth. His command consisted of elements from all parts of the Empire. The theatre of operations was from every point of view the most difficult, and imposed more hardships on those taking part, than was the case in any other theatre in which the British troops were called upon to operate.

The fact that these immense difficulties were overcome, that the mixture of elements composing the British forces worked harmoniously to a successful issue, was doubtless due to the generally excellent spirit and enthusiasm which permeated all ranks, in every unit, and above all to the personality and ability of the commander at their head.

CHAPTER II

THE town of Mombasa is situated on a small island. It is the one port and landing-place for British East Africa and Uganda. Kilindini is the name given to the southern end of the island. It is here that the mail steamers anchor and passengers disembark. At Kilindini also is the railway-station, the terminus of the Uganda railway. The Mombasa harbour is used principally by the dhows, which do a big carrying trade along the coast and with India.

The Headquarters Staff, which had sailed from Plymouth with General Sir Horace Smith-Dorrien on Christmas Eve, 1915, arrived at Mombasa on January 25th, 1916, in the middle of what is known as the hot, or at all events the dry, season. It was a pleasant surprise to find, instead of a burnt-up, khaki-coloured country, as would be expected under the equator, a green landscape.

Kilindini was to be the coast base, or rather the landing-place, for some time to come. It was by no means ideal. There was no wharf or quay alongside which a steamer could come. Everything had to be landed in lighters, which meant long delays in the disembarking of personnel and stores. A few sheds had been erected for the temporary housing of stores when they were brought ashore, but everything was passed up by rail to Nairobi or Voi as quickly as possible.

On the morning of the 26th the Headquarters Staff took the train for Nairobi, the capital of British East Africa, which had been the headquarters of the force garrisoning the colony since the outbreak of war.

The route followed by the railway runs practically parallel to the German frontier at an average distance of about fifty miles from the border line. Having crossed the bridge to the mainland, the train gradually climbs from the sea-level to the " highlands " of the interior, within sight of the mountain ranges, Usambara, South, Middle, and North Pare, and finally Kilimanjaro, within the German border.

The country to either side of the line for the first 150 miles is bush, varying in density from open, scattered trees, resembling English park land, to a close tangle of trees with thick undergrowth, which is practically impenetrable.

Here and there is a clearing where one finds a native village, which consists of a cluster of grass huts or " bandas." A few acres in the vicinity are cultivated, but the country generally is bush or jungle.

Excepting during the first climb from the coast, where the country is more hilly and broken, the general impression is of a gently undulating terrain, broken here and there by an isolated hill rising abruptly from the general level.

Voi was reached in the evening. So far the works and preparations for defence in the vicinity of the bridge joining Mombasa with the mainland, and the pickets of Indian troops with their blockhouses or entrenched posts all along the line, were the only visible signs of war. At Voi we came into touch with the actual scene of operations. It is from Voi that the old caravan route runs via Taveta between the Pare Mountains and Kilimanjaro to the German centre at Moschi. It was by this route that the German settlers in that district imported all their stores and supplies from overseas, prior to the completion of the Usambara Railway. Even latterly it had still been used to a certain extent as the trade route between British and German East Africa. Voi was the starting-point of the light field railway leading to the German frontier, and as such was a busy and important depot.

Arrival at Voi marks the change in climate between the heat of the low-lying coast district and the comparative cool of the highlands of the interior. There is no twilight in this part of the world and the sun sets at about 6 o'clock all the year round. On leaving Voi after dinner, it was dark and cold enough to make a blanket desirable.

In the morning the traveller awakes to an entirely different nature of country. As far as the eye can see, on both sides is undulating grass land, and over it are scattered herds of game, harte beest and wilde beest, gazelle, antelope, zebra, and occasional giraffe. They are sometimes within a few yards of the railway and take no notice of the passing train.

The enthusiastic East African settler had led one to expect this, but it was surprising to find that there was no exaggeration in his description of the amount and variety of game which would be visible.

The country to the south of the railway is known as " the Game Reserve."

No one is allowed to settle or to shoot within the limits of this reserve, which extends practically to the level of Nairobi. It is a sanctuary for every kind of beast.

East Africa has laid itself out to be a sportsman's paradise as an additional attraction to settlers and visitors. There are firms in Nairobi which make a business of arranging everything for the visitor arriving in the country for purposes of sport, including the provision of the " safari " personnel. As this personnel includes as a rule a " white hunter," who is not only the guide, but the general business manager for the expedition, and whose pay is about £100 a month, it is obviously only the (not necessarily idle) rich European or American who can afford to have his sport arranged for him on these terms.

Nairobi was reached about noon without incident, the journey from Mombasa having been done in something under thirty hours. At this time the enemy were still very busy with their raiding parties, laying contact mines to blow up trains. In order to minimise the risk, a loaded car was attached in front of the locomotive of each train. Through the bush country a raiding party could remain concealed till they actually reached the railway, and it was not an easy matter to deal with them. The bush had been burned and cut back for from fifty to a hundred yards to either side of the track, but the sentries still had a difficult and unpleasant task. The picketing of the line was left chiefly to the Imperial Service Infantry.

The German was not the only enemy they had to guard against. There were also the beasts of prey. At Tsavo station, a particularly vulnerable spot, owing to the railway bridge over the Tsavo River, also a recognised haunt of the lion, a little Kashmiri sentry had been taken by a lion a couple of nights before we passed through.

Major-General Sir M. Tighe, who had been in

command in East Africa for some months prior to
the appointment of Sir Horace Smith-Dorrien, in-
formed us that since he had been out they had lost
about thirty men, killed by wild beasts. The lion
and the rhinoceros were the worst enemies. Against
the latter, which charges at a great pace, the only
way is to make for the nearest tree and seek safety
by climbing. A short time previously a rhinoceros
had appeared on the scene where one of our patrols
was engaged with a German patrol. He first charged
and scattered our patrol, and then turned and went
for the enemy, who also scattered and escaped.
There was, however, a group of Masais who were
watching with interest the procedure of the opposing
parties. The rhino turned on them and one was
killed.

On arrival at Nairobi the Headquarters Staff took
possession of what had been General Tighe's headquarters and offices. General Tighe had been appointed to the command of the 2nd Division, which
was then located on the Voi-Maktau line, and had
his headquarters at Mbuyuni.

Nairobi is about eighty miles distant from the
German border. Though healthy, it is not a very
popular spot with the East African settlers, which
is unfortunate, as it is the capital of the colony.
The climate is pleasant. Being practically on the
equator there is no marked hot and cold season.
The temperature is warm, but not hot by day, as
judged by Indian standards, and the nights are always
cool.

It is the seat of government and also the headquarters of the King's African Rifles and of the railway. There is consequently a big European colony.
There are several hotels, a number of European

traders, and a big Indian bazaar.   Practically everything can be obtained in the town.

Since the war began Nairobi had been practically
the base as well as the headquarters of the military
forces in the colony. Several hospitals had been
started and all sick and wounded were brought there.
Apart from the Government hospitals, the Maharaja
of Scindia had provided two—one for European
officers, located in what was known as Scott's Sana-
torium, a settlers' hospital, some three or four miles
above the town, which he had taken over, the other
for native Indian soldiers, with accommodation for
about 100. This was established in what had been
the convent of the French nuns, from whom it had
been rented. They were both excellently managed
and run entirely at the expense of the Maharaja.

There was also a hospital and a convalescent home
provided by Captain Macmillan, an American settler.
This gentleman had joined the Royal Fusiliers, and
at his own expense ran these two institutions, particularly for members of the corps which he had
joined, but others were admitted when there was
accommodation available. In addition to the very
fine houses which were the central buildings, Captain
Macmillan had built rows of very comfortable cottages
in the grounds for the accommodation of patients and
staff. Nairobi had thus become a big hospital and
convalescent home for all sick and wounded.

The settlers in East Africa are for the most part
public-school men, and among them are a considerable number of retired officers. They had all
left their plantations and farms and were either
with units at the front or employed on one or other
of the administrative services at Nairobi, leaving
their properties to the management, in some cases

of their wives, in others of paid servants who were not eligible for service or were neutral aliens. The farms of the European settlers are all to be found to the north and west of Nairobi, in what is called " the Highlands." They have an excellent and healthy climate, nights so cool that a fire is generally desirable after sundown, and never very hot by day. This tract of country had not been affected by the war. At no time had any enemy raiding party penetrated so far.

Beyond Lake Victoria lay Uganda, marching with the German frontier from the lake along its southern border till it meets the Belgian Congo. The Uganda Railway continues beyond Nairobi to Kisumu, the terminus on Lake Victoria. To reach Uganda it is necessary to cross by one of the lake steamers, a journey of about 150 miles.

The railway from Mombasa to Kisumu is the one line of communication and traffic from the coast. There is only one branch from it, which runs to Lake Magadi, about sixty miles south-west of Nairobi, from Magadi junction, which is forty miles short of Nairobi. East of Nairobi, with the exception of the Voi-Taveta caravan road and a road along the coast, from Mombasa to Tanga, the country is practically roadless. It is not inhabited by Europeans, and the railway sufficed for all traffic between the coast and what is really the British settlement.

It is not proposed to give a lengthy geographical description of either British or German East Africa, but in order to understand the magnitude of the task which lay before the British forces and to realise the nature of the problems by which the commander of these forces was confronted, it is necessary to give a general idea of the enemy country.

German East Africa, prior to and for some time after operations commenced, was an unknown country to us. The prevailing ideas as to the area, state of development, communications, population, etc., were of the vaguest, and as a rule very inaccurate. To the reader unfamiliar with scales it is difficult to realise the actual area represented by a map. The extent of the country is actually about twice that of the German Empire in Europe, or as extensive as Germany, Italy, Switzerland, the Netherlands, and Denmark taken together. The coast-line north to south along the Indian Ocean is 470 miles, and from Shirati on Lake Victoria to where the southern border meets Lake Nyassa is about 700 miles. The distance east to west from Dar-es-Salaam to Kigoma, the Tanganyika terminus of the Central or Tanganyika Railway, is 787 miles.

This gives some idea of the extent of the country.

The frontiers are : from the ocean to Lake Nyassa on the south, where it joins Portuguese East Africa, the River Rovuma ; on the west, up the middle of Lake Nyassa, then across to the southern end of Lake Tanganyika, marching with Nyassaland and Rhodesia and subsequently Belgian Congo, up the middle of Lake Tanganyika, from the northern end of which it follows the course of the Russisi to Lake Kivu, up the middle of the lake, and from the northern end to Mount Sabinio, where it meets the Uganda frontier.

The northern frontier, with which we were most concerned to start with, marches with the Uganda to the mouth of the Kagera River on Lake Victoria, due east across the lake and then in a straight line south-west, skirting Mount Kilimanjaro, which is in German territory. There is a curious indentation to the south round Taveta, and the line then runs south-west again to the mouth of the Umba on the Indian Ocean.

The most important part of the northern frontier was that between Kilimanjaro and the sea. It is within a short distance of the Uganda Railway, the one and all-important artery, connecting the British East African and Uganda settlements with the sea, and on the German side covering the most highly developed section of their colony.

Between Mount Kilimanjaro and the lake, the country is practically uninhabited so far as Europeans are concerned, and no attempt has been made to open up communication in this district.

On the German side the slopes of Kilimanjaro and Meru had attracted a large number of settlers. The country had been opened up, and rubber and coffee plantations were flourishing. It was second in popularity to the Usambara region. The terminus of the Usambara Railway was at New Moschi, close to Moschi, the administrative centre of the district. The line ran in a south-easterly direction, skirting the southern slopes of the Pare and Usambara Mountains, till it reached the coast at Tanga, the port second in importance to Dar-es-Salaam.

Between the coast road and the Voi-Taveta road lies a waterless tract of country, practically unin-habited, even by natives. Small raiding parties made their way across from time to time, but it was impracticable for any body of troops, owing to the lack of water. From our side, once the German frontier was reached, the Umba and Lumi Rivers could always be counted on.

North of the Voi-Taveta route the valley of the Tsavo was a possible line of approach for us, so far as water was concerned, and a party of Germans had at an earlier period come by this route to the Tsavo railway-bridge; but there was no road in existence, and it was not considered as desirable a line of advance as the caravan road from Voi.

Farther north, the Magadi Lake branch of the railway, running as far as Kajiado, rendered an advance to Longido possible; but apart from this the country between Kilimanjaro and the lake is impossible from a military point of view.

Between Lake Victoria and Kivu the country is mountainous and the movement of traffic difficult.

On the lake were the German posts of Mwanza, Shirati, and Bukoba. The two latter had been occupied by us earlier in the war and subsequently evacuated. Mwanza was the trading centre of this part of the protectorate. Surrounded by hills, it was naturally strong for defence from the land side, while protected as it was by a heavy naval gun it was difficult to attack by water. It is connected with Tabora by two roads, of which the western is one of the best in German East Africa.

The country along the coast line is low-lying, but at about twenty to thirty miles inland the level rises to a plateau, of an average height of from 3,000 to 4,000 feet, which constitutes the hinterland. This plateau continues till it falls sharply to the water-level on reaching the lakes, which are at a considerable height above the sea. Lake Victoria is about 5,000, Tanganyika 2,600, and Nyassa 1,600 feet.

From the military point of view the climate is an all-important factor. Movement during the rainy season is practically impossible, and the rainy seasons vary somewhat in different parts of the country.

Along the coast line the rains begin in November
and the heaviest fall is in April, but along the northern
half of the coast there is a break and the rainfall in
January and February is comparatively light. This
does not occur to the south, where the rains continue
steadily till the end of April, which is the month of
the heaviest fall throughout the country. From
June till October is the dry and at the same time the
cool season, but the temperature is gradually rising
during the last three months of this period. The
hottest time is just before the rains break.

Malaria and dysentery are the common ailments.
Doubtless, under peace conditions, when the individual can choose his dwelling-place and is not
exposed to hardships inseparable from campaigning,
the climate is not particularly unhealthy; but on
active service, when the same choice of location was
not possible, and when men were subjected to hardships and fatigue at all hours of the day and night,
and supplies were not always procurable in sufficient
quantities, the percentage of invalids from both
fever and dysentery was very high.

The principal towns in German East Africa are
Dar-es-Salaam, Tabora, Tanga, Bagamayo, Mwanza,
and Moroguro. As towns they were of no importance, but Dar-es-Salaam and Tanga were important
as ports and as the termini of the two railways to the
interior. The other ports are Kilwa, Kisiwani,
Lindi, and Mikindani, but these, though possessing
good harbours, have not yet been developed.

Along the coast the country is as a rule flat, but
in places cliffs rise perpendicularly from fifteen to
fifty feet. Along the whole coast line there are
coral formations which render navigation difficult.
At some parts, among others Lindi, Kilwa, and

Pangam, the hills run down comparatively close to the sea-line.

Prior to the war there were fifty to a hundred Europeans at each port, other than Dar-es-Salaam and Tanga, and native populations of 4,000 to 5,000. The total adult white population in German East Africa was about 4,200, and half of these were resident in Dar-es-Salaam, Tanga, Wilhemstal, or Moschi.

The numbers in Government employ were 436 civil officials and 200 military with the Protectorate troops. Among the 4,200 there were 450 missionaries and about 1,000 women, leaving in all some 2,000 whites of all nationalities employed in business and developing the country. As over 25 per cent. of the total white population were of other nationalities than German and German East Africa ranked first among the German colonies, it is evident that the duties, responsibilities, and interests connected with the development of their colonies had not yet appealed to the German nation.

CHAPTER III

It was not till the end of 1915 that the authorities at home decided to send a force to East Africa which would be adequate to the invasion of the last remaining German colony and the subjugation of the enemy forces holding it, which till that time had not only defended their own frontiers, but were in occupation of British territory.

It is not proposed to give any account of what had happened prior to the opening of the campaign, beyond what is necessary to make clear the situation and the disposition of the forces when General Smuts took over the command.

At that time the enemy main body was concentrated between the Pare Mountains and Kilimanjaro. They had occupied the salient of British territory, which breaks the general line of the frontier just south-east of Kilimanjaro, as far as the Lumi River, and held the hill of Salaita, along the Voi road some twelve miles east of the Lumi. Along the northern frontier, between Kilimanjaro and the sea, they had detachments in the Ngulu Gap, at Mkomazi and at Jassin (blocking the coast road). There was a force garrisoning Mwanza on Lake Victoria and detachments along the Uganda frontier. There were garrisons of unknown strength at Dar-es-Salaam and Tanga, at Kigoma, and at points on the Belgian border, and posts at Tabora, Iringa, Morogoro, and other inland centres.

Prior to the war the German Protectorate Forces consisted of fourteen companies of Schutztruppen. There were no artillery units, but there were a large number of guns and machine guns. The guns were practically all of small calibre of obsolete types, and numbered about fifty-six. There were some sixty machine guns. The armament was materially increased by the dismantling of the *Königsberg*, which had been run to ground and was subsequently bombarded by our navy up one of the estuaries of the Rufiji. From her they obtained ten 4·1-inch (10·5 cm.) and some 3·46-inch (8·8 cm.) guns, besides a number of machine guns. Later they received a battery of 4·1-inch (10·5 cm.) howitzers, a battery of mountain guns, and twelve machine guns by the ship which ran the blockade and made her way into Sudi Bay in March 1916. In all, at the commencement of the campaign the enemy had sixty-four guns and eighty-four machine guns, and these numbers were increased by eight guns and twelve machine guns which were brought in the Sudi Bay ship, and some machine guns from the *Rubens*, the Mansa Bay ship.

The fourteen regular companies consisted of 162 men each. They were organised in three platoons, each consisting of fifty men. In each company was a section of two to four machine guns. The company was a self-contained unit, with its transport, consisting entirely of porters, of whom some 15 per cent. were trained and were armed with rifles, as a reserve on which to draw in case of necessity. There were 322 porters to a company. They carried, in addition to ammunition and supplies, an aluminium boat in sections and a collapsible boat for crossing

4

rivers, reserves of clothing and boots, the machine guns and the equipment connected with them, medical stores, etc., etc. Besides the porters there were what were known as Askari boys, who were the batmen to the Askaris. They were allowed in the proportion of one to every two Askaris.

There was also a training depot and a separate unit known as the signalling section.

The Askaris were enlisted for five years' service with the colours, but were allowed to re-engage if they were satisfactory. The native N.C.O.s were allowed to remain on practically as long as they were physically fit.

The troops were armed with the German Jäger rifle, M.71 and sidearms, but a sufficiently big consignment of more modern rifles was received in April, 1915, by the Mansa Bay blockade runner, to allow of the re-armament of all the regular companies.

Their uniform was of khaki drill, very similar to that worn by our King's African Rifles, a khaki jacket, khaki shorts, boots and putties, and for headdress the ordinary red tarbush with a khaki cover and sun-flap behind. Their equipment consisted of a valise, belt, and pouches, and a blanket and waterbottle.

At any distance it was practically impossible to distinguish a German Askari from one of the King's African Rifles. The only differences were that the German Askari wore white metal buttons, blue putties, and the number of his company on the front of his headdress, while our African soldiers wore brass buttons, khaki putties, and the number of his battalion was on the side of his headdress.

By way of making it possible to distinguish them, the regiments of the King's African Rifles were later provided with brassards, which were sent out from home. One battalion wore the blue-and-white bands of the Metropolitan Police on duty, another the red armlet with the letters G.R. in black, etc.

The Protectorate police force at the outbreak of war numbered 2,200, exclusive of the European officer personnel of fifty controlling them. They had all undergone military training. They wore a uniform similar to the " Schutztruppen," being distinguished by a red cross-belt and the letter P on the sleeve.

There were thus actually serving some 2,500 N.C.O.s and men with the colours of the protectorate troops and another 2,200, who were fully trained, in the police. In addition there were the men who had finished their service in the military and police and were still living in German East Africa. This number might be estimated at 3,000. The men originally enlisted in the German forces had been Soudanese, Somalis, Nubians, and Zulus, who were brought from their respective countries for military service. Doubtless a certain number of these had returned to their own countries on discharge.

These outside sources of supply had very soon been exhausted, and latterly natives of the colony had been enlisted. The majority of the men serving at the outbreak of war were natives selected from the more warlike tribes of the protectorate. The Germans had received a considerable influx of recruits from British East Africa when some battalions of King's African Rifles were disbanded a few years back, on the recommendation of the Governor at the time.

In addition to the numbers quoted above, there were the partially-trained porters and the Askari batmen with the companies, who would become efficient with a very short period of training. Their numbers might be estimated at another 2,000. The total of trained or partially trained natives would thus have amounted to about 10,000.

In addition to the Germans actually serving with the troops, there were 436 officials serving in civil employ, and at a conservative estimate there were about 1,500 Germans and Austrians living in the country who had received a military training. Of these the greater number were fit for service.

To these must be added the officers and crews of the *Königsberg*, the Sudi Bay ship, and later of the *Rubens*.

There was consequently no dearth of material for officers and N.C.O.s for the training and command of as many companies as might be raised and armed. The number would be limited by the arms and equipment available.

In January, 1914, Colonel von Lettow Vorbeck had been sent from Germany to take command of the military forces of the protectorate. He was an officer of the General Staff, and had recently served as Chief of the Staff in the Posen district. Since his arrival in the country he had done much for the improvement of the protectorate forces. He was an expert in machine gun work, and had trained the machine-gun detachments according to the latest German ideas regarding the use of that arm. Colonel von Lettow had undoubtedly gained the confidence of the forces under him.

In the course of a speech delivered by the Governor of German East Africa to the troops in Dar-es-Salaam on the Kaiser's birthday on January 27th, 1916, in reviewing the situation, he said :

Our troops in German East Africa have shown

themselves in no way inferior to their German brothers at home. In heroic struggles at Tanga, Jassin, in the Delta, and at many places along the frontiers of our colony, they have not only prevented the enemy from setting foot in our protectorate, but have also caused him serious losses in his own territory, especially by frequent mining of the Uganda Railway. It is only we who have experienced the dangers and pitfalls of the climate of our low-lying and swampy districts, we who know the waterless areas and trackless zones of dense thorn-bush, which many of our detachments and patrols have frequently to cross, who can fully realise the extraordinary performances of our brave troops. By heroic advances against a numerically superior enemy, by their steadfastness in holding out at important posts, by the cheerful endurance of the greatest physical exertions and of the ills and trials due to the climate, the heroes of the protectorate troops and the navy have raised for themselves a memorial which will endure for all time in the colony.

We are still in the middle of the conflict. We must reckon on the enemy bringing stronger forces for the attack of our protectorate. We can nevertheless look with confidence to the future. We are stronger than we were at the beginning of the war, both as regards the perfection of our organisation and the strength of our forces on land, and also owing to the arrival of reinforcements from the Imperial Navy.

Above all, we can rely on the brilliant leading of the commander of the protectorate troops, which has been tested in many conflicts, and on the subordinate commanders, especially the commandant at Dar-es-Salaam, and can trust to the proved courage and self-sacrifice of our officers and men, who are ready, one and all, to lay down their lives for the Kaiser and the Empire in defence of our colony.

Later in the day, when addressing the civil community, he said :

If we compare what is going on at home with what is being done in our colony, it would seem at first sight that what has happened and is being done is small in comparison. The numbers of our troops, our economical achievements and aims, appear small beside the armies of millions and loans in milliards. On closer inspection we find that there are many points of resemblance. We see that as at home victory is achieved by generalship and the valour of the troops, so here a superior enemy is forced back by superior generalship and the heroic conduct of our officers and men. We see that the enemy is endeavouring to cut us off from the world in the same way, but more completely than at home. We can see the enemy's blockading ships off our coasts, bent on cutting off all traffic over sea, and at the same time we are aware of his endeavours to cut off all communications by land. The enemy hopes that we here can also be destroyed by economic pressure. We have already seen, from the events of the war to date, that these hopes are doomed to disappointment. Here also the enemy cannot crush us economically. We get all we require from the country. We find all our food supplies, materials, and necessaries in our German East Africa. The value of our colony shines forth in this war. I fancy that many of those who have known the country for years doubted if we should succeed in meeting the requirements of the population, white as well as coloured. There is, however, I might say, an unexpected wealth in this country, such as we had never imagined in the past, and we find we have an adequate supply, even of such things as previously we have thought it necessary to import.

We see in other ways how favourably the colony is situated. We see with satisfaction how the German domination has set a firm foot on the natives, how even when at war our authority suffices to ensure that our natives supply all we require, porters, etc., without any attempt at rebellion or uprisings, etc., etc.

At that time Governor Schnee had some justification for this optimistic view of the situation. The dispositions of Von Lettow had proved adequate to safeguard the colony from invasion, and it was undoubtedly the case that the manner in which the offensive spirit had been fostered had kept up the morale of the German troops. They had not embarked on any big offensive, but there had been continual raids, not only against the Uganda Railway, but against the Voi-Maktau Railway and water-supply. The Germans had done wonders in the way of producing necessaries which they had been unable to bring oversea.

They were manufacturing benzine spirit for their motors, and whisky, or rather a spirit which was labelled " Ersatz Whisky," which was served out as part of their ration. They were making the cloth for the uniforms of the Askaris and managed to keep them well clothed. They were tanning leather and making a serviceable boot, and working up and turning out necessary rubber articles. They also had munition factories and were providing shell for their big guns. They were manufacturing quinine for their sick.

It was interesting to learn later where all these different industries were carried on. At the Biological Agricultural Institute at Amani, in the Usambara, (a Government institution which had always been looked upon by the settlers as expensive and useless) were produced ample quantities of quinine, castor oil, cocoa, chocolate, rubber hose, and, among other necessary articles of which they ran short, even rubber nipples for infants' feeding-bottles. Cloth as well as rope and string were being made at Morogoro, Korogwe, and other settlements, from pine-

apple, sisal, and other fibres. Bags for grain, etc., were
manufactured from the bark of trees and palm leaves.
Boots and shoes were made from locally produced
leather and from sisal at a factory they started at
Morogoro, where they were also making the necessary
nails. Tyres were produced by tapping rubber
trees direct on to rope, over which the rubber was
worked by the natives by hand up to the required
thickness. An ingenious valve for bicycle tyres was
invented and manufactured, which obviated the
necessity for the diminutive rubber tube, which they
could not produce. Benzine, paraffin, and gas were
made in large quantities from copra on a farm close
to Morogoro. Tobacco, cigars, and cigarettes were
manufactured from the locally grown tobacco.
Alcohol (92 per cent.) was distilled at the rum and
" Ersatz whisky " distilleries for medical use.
Oils, soaps, margarine, fruit juices for drinking,
and jams were produced at Morogoro and Dar-es-
Salaam. Ammunition of all natures, including 10·5
and 8·8 cm., was manufactured at Dar-es-Salaam.
They had about 30,000 pounds of sulphur in the
country at the outbreak of war, by chance or design,
and there was no difficulty as to saltpetre or charcoal.

As Governor Schnee said, owing to the war they
were thrown on their own resources, and they were
themselves surprised at what they had been able to
produce in the colony.

As regards the increase in their forces : The
original fourteen companies had been increased to
sixty-six, and there were in addition many local
detachments. Of these companies, thirty were known
as field companies, and included the fourteen regular
companies, ten were designated Schützen companies,
two were reserve companies, fourteen companies

were designated by letters of the alphabet, three were Landsturm and three naval.

They were organised in detachments, each consisting of so many companies, under a selected commander.

Immediately on war being declared a vigorous recruiting campaign had been started. New companies were formed, and the numbers in existing companies were raised considerably above the establishment. By August 11th, 1914, four additional " field " and two " Schützen " companies had been formed. By the end of the year there were twenty-four " field " and nine " Schützen " companies in existence; and by June 1st, 1915, the thirty " field " and ten " Schützen " companies were all in being. There were also fourteen companies designated by letters, A, B, C, etc., and a number of Landsturm and other detachments known by the name of the locality where they were raised.

The " field " companies were composed of the men of the regular " Schutztruppen " companies as a backbone, and brought up to strength by recruits. Prior to the war volunteer rifle (" Schützen ") clubs had been formed at different places. They used to hold Saturday rifle meetings and were similar, on a small scale, to the Swiss rifle clubs. These volunteer rifle clubs formed the basis of the " Schützen " companies. The fighting personnel was originally composed entirely of Europeans, but later they took in natives and raised their strength, till they were practically on the basis of the field companies, but retained a larger proportion of Europeans.

The " Ruga-Ruga " were enlisted during the war for porter work, but they were trained as Askaris. They were armed originally with muzzle loaders, receiving rifles as they became available from casualties among the Askaris.

The strength of companies varied, but was seldom less than sixteen Europeans and 200 Askaris. There were two large depots—one at Mwanza, where the numbers rose to 138 Europeans and 1,554 Askaris, the other at Langenburg, where fifty-seven Europeans and 600 Askaris were assembled. The actual strength and distribution of the different companies and detachments in August, 1915, is set forth in the accompanying table, Appendix B, which is a reproduction of an enemy document found later at Morogoro.

From this document it will be observed that, with the exception of the fifth company at Langenburg and the seventh and fourteenth companies on Lake Victoria, at Bukoba and Mwanza respectively, all the original companies of the protectorate troops were on the Taveta-Tanga front. Apart from the Landsturm and other local detachments, there were twenty-two companies there.

About Taveta-Mbuyuni there were four companies; two companies safeguarded the Ngulu Gap; three companies (two of which were mounted) were about Aruscha-Kampfontein, watching and ready to impede our advance from the Longido direction; one company and some detachments were in reserve about Moschi, which was also the station of General Headquarters. There was a garrison of four companies at Tanga, a post at Mkomazi, and a general reserve of four companies at Mombo, whence they could be transferred by rail to Moschi or to Tanga to reinforce either area in the event of attack. Special detachments with a large proportion of Europeans were allotted to the protection of the railway.

There were a garrison of four companies and naval and Landsturm detachments at Dar-es-Salaam, one company in the Delta and Coastguard detachments at all ports along the coast-line.

On the Rhodesian front there were four companies at Bismarckburg and two companies, of which one was 656 strong, at Langenburg.

The strength of the enemy eventually rose to 2,309 Europeans and 11,621 natives. There were in addition at least an equal number of porters, who corresponded to the non-combatants with our forces, so that their total strength might be taken as well over 30,000.

Kiguma on Lake Tanganyika eventually became the headquarters of the western command, which embraced the forces opposed to our Lake detachments and the Belgians, and included the country as far east as Tabora. At this period there were no troops detailed to oppose the Belgians beyond the naval detachments on Lake Tanganyika.

Such was the disposition of the enemy troops in August, 1915. It is probable that with the development of our preparations for advance on the Voi-Taveta and Longido lines, the enemy brought additional companies from Mombo and possibly from Tanga to the Kilimanjaro area.

The enemy were armed before the war with the M.71 rifle. There were large numbers of them in the country. They could be purchased at Dar-es-Salaam by Europeans for Rs.3.50 apiece.

Some hundreds of British rifles, sixteen machine guns, and a quantity of our small-arm ammunition fell into the enemy's hands on the occasion of the landing at Tanga in the early days of the war. These were of course used for the equipment of newly raised companies, but the supply of rifles and ammunition was mainly obtained from the ships which succeeded in running the blockade.

The *Rubens*, an English ship of 3,000 tons, which was seized by the Germans at Hamburg at the outbreak of war, was sent to Wilhelmshaven early in 1915, whence she started for German East Africa with a big supply of arms and ammunition. There were some thousands of Mauser 98 rifles, machine guns, bayonets, some millions of small-arm ammunition, and 500 rounds of 10·5 cm. shell on board. She was under the command of Captain Christianson, and with him was a Captain Albers, who had been in charge of an East African boat, and was thoroughly familiar with the coast-line of the protectorate.

It was in April, 1915, that news was received by our local squadron of the probable arrival of this ship in the vicinity of the island of Aldabra. H.M.S. *Hyacinth* went in search of her but did not find her. She then returned to port, recoaled, and as a result of further information put to sea and sighted the *Rubens* at dawn on April 4th, some four miles away, steaming for Mansa Bay. The *Hyacinth* opened fire, followed her, and from outside the bay fired a succession of salvoes. The third salvo took effect and set her on fire. The *Hyacinth* then went into Mansa Bay and dropped anchor at about 1,800 yards' range. The enemy crew had left for the shore in boats. Parties were sent on board the *Rubens* and it was found that she was " timbered up " and battened down, so that it would have taken many hours to open up the holds and get at her cargo. There was some rifle fire from the shore at the ship, which was at once silenced by gunfire from the *Hyacinth*. The party on board was recalled to the *Hyacinth*, and the Admiral, having fired a certain number of rounds into the *Rubens* above the water-line, steamed away, under the impression that she would burn herself out. It was not considered practicable to subdue the fire which was raging in the forehold and tow her out. The Germans subsequently landed the whole cargo of arms and ammunition, of which they were sorely in need.

The *Königsberg* was another source of armament for the enemy. She had been located up the Rufiji by the scout, Major Pretorius, and was effectively bombarded in July, 1915, by our ships, and abandoned and eventually blown up by orders of her captain. In this case also the German land forces were very fortunate, as ten 4·1-inch, some 8·8-cm., and lighter natures of guns, machine guns, and a large quantity of ammunition were saved, and they received a welcome reinforcement of personnel in the *Königsberg's* officers and crew. The guns were moved off to Dar-es-Salaam and Tanga, and other salvaged munitions to Kikindi.

Some small guns and machine guns were captured on board the *Adjutant*. She had been originally taken by us from the Germans in 1914. She was retaken by them near the mouth of the Rufiji in February, 1915. This ship, of 350 tons, ran the blockade from the Rufiji into Dar-es-Salaam, where she was taken to pieces and sent up by rail to Kigoma on Lake Tanganyika in 1916. It was anticipated that she would be put together again and ready for work in six months, but before that time the Germans were forced to evacuate Kigoma and on doing so destroyed the *Adjutant*.

There was one other successful blockade runner which made her way into Sudi Bay, near Lindi. This was the *Maria*, which arrived in the middle

of March, 1916, after a three months' voyage. She
had found it necessary to come via South America,
then went to East Indian waters, and eventually
made Sudi Bay, via Madagascar. She was a
German boat, built at Flensburg. She brought
with her a battery of 10·5-cm. (4·1-inch) howitzers,
two batteries of mountain guns adapted for mule
transport, 5,000,000 of 98 and a quantity of 71
small-arm ammunition, twelve machine guns (with
telescopic sights), a quantity of equipment and
clothing, both for troops and for the German women
in East Africa. She also had a quantity of stores
and provisions, medicines, etc. She was discovered
about April 10th, and fired into by our man-of-war.
Having completed the discharge of her cargo, the
Germans succeeded in repairing the damage done by
the shell, and she was shortly afterwards heard of in
the Dutch East Indies.

The Germans were making ammunition at the
Marine and private workshops in Dar-es-Salaam, both
for guns and rifles, but this source of supply would
not have been adequate. The enemy were running
short of ammunition in April, 1916, and contemplated
the necessity of surrender on that account, when the
Maria and *Rubens* arrived, luckily for them at the
right moment. The guns of the *Königsberg* and
the batteries brought by the *Maria* made a great
difference to their resisting power. Their ingenuity
and resource in providing travelling carriages for
their naval guns and the way in which they managed
to move the guns about the country, principally by
big gangs of porters, were remarkable.

The arrival of these ships was most unfortunate,
but the coast-line of German East Africa is a long
one and it was quite impossible for the few British

ships on the station to prevent an enemy blockade runner getting in.

The British forces consisted of the troops raised in South Africa and the force which had been despatched from India early in the war, known officially as " Indian Expeditionary Force B," supplemented by corps which had been raised in the colony and one or two units from the United Kingdom.

It was not till South Africa, having completed the conquest of South-west Africa, agreed to provide troops for the subjugation of German East Africa, that the vigorous prosecution of an offensive campaign was decided on by the home Government.

A small contingent, consisting of a squadron of dismounted rifles with signallers and ambulance complete, had been organised and got ready for service by the end of July, and a short time later a further contingent, the 2nd South African Horse, 1,000 strong, was raised, but it was not till the end of 1915 that it was decided that the 2nd South African Infantry Brigade, commanded by Brigadier-General P. S. Beves, which had been raised for service in Europe, should be diverted to the East African theatre.

To render the South African contingent complete and self-contained in all respects, in addition to the infantry, a mounted brigade under the command of Brigadier-General J. L. Van Deventer, a brigade consisting of five batteries of South African Field Artillery armed with 13-pounders, under the command of Lieutenant-Colonel S. S. Taylor, the necessary administrative units, supply columns, field ambulances, and railway companies were rapidly organised, and this force set sail for Mombasa at the end of December, 1915, and beginning of January, 1916.

Meanwhile another, the 3rd Brigade of South African Infantry, under the command of Brigadier-General Berrangé, and a second mounted brigade under Brigadier-General Brits, had been recruited and were well advanced in their training.

The 3rd Brigade of Infantry arrived in East Africa early in February, in time for the commencement of operations, and it was followed by the 2nd Mounted Brigade some two months later.

A separate infantry unit which also arrived early in the year was the Cape Boys Battalion under the command of Colonel Morris.

In addition to this force from the Union, a battery of naval 12-pounders of 18 cwt. and four Mark VII 4-inch naval guns with the necessary marine personnel were landed in February, 1916, from the United Kingdom. These batteries were provided with mechanical transport which arrived from home later.

The heavy guns, which weighed 4½ tons on their carriages, were landed some weeks after the lighter guns and had to be provided with wheels suited to the country they were to operate in before they were fit for the field. The original wheels sent out were not adapted to the dust and mud of the bush tracks.

The 12-pounder battery was at once provided with oxen as transport, and put through courses of instruction in land warfare and gunnery practice, and took part in the original advance.

Before the arrival of the troops from South Africa, the force in British East Africa had been drawn chiefly from India. There was but one regular British infantry battalion, the Loyal North Lancashires, and two units raised since the war began, the 25th Royal Fusiliers, better known as " Driscoll's

Scouts," and the 2nd Rhodesians, which came from outside the colony. There was also a machine-gun company formed by the Indian North-western Railway.

Within the colony the settlers had formed a corps known as the East African Mounted Rifles, and another mounted corps, Belfield's Scouts. This latter unit was composed of Boers who had settled in British East Africa. They had elected to call themselves after Sir H. Belfield, the then Governor of British East Africa. Good shots, good horsemen, and good bushmen, though not numerically strong, they were a valuable unit. There were also the battalions of King's African Rifles, the local regulars.

From India there were ten regular infantry regiments, including one battalion of pioneers, one squadron of the 17th Cavalry, and imperial service troops : Faridkot Sappers and Miners, infantry from Bharatpur, Gwalior, Jhind, Kapurthala, Rampur, and two good battalions from Kashmir.

Of the regular infantry the 40th Pathans and 129th Baluchis had already been fighting in Flanders, where they had given a good account of themselves.

There were three irregular infantry units : (1) a corps of Nandi Scouts, working with the 4th King's African Rifles. This unit was originally formed with the sanction of His Excellency the Governor in August, 1915, and then consisted of forty-six Africans under a British officer with three British sergeants. In March, 1916, however, their strength was increased to 152, the former commander, Lieutenant Hewitt, being given the rank of captain, the British N.C.O.s were dispensed with, and four white subalterns, one per fifty men, were added to the establishment. (2) The Baganda Rifles, previously known as the Uganda

5

Armed Levies, formed in July, 1915, and consisting of seven officers and 550 N.C.O.s and men. In February, 1916, a revised establishment was authorised increasing the number of officers to sixteen. (3) A small irregular force of Arabs, which had been raised and was commanded by Captain Wavell. They were Mussulmans recruited on the coast and were devoted to their commander. They were employed entirely in the vicinity of the coast, where they did excellent work till Captain Wavell was killed.

The artillery of the force, with the exception of the 4th Indian Mountain Artillery Brigade and the Calcutta Volunteer Battery, had all been improvised. The mountain artillery consisted of the 27th and 28th Batteries, armed with the 10-pounder mountain gun, and had come over from Abbottabad with their mule transport complete.

The Calcutta Volunteer Battery, under the command of Major Kinloch, was one of the first units to volunteer for service after the outbreak of war. They were armed with the 12-pounder of 6 cwt., the old horse-artillery gun. They were given oxen as transport. These three were six-gun batteries.

There was a section of 4-inch guns from the *Pegasus* for which travelling carriages had been improvised. Their personnel consisted of men of the Royal Naval Reserve, and were commanded by Captain Orde Browne, a retired artillery officer, who had left the army for employment in the Colonial Civil Service, and was serving as an assistant Commissioner in British East Africa at the outbreak of war. These guns were drawn by Packard lorries.

There was a section of naval 12-pounders of 8 cwt., such as one is accustomed to associate with the Naval Exhibitions at the Naval and Military Tourna-

ments at the Agricultural Hall. They were manned
by men of the Loyal North Lancashire Regiment, under
the command of Major D. Logan of that regiment.
They were drawn by Hupmobiles at the outset, and
later, when the Hupmobiles were required for other
work, by Reo lorries.

There was a section of 5-inch howitzers, which had
been brought from South Africa, manned by personnel
of the R.G.A. stationed at the Cape. They were
under the command of Lieutenant C. de C. Hamilton,
R.G.A. They were provided with mule transport.

In addition to the above there were four 15-
pounders, the old field-artillery gun, which were being
used as movable armament at posts on the lines of
communication, two at Maktau and two at Bissel
(Longido). They were originally manned by Indian
infantrymen and Driscoll's Scouts.

Shortly after the arrival of General Headquarters,
it was decided to form these four guns into a mobile
battery. The Indian infantrymen were returned to
their units, and the personnel was provided from a
detachment of garrison artillerymen who had come
from Mauritius under a regular artillery officer, who
was given the command of the battery. This battery
was provided with ox transport.

Such was the artillery, apart from the South African
batteries, at the beginning of 1916.

These troops, artillery and infantry, had been in
East Africa since the force landed after the ill-fated
operations at Tanga. They had taken part in such
operations as had taken place, consisting of the
advance along the coast-line, culminating in the action
at Jassin, the encounters along the Maktau line and
the landing at Bukoba, when the German garrison
withdrew and we burned the village. The net result

of the fighting so far was, as the German Governor Schnee gave forth at the end of January, 1916, that the Germans still held their colony intact and had occupied to Taveta and the line of the Lumi with an advanced post at Salaita of British territory. They were making frequent raids, for the laying of mines on the Uganda and the Voi-Maktau Railways and for the damage of our water-supply along the latter line of advance, sniping around our camps and on the lines of communication. Our troops had been considerably reduced in numbers by sickness and had consequently adopted a defensive attitude. They held the railhead at Serengeti and the post at Longido, and picketed the railway lines, along which they were distributed from Mombasa almost to Nairobi and from Voi to Serengeti. North of Lake Victoria they held the Uganda frontier-line.

In their encounters with the enemy they had failed to make headway, and while the enemy was energetic in the prosecution of raids, our troops were now confined to defensive measures. The morale of our men was none of the best, partly owing to their state of health, partly to their previous lack of success, and in a measure to the defensive attitude adopted. They had an exaggerated idea as to the fighting value of the German Askari. It is true that we were pushing the field railway on towards the German border, but the fact remained that we were still working in our own country and were still many miles from the enemy's frontier.

The best of troops, if they are tied down to defensive action, will suffer in morale. It is a confession of weakness. The troops are always on guard and never hitting back, being rushed from point to point to meet and ward off threatened attacks, but not attacking themselves. However weak the force, if a bold front is shown, if the spirits of the troops are kept up by occasional raids against the enemy, morale and with it the health of the troops is far less likely to suffer. Even when the initiative was regained, when the enemy had been defeated in more than one encounter and was everywhere retiring before us, the results of prolonged inaction were always evident. As long as troops are moving forward, no matter how great the physical strain put upon them, even when suffering from shortage of food, they retain their good spirits and morale. When it became necessary to make a prolonged halt for whatever reason, with the cessation of the excitement of the advance and with the conditions prevailing in a standing camp in the midst of tropical bush and the lack of the regular exercise, the spirits of the men would go down and the hospitals would soon begin to fill.

If you cease to worry your enemy, he will soon commence worrying you. Little raids against his lines of communication, railways, depots, for the laying of mines, etc., no matter on how small a scale, even if they do not achieve great material results, are invaluable to your own troops. At the same time they keep the enemy's mind occupied ; he does not know where you are going to hit him next. One day his wires are cut, a few days later a mine is exploded on the road or railway behind him, snipers fire into his camp by night, aeroplanes bomb a train, railway-station, or camp by day. The result is a feeling of unrest and insecurity among his troops, and while the leaders may appraise such action at its real value, the men suffer in morale. They feel that they are on the defensive.

These petty operations, though possibly not effecting much material damage, are of moral value. The enemy is not given time to evolve plans for your discomfort; he is kept constantly on the qui vive. His morale suffers, while such action keeps alive the offensive spirit of your own troops and is a physical and moral tonic.

A most important factor for the prosecution of the campaign was that of transport. From Voi to Serengeti and as far as Kajiado we had railways. The only other transport consisted of one A.S.C. company, one auxiliary and one South African Mechanical Transport company. These were supplemented by nine carrier corps, one bullock-cart and six ox-train companies. Once the force left the railway, it would be dependent for its supplies on the transport on the lines of communication; in other words, its mobility would be measured by the transport available. Even were labour and material available, the laying of a railway through such a country as we were about to enter would obviously be a very slow process and could not be reckoned on as a means of supply for a rapidly advancing force.

Added to other difficulties was the knowledge that, owing to the prevalence of tsetse fly, horse sickness and other animal diseases, apart from the question of transporting their forage over a long line of communications, animal transport was practically out of the question. The life of horse, ox, or mule would be but a short one. Apart from these obstacles to their employment, it was known that in some areas the supply of water would be a problem and the force might be dependent on what was to be found in " water-holes," which would barely suffice for the human beings.

It was obviously a matter of motor transport. The tracks fit for wheeled traffic in German East Africa are few and far between, and it was very unlikely that such tracks as existed would lead along our lines of advance. Metalled roads were known to be non-existent. During the rainy season it was realised that the movement of troops would be practically impossible, as wheeled transport would be held up by the state of the tracks. Wherever the troops were when the rains burst, supplies would have to be brought forward to them, and at that time the evacuation of the sick, if not an absolute necessity, would be especially desirable.

There were two lines of railway in the country : the Usambara line from Tanga to Moschi, and the Central line from Dar-es-Salaam to Tanganyika. Both ran at right angles to the general line of our advance. They were at an average distance of some 200 miles apart. When the former had fallen into our hands, it could be made use of as a line of supply, but there was no doubt that the enemy would do his best to render it useless and would destroy all the rolling stock when he was driven from it. When working, it would only be of use for transport from a new base at Tanga, or by connection with our own line, from Voi. It would not help us otherwise in our 200 miles advance from north to south.

The same applied to the Central line. Once it was in our hands, it would be necessary to rebuild the bridges and culverts, repair all damage done, and replace rolling stock before it would be of any use, and then, with a new base at Dar-es-Salaam, it would doubtless be of immense value for transport east and west ; but our actual lines of communication would still, for some time, run north and south, and

transport had to be provided to work on those lines
from the selected railhead.

We see, therefore, that the only transport suited to
the country was motor transport; and, on the other
hand, owing to the fact that no roads existed, and
that the routes would be by tracks cut through
primæval forest, by corduroy over extensive swamps,
and over miles of mountain tracks, motor transport
was eminently unsuitable. The transport question
was beset with every kind of difficulty, and its provision demanded considerable expert knowledge,
forethought, and imagination. The conditions would
be unlike those experienced in any previous campaign in which forces of such a size had been engaged.

The enemy's transport was a simple matter. Each
company possessed their complement of regular
porters. Before the war, when the establishment of
the company was 162, the number of porters was 322,
apart from the officers and Askaris' batmen, numbering 113, a total of 435. It is not likely that the
proportion was reduced. The advantages of this
form of transport are evident. The porter could to
a certain extent live on the country. The unit
could move through any country which an infantry-
man could traverse. They were disciplined, requiring
but little supervision, were accustomed to their loads,
and in addition formed a reserve on which to draw
to replace casualties. As a result the enemy possessed
greatly superior mobility, an inestimable advantage.
The enemy had had a vast native population on which
to draw, and later, when compelled to retire, did
not hesitate to force all the remaining suitable men
to join their porter corps. Men concerning whose
reliability they had any doubt were worked in
gangs, chained or roped together, so that escape

was impossible. Their mobility was still further added to by the portable boats which formed part of the equipment of each company, so that an unfordable stream presented no obstacle to them, while for the British forces a stream or even a deep nullah would necessitate the building of a bridge which would carry our heavy motor-lorries. Such a bridge had to possess sufficient stability to withstand ordinary floods. Heavy rains would possibly carry it away, and at all events necessitate a certain amount of rebuilding.

In the course of this narrative the extent to which our operations were hampered and delayed by transport difficulties and the immense advantage the absence of these difficulties was to the enemy will be apparent. This advantage as regards transport and mobility was possibly second in importance to those conferred on the enemy by the fact that he was operating in his own country. It is unnecessary to enlarge on the value of an intimate knowledge of the topography, resources, and population of the country. As the members of the civil administration were with the troops, the most exact information was always at the disposal of the enemy leaders.

CHAPTER IV

THE telegram containing the information that General Smuts had been appointed Commander-in-Chief of the British forces in East Africa reached Nairobi on February 9th, and he arrived at Mombasa on February 19th, 1916.

The disposition of the British troops at that time was as follows :

The 1st East African Division, consisting of the 2nd East African Infantry Brigade and the South African Mounted Brigade with Divisional troops, under the command of Major-General J. Stewart, was on the Longido line, with headquarters at Kajiado. The Mounted Brigade and the 1st and 3rd Batteries, South African Field Artillery, had not yet been pushed forward to Longido and were encamped at Mbagati, a few miles west of Nairobi.

The 2nd East African Division, under the command of Major-General M. Tighe, consisting of the 1st East African and 2nd and 3rd South African Infantry Brigades and Divisional troops, was on the Voi-Maktau line and was assembled at Serengeti, our advanced post on that line, and Mbuyuni, with Divisional Headquarters at the latter place. The 3rd Brigade was still at posts along the line from Voi to Maktau. Such was the distribution of the troops when General Smuts assumed command.

Maktau had till recently been our advanced post. It was only at the end of January that Mbuyuni and Serengeti had been occupied by the 2nd Division, practically without opposition, the former on January 22nd and the latter on January 24th.

The immediate result of this forward move was that Kasigao, an isolated hill some forty miles south of Voi and within easy reach of the Uganda Railway, was vacated by the enemy.

A party of the enemy had made their way from the Pare Mountains to Kasigao, and, established there, had for some time been a source of annoyance by their activities in laying mines on the railway.

To have directly attacked this detachment with any force would have been a troublesome business, owing to the nature of the country and water difficulties, and there was every probability that on arrival it would have been found that the enemy had disappeared.

Although they had been persistent in their mine-laying operations, our arrangements for the discovery of the mines were very satisfactory, and they had effected little damage.

The most important result of the advance to Serengeti was that it had been possible to push forward the railway and water-supply another fifteen miles.

Following the advance to Serengeti, an attack on the enemy's advanced post at Salaita had been made on February 12th by Brigadier-General W. Malleson, in which the 1st East African and 2nd South African Infantry Brigades and most of the artillery with the division had taken part. This attack had not been successful.

As regards our line of communications from Maktau

back to Voi, where it left the Uganda Railway, the field railway from Voi to Maktau followed the line of the old caravan road. Except at one or two places it led through dense bush, which was only cleared sufficiently for the road and track, so that a raiding party could make its way through the bush, by game tracks and with the help of knives, to any particular spot on the line. Here and there a derelict railway truck lying just off the line told of a successful mine. Bura, where there were mission-stations in the hills, just north of the line, was the first open space met with after leaving Voi. Here the country had been cleared for a considerable area and the hills themselves were more or less bare.

At Maktau, in the same way, the hills just north of the line were practically bare. It had been an advanced post for months and a considerable force had been assembled there. As a consequence the area about the camp had been cleared for upwards of half a mile in every direction.

The perimeter of the camp consisted of ordinary shelter trench; while a "boma," or in other words a belt of cut thorn bushes, varying from ten to thirty yards in width, formed a continuous obstacle all round. From the western spur of the isolated hill, which was about half a mile away to the north and commanded the camp and road, the two 15-pr. guns, which were taken for the battery subsequently formed and known as No. 7, had helped to keep the enemy at a distance for many months. This hill was always occupied by a strong picket.

A large quantity of stores had been pushed forward to Maktau, and there were pyramids, some thirty feet high, of hay, grain, and other supplies.

Just outside the perimeter was the cemetery, where rested those who had fallen in the encounters which had taken place when the enemy had attacked Maktau during the time that it was our advanced post.

From the time of the advance to Serengeti, Maktau was used as the practice and training-camp for the artillery, and batteries went through a course of instruction in the procedure adopted for fighting in bush country.

Maktau subsequently became the reinforcement depot for all units, and was used for this purpose till we had occupied Dar-es-Salaam. Here reinforcements from home and men discharged from hospital were assembled till such time as there were occasion and opportunity for despatching them to the front to rejoin their units.

From Maktau forward the country assumed a different aspect. The undergrowth became less dense until in the vicinity of Mbuyuni, some twelve miles on, it was what would be described as open bush while the surface of the ground was gently undulating. Mbuyuni itself was on a low ridge, running north and south across the road, and to the east of the ridge was a depression, about a mile wide, of what was practically open pasture, with hardly a tree. This was well suited to the requirements of the Air Service, and here they set up their canvas hangars and formed the aerodrome which they were destined to work from for the next three months.

Apart from the vital defect that there was no water, Mbuyuni was an excellent site for a camp. The surface land was grass and scattered trees, and the ridge was sufficiently high to ensure a pleasant breeze in the evening. It proved to be a very healthy spot, and the Medical Service subsequently selected it as a site for a stationary hospital.

Some four miles west from Mbuyuni on a similar ridge was Serengeti.

The enemy had dug good shelter trenches round both camps, and it had only been necessary to add to them, in order to enclose the areas sufficient for our requirements.

The troops were at this time disposed in accordance with the plan of campaign which had been prepared in East Africa by Major-General Tighe.

The 2nd Division was to advance on the Taveta gap, while the 1st Division, operating from Longido, moved by the west of Kilimanjaro and pushed in against the enemy's rear.

On his arrival General Smuts proceeded at once to Serengeti and made a personal reconnaissance of Salaita, obtaining a general idea of the country which the enemy was holding, from the eastern slopes of Mount Kilimanjaro on the north, to the Pare Mountains and Lake Jipe on the south.

The enemy's position was a remarkably strong one. He held a pass between practically inaccessible mountains. On the southern side were the precipitous Pare Mountains, along the base of which on the eastern side lay Lake Jipe, some ten miles long by two miles wide, surrounded by a wide belt of swamp. From it flowed the unfordable Ruwu River, skirting the northern Pare slopes.

Both lake and river were known to swarm with crocodiles. Along the northern banks of the river were the Ruwu swamps from which rose the isolated hills, Mokinni and Kingarunga, on which the enemy was reported to have posts.

The northern Pare Mountains are north to south

about twenty miles before the first break, known as the Ngulu Gap, is reached. This gap divides the Northern from the Middle Pare Group.

Naturally strong for defence, it was of course occupied by the enemy. It could only be reached by a thirty-mile tramp across a waterless tract of bush which precluded any possibility of operating by the southern flank of the position.

On the northern flank rose the majestic Kilimanjaro to a height of 20,000 feet. The slopes were rough and steep.

From north to south skirting the east of Kilimanjaro was the River Lumi, which flowed in a practically straight line across the enemy's front till it emptied itself in Lake Jipe. The Voi-Moschi road crossed the Lumi at Taveta and then ran along the lower slopes of Kilimanjaro, through the pass to Moschi.

Taveta itself lay in a basin and was commanded by an inner semicircle of heights known as the Kitowo Hills, which started close to the Lumi to the south and followed in a semicircle till they joined the slopes of Kilimanjaro, the road to Moschi passing between the Middle and East Kitowo. The south-eastern spur of Kilimanjaro, known as Chala, completed the semicircle on the north.

The hills formed a perfect amphitheatre. Taveta on the river-bank was completely shut in and commanded by them.

Chala on the north, immediately above the Lumi, was some 1,400 feet above the village and about four miles from it. To the south-west, Reata and Latema at a rather less distance had a command of about 700 feet. The occupation of Taveta, so long as the enemy held the heights around, would evidently be a very doubtful advantage, even were it possible.

The southern flank was out of the question ; Chala on the north, commanding the whole basin as it did, with an ample water-supply, not only in the Lumi down below but in the Chala Lake in the crater, was the key to the position.

Having made a personal reconnaissance of this theatre and acquired as much information as was possible of the topographical features and the nature of the country, General Smuts took train to Kajiado via Voi and proceeded by car to our advanced post at Longido, whence it was possible to look down on the intervening country as far as the near slopes of Kilimanjaro and Mount Meru. Having completed his reconnaissances of both lines of advance he proceeded to Nairobi, where he arrived on February 23rd.

If anything was to be accomplished before the commencement of the heavy rains, which were to be looked for about the end of March, there was obviously no time to be lost, and the general lines of the plan of campaign already prepared for had to be adhered to.

The enemy occupied a very strong advanced post at Salaita, which lay across and effectively barred the road to Taveta. The whole country was bush, partly dense and partly more or less open, but nowhere admitting of the advance of troops in any military formation. The strength of the Salaita position had been tested on February 12th, and it had been found that it had been prepared for all-round defence. General Smuts decided that a direct advance on the enemy's front across the gap, which would necessitate the capture of Salaita in the first instance, would not only be costly, as the enemy had evidently made all preparations to meet such an advance, but would also occupy much of the remaining time available before the rains were likely to burst.

The occupation of the Chala position was the essential preliminary to a successful forward movement. This would likewise be an expensive operation if the enemy had warning and time to prepare and occupy the position in strength. Rapidity of movement and surprise were the elements of success. These could not be obtained by infantry. General Smuts consequently decided to transfer the Mounted Brigade under Brigadier-General Van Deventer from the 1st Division on the Longido line to the Maktau line.

Orders were at once issued. Van Deventer's scouts moved across country by the eastern slopes of Kilimanjaro, the remainder of the brigade being brought round by train. The move was completed and the whole brigade assembled at Mbuyuni on March 2nd.

The ammunition column, forming part of the 2nd Division, had mainly ox transport. It had been kept in the vicinity of Nairobi till the last moment, and was also brought down now by train.

As before stated, the whole country is waterless east of the Lumi. The forces at Serengeti and Mbuyuni were dependent for their water on a 2½-inch pipe line and what could be brought by rail. Tanks had been set up at both places to allow of the accumulation of as much as possible, but the provision of sufficient water for the concentration of so many men and animals was a serious question, and for a considerable period the troops were on an allowance of one gallon a day per man. In case of any accident to the pipe, the troops had to exist on what was stored in the tanks and what could be brought up by train, till such time as the pipe was repaired.

6

Accidents had taken place frequently. An enemy raiding party would make their way to some point in the line and cut the pipe, sometimes by means of a bullet. The most serious attempt to cut off the water occurred in February when a hostile party, consisting of four Germans, accompanied by Askaris, made their way to the Bura headworks, which were situated some hundreds of feet up in the Bura Hills and miles from the road and railway. They were the source of the water-supply. The guard on the works consisted of one European.

The enemy came and, representing that they were Boers, proceeded literally to take tea with the unsuspecting caretaker, after which they bound and gagged him and got to work with dynamite bombs on the water-works.

Fortunately, by an accident, one of the Germans was seriously injured and had to be left behind. The remainder of the party made off, rightly anticipating that the explosions would give the alarm and a patrol would not be long in arriving. They had a long journey to regain their own lines at Taveta, and by wonderful good fortune the whole of the party but one were captured on their return journey. The damage that they had effected was soon repaired.

Under any circumstances it would not have been desirable or possible to have added such a water-consuming force as a mounted brigade to the troops already at the end of the pipe line any earlier. Their arrival would have been deferred till the last possible moment.

General Smuts left Nairobi on February 29th, and established his headquarters at Mbuyuni on the following day.

In addition to their position at Salaita the enemy

were known to have posts at Vilma Viwili and Mun-
yoni, isolated hills lying just east of Lake Jipe, and
a strong detachment was reported to be in the bush
to the north of the lake.

It was desirable to divert the enemy's attention
as far as possible from the northern flank. With
this object strong mounted patrols were sent each
day towards the Ngulu Gap, and on one occasion a
squadron was directed to make its way, if possible,
into the entrance to the gap, which they succeeded
in doing. At the same time reconnaissances were
being made of the route to Chala. Following the
low-lying ground, owing to the thick bush, it was
possible to move from Mbuyuni to the vicinity of
Chala without coming under observation from Salaita.
North of the road there was known to be a post in
Kilmari, while it was doubtful if Warombo was
occupied.

These reconnaissances were successfully carried
out, and the necessary information regarding the
Lumi River itself and its banks opposite Chala was
obtained. Night rides were also carried out by
strong patrols from the Mounted Brigade over the
route that was to be followed, and all was in readiness
for the advance.

On March 6th Major-General Tighe moved his
camp from Mbuyuni to Serengeti. The next day
General Smuts, accompanied by Major-General Tighe,
the brigade commanders, and the C.R.A. made a
reconnaissance of the Salaita position from the west
of Serengeti, explaining his plan of action, and in-
dicating the different points with which they would
severally be concerned.

The same afternoon the C.R.A., who had been
attached to the 2nd Division for these operations,

carried out a further reconnaissance, accompanied by the battery commanders, to whom were pointed out the positions which were to be occupied in the first instance by their units.

The actual plan for the ensuing campaign cannot be better explained than in the words of General Smuts's despatch:

" The task of the 1st Division was to cross the thirty-five miles of waterless bush which lay between Longido and the Engare Nanjuki River, occupy the latter, and then advance between Meru and Kilimanjaro to Vieh Bomaja Ngombe (Somali Häuser). My intention was thereafter to direct this division on Kahe and cut the enemy's line of communications by the Usambara Railway.

" The task of the 1st South African Mounted Brigade and of the 2nd Division was to advance through the gap between Kilimanjaro and the Pare Hills against the enemy's main force, which was reported to be concentrated in the neighbourhood of Taveta with strong detachments at the head of the Lake Jipe in the bush, east of the River Lumi, and at Salaita. The total force with which the enemy could oppose our advance into the Kilimanjaro area was estimated at 6,000 rifles with thirty-seven machine guns and sixteen guns."

Major-General Stewart's force, the 1st Division, consisted of an infantry brigade (the South African Mounted Brigade had been withdrawn from it) as mounted troops, a squadron of 17th Cavalry, the East African Mounted Rifles, the M.I. Company of the King's African Rifles, and four batteries of artillery in addition to other divisional troops, including the East African Maxim Gun Company, the Faridkot Sappers and Miners, two sections of East

African Pioneers, with two double companies of King's
African Rifles as divisional infantry.

In all converging movements the measure of
success, in fact the success or failure of the operations,
is dependent on the accurate timing of the columns.
If the enemy were driven back as was anticipated,
they would retire along their communications, that
is, along the railway west of the Pare Mountain.
The Commander-in-Chief's object was to ensure that
the 1st Division should be in time to cut off their
retreat, and he anticipated that this would be most
effectually carried out if the 1st Division could be
brought to forestall them about Kahe, where the
railway crosses the Pangani River. The enemy would
have to make their way across the river, a formidable
obstacle, and there was only one bridge besides the
railway crossing.

With this object in view the 1st Division was
ordered to move on March 5th, while the direct
advance from Serengeti would not commence till the
8th.

By the time that General Stewart's force had
arrived at Somali Häuser, the situation would have
developed sufficiently to make it clear on what point
to direct them. All routes leading west passed
through Somali Häuser, and from it Kahe could be
reached in thirty miles with a limited amount of
cross-country work.

As regards the advance into the gap, the Mounted
Brigade with the 3rd South African Infantry Brigade,
all under General van Deventer, were to make a
night march, starting as soon as it was dark on the
evening of March 7th for Chala. Having crossed
the Lumi as early as possible on the morning of the
8th, Chala Hill was to be seized. The 2nd South

African Infantry Brigade was to follow the 3rd to the Lumi, and, holding the crossing of the river, would form a general reserve, which could be used to reinforce General Van Deventer or, by moving along the north bank, could support the 2nd Division.

The 2nd Division with the bulk of the artillery was to advance at dawn on the 8th. The infantry, covered by the fire of the guns, was on that day to take up and entrench a position opposite Salaita, with a view to attacking the following day.

The preliminary movements were carried out as planned.

The 1st Division from Longido had to cross some thirty miles of open undulating country before they reached water, which was first to be found at the River Engare Nanjuki. As their advance would be visible from the slopes of Kilimanjaro, General Stewart's initial movement was made by night.

The advanced guard reached Nagasseni, a small hill on the eastern bank of the Engare Nanjuki, on the 6th, having started as soon as it was dark on the evening of the 5th. They met with no opposition. The remainder of the column closed up to this point by 2 p.m. on the 7th. On the 8th the advance was continued and the column reached Geraragua. The further advance lay through the valley which separated Kilimanjaro from Mount Meru.

There are numerous streams flowing down the southern slopes of Kilimanjaro, and with the Sanna, which flows down the valley practically parallel to the road to Somali Häuser, there was no longer any cause for anxiety as regards water.

From Engare Nanjuki to Somali Häuser is twenty-six miles, thence to Kahe about thirty, and to Moschi about fifteen miles.

It is not necessary to point out what the effect, both material and moral, would be on the enemy when he realised that a column of all arms was pushing in against his rear and his communications. Assuming that he would not be strong enough to give battle in both directions simultaneously, there were two courses open to him. Either he could hold up one column with a detachment while he dealt a decisive blow to the other, and then transfer his main force and repeat the operation against the contained force; or he could retire along his line of communications, fighting delaying actions in both directions, to retard our advance as long as possible.

The country was well suited to the latter course. The advance of the attacking forces would be confined to valleys, the routes being further limited by bush and swamps, while the lower slopes of Kilimanjaro, forming a succession of ridges at right angles to the line of advance, with numerous rivers flowing between them, could be converted into a series of defensive positions, which could only be occupied or turned at a great expense of men and time.

As regards the advance from the east, the Salaita position effectually barred the Voi-Taveta road and commanded the surrounding country. The strength of the position had been tested on February 12th. To north and south of Salaita Hill the bush was dense. From the time that the troops left the water-pipe at Serengeti there would be no water till they reached the Lumi River. The enemy had disposed water-tanks behind the crest of the hill, which they kept filled by a constant service of porters over the fourteen miles from the river, but there was no doubt that they would have destroyed the tanks before they vacated the position.

Aeroplane photos showed the lines of trench running across the face of the hill from north to south. These were also plainly visible from the ground-level. The photos also showed the communication trenches running back from the crest on the reverse slope of the hill, but they gave no indication of the preparations which had been made under cover of the bush along the base and to the north and south of the hill, where the real defences were to be anticipated. In the action of February 12th the infantry advance had been made through the bush on the northern side of the hill, and they found themselves opposed by formidable entrenchments on that side, well provided with machine guns; while the machine guns and snipers, well concealed in trees in advance of the trenches, had done effective work and had been impossible to locate. The work of our guns on that occasion had been confined to the trenches along the face of the hill and the sangars on the crest.

The information regarding Taveta had not been very definite. Aeroplane and scout reconnaissance reported the existence of formidable lines of entrenchment on the far side of the Lumi and that the Mission Hills had been converted into a redoubt for all-round defence. As regards the strength of the enemy forces, a camp of " bandas " of considerable extent had been located in the vicinity of the Mission Hills, but there was no information as to the actual strength of the enemy forces. Several bridges were reported to have been thrown over the Lumi to the south between Taveta and Lake Jipe.

Before dawn on March 8th the advanced guard of the 2nd Division under General Malleson left Serengeti and advanced towards Salaita, followed by

the main body at 5.20 a.m. The advanced guard
deployed on a line running north and south, a little
to the west of the Njoro Drift. The artillery came
into action in the positions as previously arranged :
No. 10, the 4-inch (" Peggy ") naval guns, commanded by Captain Orde-Browne, behind a low ridge
to the south of the road, about a mile to the east of
the drift ; No. 9, the 12-pr. 18-cwt. guns, under Major
Russell, to the north of the road in a position screened
by bush. The remaining batteries (including No. 6
Battery, the 12-prs. of 8 cwt., under Major D. Logan,
of the Loyal North Lancashires, which had accompanied the advanced guard till such time as they
had deployed and were established in their position,
and had then joined the other batteries), came into
action ready to open fire to the front or to deal with
counter-attacks from either flank.

The sun rose at about 6 a.m., but owing to a thick
mist it was not till much later that the aeroplanes
appeared and were able to direct the fire of the
guns on the previously arranged registration points
Throughout the day fire was kept up in short bursts,
being mainly directed to searching the bush at the
base and to the north and south of Salaita, the reverse
slope of the hill and the road leading on to Taveta.
Soon after dusk the guns returned to Serengeti camp, a
strong infantry screen remaining on the line which had
been occupied by the advanced guard during the day.

A few small parties of the enemy had been seen
about the position during the day, but there had been
no hostile action.

Before dawn on the 9th the force again advanced.
Our infantry screen had pushed forward to a
position running north and south on the west side
of an open belt, about one and a half miles to the east

of the base of Salaita Hill. This belt, though covered with low bush, was practically without trees, and from the edge of the bush there was an unrestricted view of the enemy's position. The 130th Baluchis, who were holding the line to either side of the road, stated that at dawn large numbers of the enemy had been visible about the position.

The light batteries, Nos. 6 and 8 (the battery commanded by Major Kinloch), were at once pushed forward to concealed positions near the edge of the bush to the south of the road, No. 10 Battery occupying the same position as on the previous day. The 134th Howitzer Battery, commanded by Major F. Oats, and No. 9 Battery were brought to positions north of the road, under cover of a low ridge running north and south, about a mile to the west of the Njoro Drift. From the positions occupied, the batteries were capable of dealing with counter-attack from either flank and could effectively cover the infantry advance.

Major-General Tighe decided to make a direct attack across the open. The guns having registered, a heavy bombardment was ordered on the enemy trenches, under cover of which the infantry advanced soon after 2 p.m. Officers from the batteries, with distinctive flags on long bamboos, accompanied the infantry firing-lines in their respective zones, and at about a quarter to 4 word was received from Colonel Graham, commanding the 3rd King's African Rifles, which was the leading battalion in the attack, that the enemy had evacuated the position and retired. The position was occupied by our infantry without opposition, and No. 6 Battery was sent forward to join them. The remainder of the force returned to the tanks which had been set up at railhead, now about half a mile to the east of the drift, where they bivouacked. Water was sent forward in carts to the troops at Salaita.

The enemy's position was found to be very strong. The trenches which ran through the bush at the base of the hill were covered by a parapet of built-up stone, with dugouts at intervals, roofed and lined with stone which would give protection against all but the heaviest shell. The main line of defence had been skilfully sited. It allowed a good field of fire to the front, and cross-fire had been arranged from well-concealed machine-gun emplacements. There were also observation posts provided in every sector of the line. The entrenchments, which ran irregularly at a height of ten to twenty feet above the general level of the plain, were well concealed with foliage and creepers. At forty to fifty yards from the firing-line was a " boma " of thorn bush, averaging about thirty yards in width, concealed in which was an elaborate barbed-wire entanglement, stoutly picketed. Tin cans containing stones were slung to the wires at intervals along the whole perimeter. A certain amount of stores, meal, tools, ammunition, etc., which had been left by the enemy, whose departure had evidently been sudden and unpremeditated, fell into our hands. The observation sangar at the summit and the iron water-tank in rear of the southern end of the crest had been demolished by the guns, and the whole ground, including the reverse slope, was pitted with shell craters.

At daybreak on the 10th the division advanced by the Taveta road, skirting the southern end of Salaita, through the Lumi Forest. The road, though not metalled, was in fairly good order, but at intervals the enemy had prepared a form of " booby trap," consisting of a grid of trenches, four or more, extending more than half-way across from alternate sides. The trenches were about three feet deep and about two feet wide and skilfully concealed. Wire netting was spread, over which was a thin layer of brushwood supporting a covering of earth. Fortunately every one of them was discovered. The enemy had evidently hoped that an armoured car or some other form of motor vehicle would have been in advance. As it was, the only effect was to necessitate a short detour through the bush to avoid the trenches till such time as they were filled in.

The enemy field telegraph ran alongside the road. The wire was supported on twenty-foot poles, on which a beer-bottle, with the bottom broken out, served as insulator. This was the form of insulator always used for the German field telegraph, except on main routes. There was evidently no lack of empty beer-bottles in German East Africa.

From Salaita the road gradually descended through the Lumi Forest to the river. This tract of country had the reputation of being one of the best districts for the lion hunter in the country. As the river was approached the country became more and more swampy, and although there had been no rain recently, the road was muddy in places. It was obvious that with very little traffic it would become impassable for heavy vehicles.

The river was reached at about noon. Its course was marked by the exceptionally high trees which lined its banks. A halt was made in a bend of the river, which enclosed an area, evidently a swamp in wet weather. Though dry at the time, there was the hot, steamy, unhealthy atmosphere associated with tropical swamp-land.

The drift by which we were to cross and the old bridge were both situated in this loop of the river. At the drift the banks were some fifteen feet above the bed of the river, and the approaches were steep and muddy. The water was about thirty feet wide and two feet deep. The bridge was a rickety old structure, unsafe in its present condition for anything heavier than a bullock cart. It was necessary to get to work at the bridge and to improve the slopes of the drift and corduroy them before motor and other heavy vehicles could be got over.

The animals had had a hot and tiring march, and as it was cold when they started and water had not been plentiful, they were badly in need of a drink. Besides the drift there was only one other spot about half a mile down-stream where they could be watered. The work on the approaches was consequently much delayed by the stream of horses, mules, and oxen coming to water. The advanced guard infantry was already across the river, and the 8th Battery, which had ox transport, was sent over as soon as their animals had watered.

Although patrols had previously made their way round Salaita, they had not been able to get to the river crossings, and their condition had not been anticipated.

Information had been received that the enemy had evacuated Taveta and retired towards the Latema-Reata neck, and that a squadron of the South African Horse had occupied the Mission Hills.

At about 3 p.m. Major-General Tighe received a report from some source that the enemy were advancing in force on Taveta from the direction of the neck. The remaining infantry of the division, except the King's African Rifles, who were detailed as escort to the guns and train which could not cross in the existing state of the passages, was ordered to move at once and take up a position about the Mission Hills. There was no difficulty about the passage of the infantry, but the only other artillery which could be got over at the time was the 134th Battery, also ox transport. The remainder of the artillery was ordered to cross as soon as the bridge, which was being repaired, or the drift would allow of their passage. Meanwhile the position was reconnoitred, and the 8th and 134th Batteries took up positions in rear of the Mission Hills. At this time the Commander-in-Chief arrived at the Mission House, after a rough cross-country journey from Chala, partly by motor and partly by horse. The report as to the enemy's advance was unfounded, or rather belated, as the enemy had advanced in the morning but had retired again almost immediately.

The Commander-in-Chief then rode forward to Taveta village, about a mile in the direction of Latema, through the empty German camp, to make a reconnaissance of the enemy's position. The 130th Baluchis had already occupied the village and a knoll about a quarter of a mile beyond the village. General Smuts took up his position on this knoll. The enemy was known to be about the neck, but there was no sign of them or of any defensive preparations. Ranges were taken to different conspicuous points in the position, which varied from 4,000 to 5,000 yards, and the Commander-in-Chief then returned to the Mission House, where General Headquarters were established for the night, the 2nd Division being in rear, at the foot of the hill, where the division encamped.

By this time ox carts were streaming across, but

the ground from the river to the Mission Hills and all round them was low-lying and swampy, and traffic was confined to the road running from the drift. There was water running from the Chala direction in a ditch about four feet wide, and from this the thirsty troops got water, but it was none too tempting.

While the 2nd Division had been advancing by the direct road, the bulk of the force had carried out the turning movement in accordance with the plan of operations.

As soon as it was dark on the evening of the 7th, Brigadier-General Van Deventer's column started, by the route which had been previously reconnoitred, for the Lumi. The 1st South African Mounted Brigade started from Mbuyuni, and the 3rd South African Infantry Brigade from Serengeti camp. The General Reserve, consisting of the 2nd South African Brigade, under command of Brigadier-General Beves, followed the 3rd. The artillery with the force was distributed as follows : the 2nd and 4th Batteries of the South African Field Artillery, under command of Lieutenant-Colonel S. S. Taylor, moved with the Mounted Brigade and the 28th Mountain Battery, under Major L. Davies, R.G.A., and the 12th Battery of 5-inch howitzers, under Captain C. de C. Hamilton, R.G.A., with the 3rd South African Infantry Brigade, all of which were under Brigadier-General Van Deventer, while the 5th South African Field Battery, commanded by Captain Adler, was attached to General Beves's brigade. The Commander-in-Chief accompanied the Reserve.

Having made a halt of some hours en route, the Mounted Brigade reached the Lumi at about 6 a.m. on the 8th, near the southern end of the Ziwani swamp ; and the 3rd Infantry Brigade, under

Brigadier-General Berrangé, struck the river a little lower down, opposite Lake Chala, with the 2nd Brigade close behind it.

Having made good the high ground between the Rombo Mission and Lake Chala, the 1st Regiment of South African Horse with the 2nd South African Battery occupied Chala Hill without opposition, and bivouacked on the western slope. The small detachment of enemy which had been at Chala had retired a short distance before the advance of our troops. A detachment of mounted troops sent out to threaten their line of retreat to the south caused them to retire on Taveta. They were followed up a short distance, but as the enemy were known to be in considerable strength at Taveta, this detachment was recalled to Chala before nightfall.

Meanwhile, the infantry brigades had taken up a position astride the Lumi and thrown out a strong outpost line. Under the Commander-in-Chief's orders, a regiment of South African Horse, under Lieutenant-Colonel Kuhn, had been sent to make good Kilimari Hill, on which there was a small fort, but encountered considerable opposition. By General Smuts's orders, Colonel Kuhn gradually fell back, followed by the enemy, who were especially strong along the river-line, where they had good cover in the dense bush. When they reached the infantry outpost line they made several determined attacks, but were repulsed with considerable loss, while our troops also sustained a certain number of casualties. The enemy then withdrew in the direction of Kilimari.

The following morning, the 9th, infantry, supported by the 4th and 12th Batteries, moved out against Kilimari and the ridges to the west of it. The enemy retired and the fort was occupied.

The enemy force was subsequently found to have numbered some 500. From information obtained from prisoners and captured documents, it appeared that the enemy, owing to our demonstrations towards the Ngulu Gap and in the direction of Lake Jipe, had come to the conclusion that our attack would be made to the south of the road. They had consequently disposed their forces to meet the main attack in this area and had detached the Kilimari force to make a counterstroke by the northern flank against Mbuyuni. Our advance against Chala had taken them by surprise, and this detachment found itself entirely cut off from the main body about Taveta and to the south of it. As the Mounted Brigade effectually prevented them traversing the ground between Rombo and the river, they moved off to the north, and it was not till two or three days later that they found their way to Moschi.

On the same day, the 9th, General Van Deventer sent mounted troops, accompanied by the 2nd Battery, to get astride the Taveta-Moschi road, recalling them to Chala at nightfall. At the same time he sent the 12th South African Infantry to make good Ndui Ya Waromba Hill and the bridge over the Lumi to the east of Taveta. This movement, combined with the effect of the bombardment of the position, doubtless decided the enemy to withdraw from Salaita. They just avoided encountering a couple of squadrons of South African Horse, sent to intercept them.

During the day the 2nd Battery, with the section of ammunition column of the 2nd and 4th Batteries, crossed the Lumi and bivouacked that night with the remainder of the Mounted Brigade.

On the morning of the 10th the 2nd South African

7

Horse, accompanied by the 2nd Battery, advanced on Taveta. They arrived in time to forestall a large force of the enemy which was observed moving down from the direction of Latema. It was doubtless this movement of which General Tighe received information later in the day. The mounted troops pushed on, and the battery came into action about 100 yards west of Taveta in support of the regiment which advanced towards the Latema-Reata neck. The enemy withdrew into the bush, from which they opened fire on our advanced troops. The guns meanwhile directed their fire on small enemy parties which were visible from time to time about the neck, and searched the slopes at ranges of 4,000 to 5,000 yards with good effect. At 4 p.m. the regiment and battery were withdrawn and rejoined the brigade at Chala at about 8 p.m.

While these events were taking place on the Taveta front, the 1st Division had started their advance from the west. General Stewart had reached Geraragua on March 8th. A halt was made on the 9th to allow supplies to come up and to carry out certain reconnaissances of the routes ahead. The result of these reconnaissances was that the road on to Somali Häuser was reported to be impassable for wheeled transport, as all the bridges had been destroyed by the enemy. The halt was prolonged till the afternoon of the 10th, the mounted troops moving off at 4 p.m. They came into contact with an enemy force and sustained a few casualties. There was nothing further to record with reference to the advance of the 1st Division during the next few days. The road eventually selected was found to be very difficult, owing to the obstacles which the enemy had put in their way, mainly of the nature of felled trees. The enemy opposed to them was obviously of the nature of a containing force, and did not offer any serious resistance. The mounted troops eventually joined up with the division on the night of March 12th/13th at the Sanja River, and on the 13th the force advanced to Somali Häuser.

The situation on the evening of the 10th was : General Headquarters at the Taveta Mission, with the 2nd Division holding the Mission Hills and an outpost line running through Taveta village ; the Mounted Brigade at Chala and the 2nd and 3rd South African Infantry Brigades astride the Lumi about Chala ; detachments from the 2nd Division holding Salaita and the Serengeti and Mbuyuni camps. The heavy guns (except the 5·4-inch howitzers) and the motor transport of the 2nd Division train, with the King's African Rifles as escort, were still east of the river, awaiting the necessary work on the crossings before they could be brought over. The 1st Division was a short march to the east of Geraragua.

As regards the enemy : The Taveta force had retired to the Kitowo Hills, and as far as was known were in the vicinity of the Latema-Reata gap ; a detached force had been driven in a northerly direction from Kilimari Hill and the ridges to the west of it ; a reserve was to be anticipated to the west in the direction of Moschi; while a containing force, evidently not very formidable, was opposed to the 1st Division to the west of Moschi. These were the forces in the immediate vicinity, and as a result of the demonstrations to the south, a certain force was probably in the neighbourhood of the Ngulu Gap, which would doubtless be brought to this theatre as quickly as possible.

The first move in the game had been won by our

side. The enemy had been misled, and in consequence
his dispositions, based on what he had assumed to
be the plans of our commander, were wrong, and given
that our pressure was not relaxed, it would not be
possible for him to readjust them during this phase
of the operations.

CHAPTER V

THE Commander-in-Chief was determined to follow up the success already gained, and to allow the enemy no opportunity to rectify his original faulty dispositions. The enemy force definitely located about the Latema-Reata neck, the exact strength of which was unknown, had to be dealt with before any further advance could be made from Taveta. This force covered the line of retirement to Kahe. At the same time there was probably a force covering Moschi and barring the line of advance to that centre. It was desirable that pressure should be exerted on this latter force to prevent it being used to reinforce the enemy in the neck, or operating against the flank of the force engaging them. The southern Kitowo Hills run from Reata, the south-eastern extremity, for about two miles in a north-westerly direction. The hills, rising to about 1,000 feet, are steep, covered for the most part with bush and difficult to climb, except at the neck, through which the route to Kahe runs. Beyond the hills the country was alternate forest and swamp as far as the Ruwu River, which was known to be unfordable, full of crocodiles, and consequently an impassable obstacle except where bridged.

Early on the morning of the 11th General Van Deventer with the Mounted Brigade and the 2nd and

4th South African Batteries advanced as far as Baharias. The country was rough and broken, and movement was very difficult. Immediately on his left the 4th South African Horse, supported by the 12th South African Infantry, advanced to East Kitowo Hill, which they occupied. The Force Reserve was ordered to advance from Chala to Taveta.

General Smuts had decided to attack the force holding the neck with the 2nd Division. Owing to the necessity for garrisoning Serengeti and Salaita, the infantry of this force consisted of but three battalions, while part of the artillery was still on the north side of the river; but these batteries might be expected shortly, as the work on the crossings had been carried on vigorously during the night.

The Commander-in-Chief moved forward to the knoll beyond the village about 8 a.m., and the infantry was then assembling at Taveta. The force available on the spot consisted of: Belfield's Scouts and the M.I. Company, Nos. 6, 8, and 134 Batteries, 2nd Rhodesians, 130th Baluchis and 3rd King's African Rifles, Loyal North Lancashire and Volunteer Machine-gun Companies.

Belfield's Scouts had been in touch with the enemy along the lower slopes from early morning. As soon as orders were received for the attack, positions were reconnoitred for the batteries. No. 8 was already in action in the vicinity of the village, and the 134th and 6th were ordered forward to Taveta. Brigadier-General Malleson, commanding the infantry brigade, decided on the spur, running about 100 yards towards Taveta from Latema, as the objective for the attack. This spur commanded the neck, and from it it would be possible to reach the crest of the hill and command the enemy's line of retirement.

The infantry were to advance with the King's African Rifles on the left, the 130th Baluchis on the right, and the Rhodesians following the latter in reserve, to the north of the road or track. The batteries were disposed, the 8th on the left supporting the King's African Rifles, the 6th Battery on the right supporting the 130th and the 134th about midway between them, the guns being at ranges of about 3,500 yards from the crest. The remaining batteries would be brought into action as they arrived.

The infantry advanced at about 11.30 a.m. under cover of the fire of the guns. On either flank were the mounted troops.

For the first 1,000 yards from the village the country was open, but beyond that was bush. As the infantry approached the bush a heavy fire from rifles and machine guns was opened, and guns which were located on the ridge on either side of the neck came into action. Our guns concentrated on the enemy guns on Reata and they were very soon silenced. One gun was subsequently found to have received a direct hit, which smashed an axle, and consequently had to be abandoned and fell into our hands. The 134th opened fire on the Latema spur, and as the first of the 60-lb. shell burst just in rear of the highest point, parties of enemy were observed dispersing in all directions.

The advance of our infantry was held up by the enemy, who were well concealed in the folds of the ground, along the edge of the bush, in positions artificially strengthened, and at the same time hidden by the long grass. They had a number of machine guns in action and snipers in the trees in advance and on the flanks. Our progress was slow, and there were a certain number of casualties. Having

made their way through the first belt of bush, which
proved to be about 100 yards wide, the infantry
dug in, while subjected to a continuous fire. In
front of them was an open space about 200 yards
in width. The artillery officers with the firing-line
were trying to locate the positions of the machine
guns, in order to turn the fire of our guns on to them.
Meanwhile the gun fire was distributed along the
whole enemy front. An early round from the
howitzers had set fire to a " banda " on the Latema
spur, and the fire was rapidly spreading up the crest.
The heat was intense and water-carts were going as
near as they could to the firing-line, but it was a
difficult problem to get the water to the troops in
action, who were suffering greatly from thirst.

At about 4.30 p.m. No. 9 Battery crossed the
river and was brought into action on the south side
of the village. Shortly after their arrival the 5th
South African Battery came up with the 2nd South
African Infantry Brigade from Chala, and were
brought into action on the right of No. 9. Meanwhile, the infantry were gradually pushing forward.
On the left the King's African Rifles had made
considerable progress. At about 5 p.m., as they
were making a rush led by their Colonel, a voice was
heard shouting : " Come on, the King's African
Rifles, this way ! " Colonel Graham turned in the
direction indicated, and fell, having received five
bullets from a machine gun. It was the German
machine gunner who, in excellent English, had been
cheering them on. It is gratifying to know that
the cunning German and the whole of his crew were
wiped out later, and that the gun fell into our hands.
At nightfall, by the Commander-in-Chief's orders, the
advanced batteries were brought back and bivouacked

just north of the village, Nos. 5 and 9 remaining in
action. The infantry were now holding an irregular
line extending from half-way across the neck to the
lower slopes of Latema spur. On the arrival of the
South African Infantry, the 5th Regiment had been
placed at General Tighe's disposal. (Owing to indis-
position, at about 4 p.m. General Malleson had been
forced to withdraw, and his place had been taken by
General Tighe.) General Tighe had, on taking over
command, ordered the Rhodesians to support the
King's African Rifles on the left, and the result of
the determined push, which had then been made,
had been a considerable gain of ground, but it had
not been possible to make the upper slopes. The
Baluchis supported by half of the 5th South African
Infantry had simultaneously pushed in on the right,
and the whole line had dug in and were holding the
ground which they had gained.

The 7th South African Infantry were then placed
at General Tighe's disposal. They reached him at
about 8 p.m. The sun had set at about 6 p.m., and
in the darkness which immediately followed, it was
no easy matter to keep up communication and to
determine the exact whereabouts of the widely
deployed infantry. As was afterwards learned, a
party of Rhodesians and King's African Rifles had
made their way through to the crest of the Latema
slope, where they had hung on, but they had not been
able to pass back word of their situation. To send
a messenger back through the bush in the darkness
meant that if he succeeded in finding his way through
the bush, he would have to make a very wide circuit
if he was not to be exposed to the fire of his own men.
General Tighe then decided to push in and endeavour
to clear the ridge with the bayonet. Half of the

5th South African Battalion had already been put
in in support of the Baluchis.   From what had been
seen of the upper slopes, they appeared to be covered
with open bush.   To keep touch in an advance without even the reports of the rifles to act as a guide to
the whereabouts of the extended line would be a very
difficult matter, but it was the only means of securing
the position that night.   A postponement would
mean that the enemy were to be allowed to have the
whole night to prepare and strengthen the position
they were then holding, forcing on us a repetition of
the attack the following day, under conditions if
anything more difficult than those already experienced, with the possibility of the enemy being reinforced during the night.

The bayonet attack was entrusted to the South
African Infantry. Colonel Byron, the commander
of the 5th Battalion, arranged that the 7th Battalion
should form the first line and that the 5th should
follow them closely in support.   The plan was that
on arrival at the crest Lieutenant-Colonel Freeth,
who commanded the 7th Battalion, was to wheel to
the right, and Major Thompson, the 2nd in command,
to the left, clearing the crest to north and south,
while the 5th were to close in and secure and hold
the neck itself.   The two wings of the 7th Battalion
pushed in as directed, gradually making their way
up the slopes, and parties, under Colonel Freeth
and Major Thompson respectively, reached the crests
on either flank.   Colonel Freeth had with him a
small party of under twenty, and he found a small
party of Rhodesians and King's African Rifles
already there.   They dug in where they were. Major
Thompson on the Reata slope similarly dug in in
a position from which he hoped that he would be

able to command the neck. Colonel Byron, in the
neck itself, found the enemy in a strong, prepared
position, from which they were able to sweep the
approaches with the fire of their rifles and numerous
machine guns. Finding that the position which he
had gained was absolutely untenable, he decided to
retire. Meanwhile General Tighe had ordered the
130th Baluchis to advance to the support of the 5th
South Africans. On advancing at about 1.30 a.m.
they met Colonel Byron, who explained that he
had been compelled to order his men to withdraw.
Major Mainprise, R.E., putting himself at the head
of a party of Baluchis, charged at the middle of the
enemy's position. He fell, riddled with bullets,
having come under the concentrated fire of three
machine guns. Of the party with him, over twenty
were killed. General Tighe then ordered that the
troops should dig in where they then were, astride
the road, and await daylight.

General Tighe then reported to the Commander-
in-Chief what the situation was so far as he was able
to judge. He had received no word from Colonel
Freeth or Major Thompson, and all efforts to get in
touch with them had failed. As a result of this
report the Commander-in-Chief decided that it was
inadvisable to press further with the direct attack
on the neck and determined to await the effect of
the turning movement by the mounted troops, which
was to be carried out on the 12th, and which would of
necessity cause the enemy to evacuate their position.
Orders were accordingly issued to General Tighe to
withdraw his force before daybreak and take up a
position farther from the neck. The troops were
gradually retiring from their advanced positions in
accordance with these orders, when one of the patrols,

sent out to gain touch with Colonel Freeth and Major
Thompson, sent word by a motor-cyclist that Colonel
Freeth and Major Thompson were in occupation of
the ridge on either side of the neck, and that the
enemy were retiring in the direction of Kahe. At
this time Nos. 5 and 9 Batteries were standing to
their guns and No. 8 Battery had come into action
to the south of the village. The Commander-in-Chief
at once ordered the 8th South African Infantry forward, and the 9th and 5th Batteries were sent with
all speed to the neck, the Commander-in-Chief
accompanying them. The enemy were seen retiring
in the distance, or rather the dust of their column
was visible above the trees, as beyond the neck as
far as the eye could see was dense forest. The 9th
Battery, which was the first to arrive, opened fire on
the column, and, from the disappearance of the dust-
clouds, it was evident that the column at once dispersed to either side of the road. The batteries were
then ordered back to Taveta.

Throughout the previous evening and night the
ambulances and stretcher-bearers had been coming
in to Taveta village in a steady stream. By midday
our wounded and dead had all been brought back.
The house of the Assistant Commissioner had been
converted by the Germans into a hospital, and in
addition a number of huge "bandas" had been erected,
which provided the necessary accommodation for our
casualties. That evening the chaplains of the different denominations performed the funeral services
over the remains of those who had fallen, the cemetery
chosen being alongside the burying-ground which
had been used by the enemy during the time they
had occupied Taveta. The inscriptions on their
graves showed that, apart from losses in action, they

had suffered from an outbreak of typhoid. Taveta, being surrounded by hills, is exceptionally hot, and lying as it does in the proximity of the swamps of the Lumi, is an unhealthy spot.

During the next two days the battlefield was cleared up. A number of the enemy were buried, a naval gun, machine guns, and a number of rifles and ammunition were brought in and handed over to the Ordnance. In the vicinity of the Latema spur the results of the high-explosive shell were evident from the effect on the victims, who were in some cases literally blown to pieces. On the body of an officer in the neighbourhood of the abandoned gun was a half-written letter, in which he had given a description of the bombardment of Salaita on the 8th and 9th. He said that the British had brought up heavy naval guns, and that it was impossible for them to hold out against them.

They had further experience of the effect of heavy guns at Taveta, as the fire of the heavy howitzers had evidently been most effective. The field-guns had also done good execution. In a machine-gun emplacement, with the machine-gun stand and boxes of ammunition, were the bodies of a German officer and four Askaris, all killed by shrapnel bullets. This was the first occasion on which the enemy had left any German dead behind. It is true that in the previous fighting we had not actually occupied the ground on which a stand-up fight had taken place, but in the case of patrol encounters they had always carried off their casualties.

Our losses were less than might have been anticipated. The total did not amount to 300. Among them were five officers. A serious loss was Lieutenant-Colonel Graham, the commander of the 3rd King's

African Rifles, a gallant officer, idolised by his men. Major Mainprise, the Brigade-Major of the 1st East African Brigade, was an officer who had, though comparatively young, already achieved considerable distinction by work he had done across the frontier in India, prior to the outbreak of war.

The heaviest losses among the men were borne by the King's African Rifles, who had pushed in with the greatest gallantry, notwithstanding the heavy enemy fire to which they were exposed.

When the enemy retired, the troops bivouacked in the vicinity of Taveta and the recently evacuated German camp, a detachment remaining in occupation of the neck and Latema Hill.

The force occupying West Kitowo had been subjected to some gun fire, but had not been attacked.

We were now in possession of the amphitheatre of hills around Taveta and the enemy had been driven off British territory. They had been defeated in a pitched battle and forced to retreat, leaving a large number of their dead behind them. It was first blood in the new campaign. The effect on the German Askaris, of seeing their forces turned out of a strong prepared position, for the first time, and their experience of high-explosive shell were likely to reduce considerably their future fighting value.

CHAPTER VI

THE OCCUPATION OF MOSCHI AND ARUSCHA DISTRICTS

AT daybreak on March 12th the Mounted Brigade, which had bivouacked at Baharias, after a trying march over the roughest of ground, continued their advance. Their first objective was Spitz Hill, which they occupied about noon, having driven before them the enemy patrols. After a short halt they moved down to the Taveta-Moschi road, reaching the banks of the Himo River, where they encamped soon after dark. It was found that the retiring enemy had blown up the bridge, and the river, flowing between steep and rocky banks, from thirty to fifty feet above the level of the water, was a serious obstacle for wheeled transport. There was, however, an old drift a short distance above the site of the bridge, and the following day the brigade crossed by it and pushed on to New Moschi, the terminus of the Usambara Railway. Here they halted for a day, moving up to Old Moschi, the military and administrative headquarters of the district, on the March 15th.

On that day General Headquarters came forward to the Himo, occupying the site of a recently vacated German camp in a rubber plantation. The " bandas," which the German porters construct exceptionally well, were most useful. The " banda " is a grass hut which is constructed on a skeleton of woodwork.

The plan having been decided on, the porters go off into the bush and collect all the necessary wood, grass, and bark. The outside walls are outlined by the trunks of small trees, forked at the top, which are stripped bare and planted in the ground. Extra high trees are used for the support of the tree which is to form the gable roof. Stout cross-pieces rest in the forks of the uprights, to which they are secured, and thin branches are then tied with tree bark from the gable to the top of the side walls. Still thinner branches are then tied at intervals down the slopes of the roof to which the grass is subsequently attached. The sides and ends of the hut are then treated in a similar manner, the walls being carried up or half-way up to the roof, according to the taste of the prospective resident. The African " banda " is an excellent shelter against both rain and sun. As regards the sun, it is far superior to any but the stoutest of tents.

The 3rd South African Brigade with the 28th Mountain Battery and the 2nd South African Brigade with the 5th Battery had already moved forward, and were encamped on the west and east banks respectively of the river. On the following day, March 16th, the 2nd Brigade shifted their camp from the river and bivouacked in a perimeter camp outside of the rubber plantation, a few hundred yards south of General Headquarters, about half a mile from the river.

The 2nd Division, which was holding the Latema neck, remained with the rest of the artillery at Taveta.

We were now in a settled area. The plantation in which General Headquarters were encamped belonged to an Italian, who had been interned by the Germans. His son was reported to be fighting on the side of the enemy. There were other plantations belonging to European settlers dotted about on the mountain-slopes. Two or three miles up was a Bohemian coffee planter who had come to the country originally as a missionary, but had decided that coffee planting offered more attractions than the saving of African souls. Soon after our arrival he presented himself at General Headquarters camp, begging for protection for his house and property against the natives, whom he feared would not hesitate to loot his belongings once the Germans had departed. (Incidentally he also offered to sell his estate at what he assured us was an alarming sacrifice.) He evidently had not much confidence in the permanence of the respect for law and order instilled into the native mind by their late rulers. Another plantation close at hand belonged to an Englishman, who had been interned by the enemy at the outbreak of hostilities; while to east and west up the hills were the residences and plantations of other European settlers, either fighting or interned. There were German mission-stations, Catholic and Protestant, with imposing churches, in the vicinity, and the missionaries were still there. At New Moschi was a colony of Greek traders. On beyond, in the vicinity of Mount Meru, the settlers were nearly all Boers who had migrated from South Africa. Every settlement was found to have its proportion of native " banyas," or shopkeepers, from India; in fact, the trade with the native Africans in German East was practically in their hands all through the country.

It was now necessary to put in order the road over which we had come. Between Taveta and Himo there were several nullahs to be crossed, and in each

8

case the bridge, if there was one, had been destroyed by the enemy, and the drift, where there was no bridge, required a certain amount of work before it would be fit for motor traffic. The bridge over the Himo had also to be rebuilt. It had originally rested on stone piers, which had been dynamited, and the whole of the superstructure had disappeared.

Information was received that the enemy force which had been opposed to General Stewart, consisting of six companies, had withdrawn and had passed through New Moschi, moving towards the Ruwu on the night of the 12th/13th. It was learned later that the commander of this detachment had committed suicide, owing to his failure to offer effective opposition to the advance of the 1st Division. His conduct had been adversely criticised by the German Commander-in-Chief, and he was so affected thereby that he straightway shot himself.

On March 14th the advanced guard of General Stewart's force joined hands with the advanced troops of the Mounted Brigade at New Moschi.

The situation of our troops was now as follows : On our left, to the east, was the 2nd Division, under General Tighe, with Colonel Byron, who had taken Brigadier-General Malleson's place when he was invalided, in command of the 1st East African Brigade, holding the Latema neck, the headquarters of the division being at Taveta ; in the centre, in the vicinity of the Himo River, about the level of the Taveta-Moschi road, was General Headquarters, with the 2nd and 3rd South African Infantry Brigades ; the 1st Division, now under the command of Brigadier-General Sheppard, R.E., was at New Moschi ; General Van Deventer with the Mounted Brigade was at Old Moschi, with one regiment, the 4th South African

Horse, at the Mue River crossing and one regiment watching the right flank on the Weruweru.

The enemy had retired towards the Ruwu and were known to be holding positions to the north of the river. The intervening country was very difficult. From Lake Jipe to the Mue River there was a line of isolated hills : Kingarunga and Mokinni on the east, rising from the Ruwu swamps ; on the west, Unterer Himo, Euphorbien, Kifumbu, and Rasthaus, and between Mokinni and Unterer Himo some bare, low hills not marked on the maps. Mokinni and Kingarunga, rising from the midst of the swamps, were bare and rocky. The hills to the west, situated in the midst of dense forest, were covered with bush. The enemy line of communications was the railway running down the west side of the Pare Mountains towards Tanga. This route was also his best line of retirement, but there was an alternative line of retreat by the road west of Lake Jipe, on the east side of the mountains, which led to the Ngulu Gap and there was a road along the base of the mountains, on the south bank of the river, by which this road could be reached.

It was essential to the enemy to retain possession of the crossings of the Ruwu to ensure the possibility of retirement. The passages of the Ruwu were : A bridge just south of Kingarunga, approached by a causeway through the swamp to the north of the river ; a bridge just south of Rasthaus Hill ; the wagon-bridge at Kahe Kwa Ruwu, about two miles east of Kahe station, approached by the Mue-Massai Kraal road ; and on the extreme west the railway-bridge, about a mile to the south of Kahe station.

For the protection of these passages the enemy's troops were distributed as follows :—a detachment

holding Kingarunga covered the causeway and
bridge there; the Rasthaus bridge was protected by
a force on Rasthaus Hill, with advanced posts on
Unterer Himo and Euphorbien; the wagon-bridge
was covered by forces astride the Mue road, the
whereabouts of which were not definitely known;
and a force in the neighbourhood of Kahe station
safeguarded the railway-bridge. A strong force
of the enemy was reported to be on the south bank
of the river in reserve. Aeroplane reconnaissances
had located lines of earthworks to the north of Rasthaus and astride the wagon-bridge road; but owing
to the density of the bush, the information as to
their extent and the number of lines existing was
vague.

For the forwarding of supplies, the advance of the
heavy artillery, etc., it was imperative that the road
from Taveta should be made fit for heavy traffic as
speedily as possible. There was a consequent lull
in the vigour of the pursuit, and the enemy, having
completed his preparations for the barring of our
further progress, became aggressive. At about midnight of the 16th/17th he made a night attack on
the camp of the 2nd South African Infantry Brigade,
situated just south of General Headquarters. Having
made their way to the edge of the bush just south
of the camp, the enemy suddenly opened a heavy rifle
and machine-gun fire. This was continued with
short pauses for about half an hour. Not a shot was
fired in return by the South African Infantry, who
remained under cover of their trenches awaiting the
advance of the enemy to closer quarters, as they had
an excellent field of fire for some hundreds of yards
immediately outside the perimeter of their camp.
The enemy, however, was in doubt as to what was

awaiting them, and having discharged a large quantity
of ammunition, they eventually retired without
venturing into the open. There was not a single
casualty among our troops. The South Africans
were well dug in, and the enemy were firing uphill.
There were considerable numbers of horses and mules,
belonging to the battery and the transport of the
brigade, within the perimeter, their lines sheltered
by the lie of the ground. By wonderful good-fortune
not one of them was killed. On our right also enemy
patrols were active in the vicinity of the Mue River
and to the south of New Moschi.

Orders had already been issued for the railway to
be pushed on across the Lumi to Taveta, and it was
necessary that the enemy should be cleared from
the north bank of the Ruwu as soon as possible, with
a view to continuing the line and joining it up with
the Usambara line. The Commander-in-Chief accordingly determined to make a general advance southwards forthwith. According to local information,
the rains might commence any day, and it was all-
important to carry out these operations, in which
our troops would be working in low-lying ground,
with the least possible delay.

Orders were accordingly issued for a general
advance. On the night of the 17th/18th Belfield's
Scouts were sent forward from the Himo to occupy
Unterer Himo Hill. They succeeded in gaining
the crest, driving off an enemy picket, but in the
morning were attacked by the enemy in strength
and forced to retire. At about 8.30 a.m. on the
18th the 2nd South African Brigade with the 5th
Battery advanced on Unterer Himo. The 1st East
African Brigade (less two battalions), supported by
the 9th Battery from Latema neck, had been ordered

to co-operate in the attack on Unterer Himo; while the 3rd South African Brigade with the 28th Mountain Battery, covered to the west by the 4th South African Horse, was to advance simultaneously on Kifumu and Euphorbien Hills on the west of the Himo. Farther west, on the extreme right, the East African Mounted Rifles, with the squadron of the 17th Cavalry, were to advance via Mue and Massai Kraal.

The 2nd and 3rd Brigades accordingly advanced simultaneously at 9 a.m. Shortly before noon the 5th Battery came into action and searched the crest and summit of Unterer Himo, and a section of the 28th Battery co-operated from the west of the river. The infantry advanced under cover of the fire of the guns. By about 4 p.m. the 2nd Brigade had occupied Unterer Himo and the 3rd Brigade had driven back the enemy and were in possession of Euphorbien. Meanwhile, the 1st East African Brigade had advanced to and occupied the bare low hills which lie between Unterer Himo and Mokinni.

On the right the Mounted Rifles and 17th Cavalry found Massai Kraal occupied by three strong enemy companies. Behind them was the 2nd East African Infantry Brigade, which early in the day had been ordered forward by the Commander-in-Chief from New Moschi to Mue. The 9th and 5th Batteries returned to Latema and Himo respectively, when the forces which they were accompanying had gained their objectives. The 3rd Brigade made good Euphorbien, the 28th Battery having engaged and silenced enemy field guns which had opened fire on the advancing infantry from the summit of the Rasthaus Hill. The main body of this brigade encamped for the night on Kifumu.

In the course of the day the 10th and 12th Batteries,

the 4-inch naval guns and 5-inch howitzers, were brought forward from Taveta to Himo, where they arrived at about 5 p.m.

The results of the day's fighting had been very satisfactory. In the morning the enemy had been in possession of Unterer Himo and Euphorbien as advanced posts to the Rasthaus position. Our troops had driven them out of these advanced posts, and had also occupied the lower hills farther to the east, which commanded and effectually barred any advance to the Kingarunga crossing by the north bank of the river.

The Commander-in-Chief determined to attack Rasthaus and push on down the wagon-bridge road on the 19th. The 2nd and 3rd South African Infantry Brigades, the latter supported, if necessary, by the 1st East African Infantry Brigade, received orders to make a concentric attack on the Rasthaus position, and General Sheppard was ordered to make a simultaneous advance with the 1st Division from Mue via Massai Kraal towards Kahe Kwa Ruwu.

The 2nd South Africans, who had been rejoined by the 5th South African Battery, set out from Unterer Himo in the early morning, but were soon brought to a practical standstill. The bush to the east of the Rasthaus position, consisting principally of dense thorn, was found to be impenetrable, even for individual men on foot.

The 3rd Brigade advanced about the same time, the 12th South African Infantry leading. Enemy guns from behind the Rasthaus crest again opened fire on the advancing infantry, but, as on the previous day, were soon silenced by the guns of the mountain battery which continued in action covering the infantry advance. The movement through the bush was very slow and the leading troops were much harassed by the fire of enemy snipers, who could not be located. About midday a halt was made. The advance was resumed about 4 p.m. The 12th South Africans again pushed on, covered by the artillery, until they suddenly found themselves confronted by a well-concealed prepared position from which the enemy opened a heavy rifle and machine-gun fire. They were then about 2,500 yards south of Euphorbien Hill.

The South Africans gradually built up a firing-line at close rifle range, and remained in action till about 5.30 p.m. The enemy had meanwhile succeeded in working round through the bush to a position on their right or western flank, from which they were able to bring a punishing enfilade fire on the advanced line of the South Africans. There was no possibility of holding on to the position through the night, and the order was issued for them to withdraw to Euphorbien Hill. This was not an easy operation under the conditions in which they were then placed. The retirement was, however, ably carried out by the infantry under Major Breytenbach, the battalion commander, the successful withdrawal being rendered possible largely owing to the well-directed covering fire of the guns, controlled by Lieutenant Eden, the artillery officer with the infantry firing-line.

In the course of the retirement Major Breytenbach and his adjutant, Captain Kruger, were both severely wounded. Lieutenant Eden and several of the gunners, who were engaged in rolling up and bringing in their telephone wire, were also wounded, but succeeded in bringing in all the equipment. The infantry suffered some forty casualties. On the right the 1st Division, under General Sheppard, had

made considerable progress, having fought their
way forward through the dense bush through which
the road passed, through Massai Kraal, as far south
as a level with " Store," where they bivouacked for
the night.

The Commander-in-Chief now decided to withdraw
the 2nd South African Brigade from Unterer Himo
and reinforce the 1st Division, who were undoubtedly
confronted by the enemy's main body. Till such
time as he was reinforced, General Sheppard was
ordered to fall back to Massai Kraal. On the 20th
General Beves's brigade passed through Himo camp,
where they were joined by the 12th Howitzer Battery,
on their way to join the 1st Division. Orders were
issued to General Van Deventer to proceed with the
Mounted Brigade by a night march through the bush
to the west of the railway, cross the Pangani to the
south of Kahe, and get in rear of the enemy's position.

At this time one mounted regiment, the 4th, was
on the Weruweru River, another was operating with
the 3rd Brigade, the remainder of the Mounted
Brigade was at Old Moschi. Soon after 2 p.m. the
force at Old Moschi were on the move and the brigade
concentrated west of New Moschi before dark.

That night, the 20th/21st, General Sheppard's
force was in an entrenched perimeter camp, in an
open space in the vicinity of Nassai Kraal, in the
midst of what was otherwise a densely wooded tract
of country. At about 9.30 p.m. the enemy made a
determined attack on the camp and, pouring in a
heavy fire, gradually pushed in to within twenty yards
of the trenches. It was intensely dark, there being
no moon. The infantry met the assault with fire
from rifles and machine guns, and the enemy withdrew to the cover of the bush, but only to rally for a

fresh onslaught. Again they tried to rush the camp and were again driven back. They made no less than four determined attacks before they actually withdrew at about midnight. Our losses were comparatively light. We had some thirty casualties, but the enemy lost heavily, both in Askaris and Europeans. The actual figures were subsequently learnt from the German newspapers. When they retired they left no whites and very few Askaris on the ground, but their losses amounted to over 150. According to the statements of prisoners, the attacking force numbered over 2,000.

By daylight the following morning, the 21st, General Van Deventer with the Mounted Brigade and the 2nd and 4th South African Batteries was approaching the Pangani River, to the west of Kahe Hill. There had been no opportunity of making a previous reconnaissance of the route through the bush, but the force had succeeded in making their way over some twenty-five miles during the night, and at daybreak were at the spot designated, within gun range of their first objective, Kahe Hill. They had made one considerable halt of about three hours, in the vicinity of Misinga's, about ten miles west of Kahe, and the leading troops arrived at the riverbank as the sun rose.

They were now confronted by an obstacle, the magnitude of which had not been anticipated. According to the map there should have been a bridge, but no bridge existed, and the river was found to be over twenty yards wide, of considerable depth, and the current was swift. The engineer officers with the force decided that it would be impossible to bridge it in the day, and that a raft could not be constructed in the time available.

General Van Deventer then ordered the 1st South African Horse to swim the river. At the same time the 2nd Battery came into action and opened fire on the summit and northern slopes of Kahe Hill. The dismounted cavalrymen made their way up the southern slope, which was covered with thick bush, and by 11.30 a.m. the enemy had been driven off and the hill was in our hands. The enemy had not anticipated any attack. One company had been detailed to hold the hill and there were no supporting troops in the immediate vicinity. The hill was undoubtedly the key to the Ruwu position. Presumably the enemy had looked on any turning movement from the west as out of the range of possibility, particularly having regard to the nature of the obstacle offered by the Pangani River, and had concentrated his attention on the dangers threatening from the columns advancing towards the Ruwu from the north.

Von Lettow, the German commander, was at the time at the wagon-bridge over the Ruwu, while his trusted lieutenant, Major Kraut, who had been in command at Latema, was in charge of the Rasthaus section. As soon as it was realised that Kahe Hill had fallen into our hands, the enemy evidently appreciated its importance and made several determined attempts to retake it, but it was too late. Major Koen and his men were firmly established; the artillery had sent forward an officer, Lieutenant Court Smith, who had swum the river and had established communication with his battery on the west bank, and all attempts to retake the position were beaten back with loss by the dismounted South Africans and the fire of the guns. A 4.1-inch naval gun co-operated in the German counter-attacks from a position about 5,000 yards away on the south bank of the Ruwu, and caused a few casualties among our troops, but the hill remained in our possession.

Meanwhile, General Van Deventer advanced and occupied the station, the enemy retiring. The enemy meanwhile blew up the Kahe railway-bridge. It was now all-important for him to delay the advance of General Sheppard's force. He found his line of retirement by the west of the Pares threatened, and if he could hold the line of the Ruwu he could still withdraw by the Jipi route.

Two dismounted squadrons were then sent forward, under Major Wilkins, to interrupt the railway and bar the enemy's line of retreat by the road alongside it. At the same time a detachment was sent to occupy Baumann Hill. The distance was not very great by the map, but when Major Wilkins's force had proceeded a short way from the base of the hill they found themselves confronted by a line of dense, low thorn bush. They sought in vain to northward and southward for a way round, but it extended apparently indefinitely. They then tried to make their way through it. It was quite impassable, and they eventually made their way back to Kahe Hill, just before dusk, with their clothing torn to ribbons, some men being practically naked. The Baumann Hill detachment succeeded in reaching the summit, and were recalled when General Van Deventer decided to concentrate his force for the night on the west bank of the river. They encamped a short distance to the north-west of Kahe Hill. The force on the hill and No. 2 Battery remained in position after the repulse of the enemy's final attempt to retake the hill, till dark, and opened fire on any enemy parties observed from the summit. The enemy had kept

up an intermittent fire on them, and shelled any
cloud of dust to be seen on the west bank, but the
effect had been negligible.

General Sheppard's force had been hotly engaged
from noon. On receipt of information that the
Mounted Brigade were nearing Kahe, the Commander-in-Chief had ordered General Sheppard to
push on towards the Ruwu.

He had at his disposal the 1st Division, consisting
of the 2nd East African Brigade (25th Royal Fusiliers,
29th Punjabis, 129th Baluchis), the East African
Mounted Rifles, a squadron of the 17th Cavalry, the
1st and 3rd South African Batteries, the 27th Mountain
and 12th Howitzer Batteries, the 1st King's African
Rifles and two naval armoured cars, and the 5th, 6th,
and 8th Battalions of the 2nd South African Brigade.

At 11.30 a.m. the advance commenced. The
South Africans were to the west and the East Africans
to the east of the road, the right and left flanks resting on the Defu and Soko Nassai Rivers respectively.
Farther to the east was the 3rd South African Brigade,
which had received orders to advance from Euphorbien
Hill.

General Sheppard's intention was to turn the
enemy's right or east flank, and so cut him off from
the River Ruwu. The enemy fought a stubborn
delaying action, taking every advantage of the thick
bush and his intimate knowledge of the ground
through which he was retiring. Shortly before
1 p.m. the leading troops arrived at the edge of an
open tract about half a mile in width, from the far
side of which the enemy poured in a heavy rifle
and machine-gun fire. They found that they were
face to face with a strong prepared position.

The mountain guns were gradually worked forward

into the firing-line, and the South African batteries
came into action at about 1,500 yards in rear, with
their forward observing officers up with the firing-
line at the edge of the clearing. The infantry made
repeated attempts to cross the fire-swept zone,
covered by the fire of the artillery, but were driven
back. The enemy's position was well chosen. In
addition to the irregular line of trenches along the
north side of the bush beyond the clearing, they had
a line on the east, where the bush was continuous,
along the west bank of the Soko Nassai, starting from
the river and curving back towards the main line
of defence. On our side, the bush at this part was
so dense that it was only from the very edge that
anything could be seen. The artillery officers were
compelled to climb trees in some cases to see anything of the targets on which they were directing
their fire, while it was quite impossible to locate
the enemy's flanking position along the Soko Nassai,
and it could only be guessed at. In addition to the
4·1-inch gun to the south of the Ruwu, which when it
was not directed on the Mounted Brigade was turned
on the attacking infantry, there was a second 4·1-inch
gun mounted on a railway-truck, some distance
south of the river, which kept up a continuous fire
on the dust caused by the advancing infantry, and
later by the vehicles (ambulance, ammunition, etc.)
working in rear of the advancing troops. The enemy
had in addition pom-poms and field-guns at different
points along his position which were in action throughout the day, but were not located.

· The bush between Euphorbien and the Soko
Nassai was so dense that the 3rd Brigade were
practically held up and never succeeded in reaching
the scene of the fighting. General Sheppard, who

had the whole of his force in the space between the
Defu and Soko Nassai Rivers, a breadth of about
one and a half miles, then sent half the 129th Baluchis
across the Soko Nassai with orders to turn the enemy's
right.   They crossed the river and advanced a certain
distance, but were held up by enemy fire, directed
on them from the vicinity of the river-bank.

The work of the 27th Mountain Battery, of which
two sections were in action to the west and one to
the east of the road, was remarkably good.   From
the commencement of the attack on the enemy's
position they were in action in the infantry firing-line.
Their shields were covered with the marks of the
enemy bullets.   They kept up a heavy fire till darkness put an end to the fighting.

It was unfortunate that General Sheppard never
learned that General Van Deventer had occupied
Kahe station, some two to three miles in advance of
his right flank.   Owing to the dense bush, communication was never opened between them.

At 6 p.m. the 1st and 3rd South African Batteries
were ordered back to camp.   The infantry dug in
where they were, the 27th Battery remaining " in
action " throughout the night.   General Sheppard's
intention was to renew the attack at dawn, but it
was found that the enemy had slipped away under
cover of darkness, and patrols reported that he had
retired by the road alongside the railway towards
Lembeni.   The 4·1-inch gun which had been in
action just south of the Ruwu was on a fixed mount-
ing, and was blown up and abandoned by the enemy.
The wagon-bridge over the Ruwu was left intact.
During the night the Rasthaus force had also been
withdrawn, and we were now in possession of all
the country to the north of the Ruwu River.

The casualties in General Sheppard's force amounted to about 300. The enemy's losses were not known, but he had undoubtedly suffered heavily. At the foot of Rasthaus Hill, which was occupied by us on the 22nd, there were a number of graves, the result of the fighting on the 18th and 19th.

In the vicinity of Kingarunga, near where the Ruwu flows out of Lake Jipe, there was a causeway which led through the swamp from the Kingarunga Hill to a narrow bridge across the river. The enemy had put up a blockhouse on the south bank, and was still in possession of this crossing. It was necessary to drive him out of this position, which was rather close to our line of communications. Accordingly on the 22nd, the day that Rasthaus was occupied, a detachment of Kashmiris, supported by a section of No. 8 Battery, was sent from Taveta. The guns took up a position in the vicinity of Kingarunga, and, covered by their fire, the infantry advanced to the river. They were met by fire from the blockhouse and the edge of the bush on the south side of the river. The infantry took up a line close to the river-bank at close rifle-range, and, aided by the guns, the enemy was soon forced to retire and the bridge was destroyed.

Posts were now established along the Ruwu from Lake Jipe to Kahe. The river is a considerable obstacle, being about thirty feet wide and fifteen to twenty feet deep, in addition to which it abounds with crocodiles.

On the 21st Aruscha was occupied by Major de Jager with Van Deventer's Scouts.

The whole area to the north of the Ruwu, including Kilimanjaro and Mount Meru and the Moschi and Aruscha administrative districts, was now in our

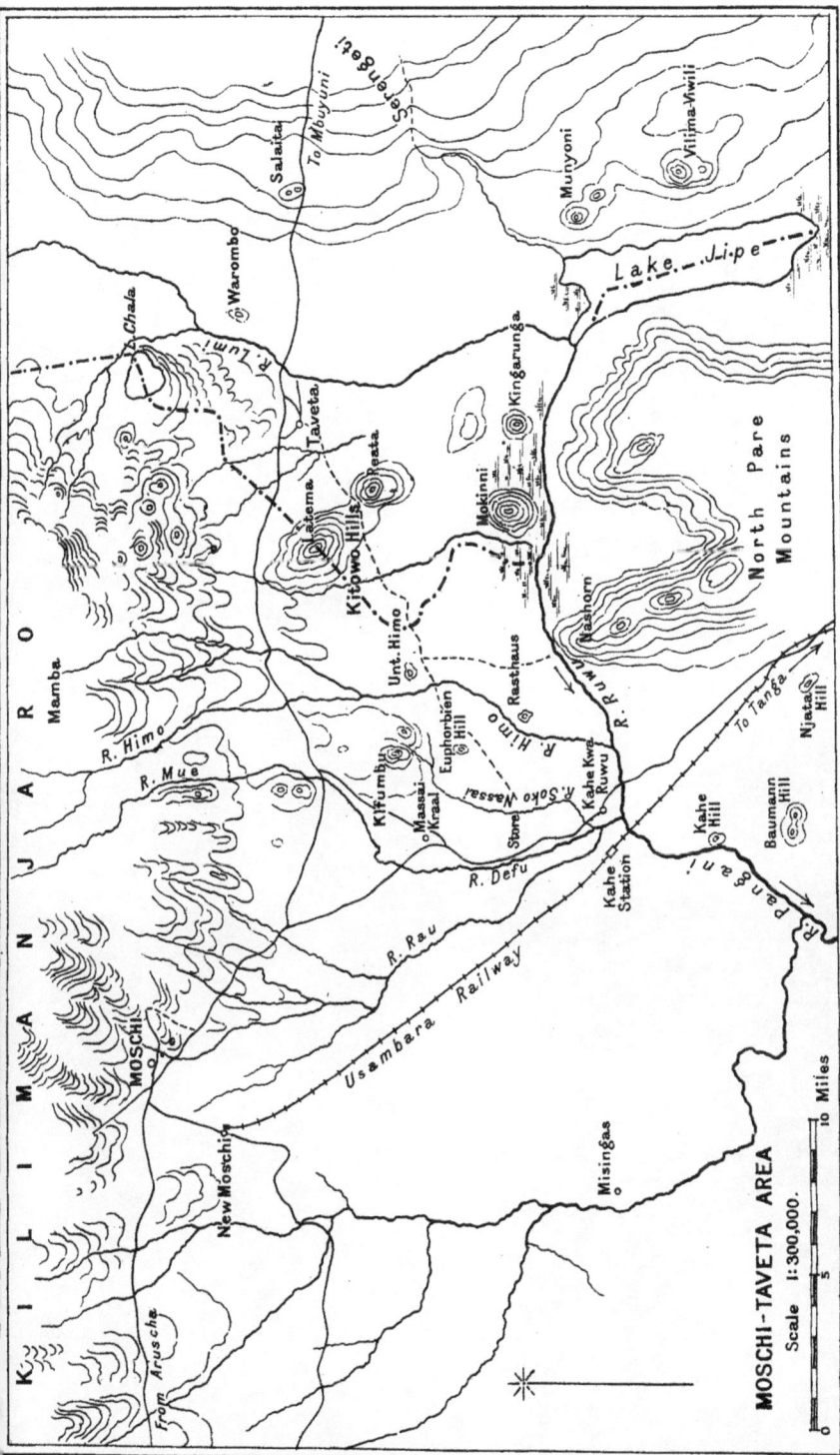

MOSCHI–TAVETA AREA

Scale 1:300,000.

0   5   10 Miles

hands, and, what was important, the railway from New Moschi as far as the Pangani. A firm footing had been obtained in the enemy's country (about 4,500 square miles were in our possession), and a suitable forward base for carrying out the necessary preparations for a forward move when the climatic conditions rendered it possible had been secured.

CHAPTER VII

As regards the immediate future, our operations were dependent on weather. The important point to be determined was when the rains would begin, and when they did begin how long they would last. In a normal season the rains burst about the middle of March. It was the first week of March before operations commenced. General Smuts had determined to take the risk, make his first push, and endeavour to occupy Moschi and drive the enemy out of British territory before the rains burst. Providence had been on his side. He had not only occupied Moschi, but the whole of the Aruscha district, and had driven the enemy beyond the Ruwu River. We were at the end of March and the rains had not yet come. The British forces must, of course, remain in occupation of the territory gained, and it was necessary to make good the line of communications in rear, to ensure their supply during the rains, while they would presumably remain stationary.

The transport question was the great problem throughout the campaign. Once the rains commenced, there would no longer be any possibility of using motor transport. From the experience we already had, we knew that the roads, or tracks, became absolute quagmires, not inches, but feet deep in mud as the result of heavy rain. It was essential that the railway should be pushed on from Serengeti over the Lumi and the low-lying swampy country on either side of it. We were in possession of the Usambara line from New Moschi as far as the Pangani. Once our own railway was joined up with it, there would be little difficulty in supplying the troops holding the line of the Ruwu and spread along the slopes of Kilimanjaro and Meru.

The railway engineers at once proceeded to make surveys of the intervening country. It was decided that the best line to take was some distance below the road, and consequently nearer the river. The ground was naturally more swampy, but it was considered that it would be easier to deal with this than with the earth work and the considerable obstacles offered by the tributary rivers, which flowed through deeper channels higher up the slopes.

The road from New Moschi on to Aruscha also promised to give trouble. Here, again, there were many stream and river beds to be crossed and long stretches of swamp to be negotiated by the transport which would have to be used on this section. There was, however, an alternative on this side in the line which ran to the west of Kilimanjaro from Longido, the route which had been followed by the 1st Division in their original advance. Although this area was not very far away, the rains there were known to be very slight, and it would be rarely that transport could not move by this route.

All transport, including that of the artillery, was now hard at work getting forward supplies. Troops west of the Himo River were dependent on the crib pier bridge, which had been put up as a makeshift till such time as the proper bridge, which the enemy had very thoroughly demolished, could be made good. The crib bridge was at the site of the old ford, which was approached by steep and circuitous deviations from the road. There was consequently considerable delay at this veritable defile. The stone piers of the old bridge had been dynamited, and the whole of the superstructure destroyed. The engineers were hard at work, night and day, having quickly installed electric light. Although there were other bad spots along the road, the Himo bridge was the neck of the bottle and causing considerable delay.

General Smuts now decided on a reorganisation of the force. The troops had till this time been organised in two divisions, the 1st under General Stewart, consisting virtually of a mixed brigade, while the 2nd, under General Tighe, had been considerably added to and embraced the remainder of the force, except what was with General Van Deventer, whose command was detached.

Under the new organisation there were three divisions: 1st Division under Major-General Hoskins, who had just arrived in the country, consisting of two infantry brigades, composed of British, Indian, and East African units, with artillery and the mounted troops not from South Africa.

2nd Division under Major-General Van Deventer, consisting of the 3rd Mounted Brigade, commanded by Brigadier-General Manie Botha, and the 3rd South African Infantry Brigade.

3rd Division under Major-General Brits, comprising the 2nd South African Mounted Brigade, which was then on its way from the Cape under General Brits, and the 2nd South African Infantry Brigade. The details of the force according to this reorganisation will be found in Appendix A.

It was now necessary to find quarters for the troops

with a view to the approaching rains. The principal points to be considered were, the health of the men, facility of supply under all eventualities, and the defeating of any attempts of the enemy to interfere with our lines of communications.

It was all-important to encamp the men as far as possible from the well-known malarial swamps in the vicinity of the rivers, and the animals, where practicable, above the level of " fly." It was, of course, necessary to hold the line of the Ruwu against the enemy, who were in the mountains on the far side.

On March 23rd the Mounted Brigade had been moved back from the Pangani, where they had encamped in the vicinity of Kahe, to New Moschi, and on the 28th they moved on to Aruscha, where the headquarters of the 2nd Division were established. The 3rd South African Infantry Brigade followed a few days later.

The headquarters of the 1st Division were established at Mbuyuni, which had already proved itself to be a healthy spot, and was later selected as the site of one of the lines of communication hospitals. The 2nd East African Brigade was ordered to remain at New Moschi for the time being, and the 27th Mountain Battery was kept in a camp which was selected at the Mission Station about a mile above the fort at Old Moschi. The remainder of the division was concentrated at Mbuyuni.

Brigadier-General Beves with the 2nd South African Infantry Brigade camped in the foot-hills about a mile above the Himo crossing, and with them the Army artillery.

General Headquarters were established at Old Moschi, which they occupied on March 27th. The offices, which had just been vacated by the civil administration of the district, were well suited to the requirements of headquarters. There were a German hospital and a block of hotel buildings which were taken over by our medical officers for a hospital and were unfortunately very soon filled by our sick. The outpost work along the Ruwu and the days which had been spent in the low ground about Taveta accounted for the influx of fever cases.

Old Moschi is charmingly situated on a spur of Kilimanjaro. It is 4,800 feet above the sea, and the climate is cool and very healthy. Beyond the old fort and some half-dozen small bungalows, there are no buildings except the hotel and hospital and a few native huts, with the usual stores kept by the Hindoo traders to be found all over German East. The scenery reminded one of that of a Himalayan hill-station, but there is much more ground under cultivation than is usual in the Indian hills. Looking up the mountain as far as one can see, the slopes are covered with native "shambas," plantations of bananas, beans, and sweet potatoes. The lower slopes are not cleared and are still covered with thick bush. At and above the level of the settlement there are no mosquitoes and it is beyond the range of " fly."

Old Moschi had been the scene of some bloody engagements in the early days of the German occupation. The old Wajagga Chief had a fort on the site of the present building. The Germans came with a strong force, backed by guns, demolished the fort, and massacred the Chief and all his relations. They then built the fort which we now occupied.

It consisted of a wall, about twelve feet high, of stone and clay, rectangular in plan, loopholed all round, and enclosing the offices, stores, guard-room, etc. The offices and the officers' mess were in the upper story, which is surrounded by a wide verandah, from which there is a glorious view of the country round. To the west lay Mount Meru, to the south-west the steep slopes of the Lossongoi Plateau, and to the south and south-east the Pare Mountains, with the valley of the Pangani between them, stretching away towards the sea as far as the eye can see.

Old Moschi was at one time the headquarters also of the military district, but latterly they had been transferred to Aruscha.

New Moschi, the terminus of the railway, is some five miles away in the plain below. Old Moschi was destined to be the seat of General Headquarters for some weeks. Exhaustive reconnaissances had to be carried out, the line of railway to be joined up with the Usambara line, supplies, stores, etc., to be accumulated for the next advance as soon as the weather should render it feasible. New Moschi, the railhead, was naturally the spot selected in the first instance for an advanced depot, and here the motor transport and engineers set up their shops.

According to the information obtained, the enemy's forces were now assembled in the Pare Mountains and along the line towards Tanga. A small force had been located by the patrols of the Mounted Brigade, holding a position at Lol Kissale, but there was no sign of any other enemy force in the Aruscha district. General Smuts determined to send the Mounted Brigade to clear out this enemy detachment from Lol Kissale, which is about thirty-five miles south of Aruscha.

On April 2nd the 4th South African Horse were ordered to Engare Olmotoni, to protect the depot which had been formed there; and on the following day the remainder of the Mounted Brigade, with the

2nd and 4th South African batteries, marched at noon for Lol Kissale. It was known that the enemy position covered the springs on the hill and there was no other water to be had in the neighbourhood. Consequently, before any forward move could be made on this line it was essential that we should occupy the hill.

At about 8.30 a.m. on the 4th, General Van Deventer was in touch with the enemy. They were found to be occupying positions on the northern and north-western slopes of Lol Kissale Hill. They were well concealed and difficult to locate. The northern slopes were covered with huge boulders, trees, and bush. The perimeter of the base of the hill was about six miles.

The 2nd and 4th Batteries were brought into action from the north and north-east respectively. As the dismounted cavalry approached, the enemy opened a heavy machine-gun fire.

One of the machine guns was silenced at about 10 a.m. by the fire of No. 2 Battery. It was afterwards found that the whole detachment had been either killed or wounded. A second machine gun, though not definitely located, was silenced a little later by sweeping and searching fire. The 1st and 3rd South African Horse advanced and engaged the enemy, covered by the fire of the two batteries. Meanwhile, the 2nd South African Horse made their way round to the south of the hill and commenced the ascent with a view to encircling the enemy. They received information of what was happening, and made several attempts to occupy the summit and secure a line of retreat, sending small parties up the northern slope, but they were always barred by the fire of our guns.

The following day the guns were in action again at 4.30 a.m. A machine gun, which opened fire from a new position, was quickly silenced by No. 2 Battery. The 2nd South African Horse during the day succeeded in establishing themselves on a line to the south of the position, and during the night of the 5th/6th gradually closed in.

At dawn the following day the enemy surrendered, and men and animals were able to get to the water. They had had none since leaving Aruscha.

The force taken consisted of seventeen whites and 414 natives, with two machine guns.

In addition to the prisoners, a considerable quantity of stores, ammunition, and pack animals fell into our hands.

The Mounted Brigade ammunition column, which had followed behind, joined up on the night of the 5th/6th.

On April 7th the first two battalions of the 3rd South African Infantry Brigade, which had followed the Mounted Brigade, arrived at Aruscha.

From the reports of prisoners and from captured documents it was learned that the enemy was about to reinforce the garrisons at Kondoa Irangi and Ufiome, with the object of barring our advance by that route to the Central line. It was obviously very advisable to occupy Kondoa Irangi, the most important road centre and junction east of the Central railway line, which it directly threatened, and if possible to forestall the enemy there. They were bound to protect the Central line, and to do so would of necessity be compelled to withdraw troops from the mountain region to the north.

We were in possession of the official German weather reports, according to which the average rainfall for a number of years in the Kondoa district was rather less than three and a half inches. General Smuts accordingly decided to push on the 2nd Division and occupy Mbulu, Ufiome, and Kondoa Irangi before the enemy's reinforcements could arrive.

Orders to this effect were issued, and on the 8th, at 6 p.m., the mounted portion of the 2nd Division started from Lol Kissale, arriving at Tarangire at 1 p.m. on the following day. Enemy patrols were active, and each day a certain number of enemy were disposed of or captured. The force halted at Tarangire till the 11th, when the march was resumed at 9 a.m.

They encamped that night about ten miles north of Ufiome, which was reached at 3 p.m. on the 12th. Meanwhile, the 4th South African Horse was ordered forward from Engare Olmotoni, and a battalion of the 3rd Infantry Brigade joined the mounted troops. On the 12th the rain began to fall and it poured incessantly from that time onwards. The consequence was that progress was slow and very difficult.

On April 13th the march was resumed, and Galai was reached at 7 p.m., after a fourteen-hours march. Here the force halted till the 16th.

Meanwhile, the 10th South African Infantry, accompanied by the 28th Mountain Battery, had been called up from Engare Olmotoni to Umbugwe, and were ordered to attack the enemy post commanding the pass over the Iraku ridge on the road leading from Umbugwe to Mbulu.

Lieutenant-Colonel Montgomery, the officer commanding the 10th Infantry, decided to make a wide turning movement with the bulk of the force, while Lieutenant-Colonel Davies, the commander of the battery, with a company of the infantry and a section

of machine guns attacked in front.   The frontal attack
was developed at about half past three in the afternoon of the 9th.   The infantry advanced, subjected
to fire from snipers who were in position along the
crest of the Iraku Hills.   The advanced guard occupied
a position at less than 1,000 yards from the enemy's
position, but could not get on, as the fire of the snipers
was accurate.   At sunset the advanced guard commander withdrew his men to the ridge occupied by
the guns, at about 1,000 yards' range.

At about 10 p.m. Lieutenant-Colonel Davies decided
to make a night attack, and the infantry were ordered
to endeavour to cross the exposed tract of ground
and occupy a position beyond it.   At the same time
a few scouts were sent forward to make a close
reconnaissance of the enemy's position.   By 1.30 a.m.
the infantry were in possession of the ridge, the
enemy having retired, abandoning their camp.   The
main body under Lieutenant-Colonel Montgomery
arrived about noon.   The enemy had made off in
the direction of Tabora.   They had suffered a certain
amount, according to the natives, both among their
whites and coloured troops.   They evacuated Mbulu
fort at 11 a.m. on the 10th, and it was occupied by
our troops.

The Mounted Brigade resumed their advance on the
16th, and on the 17th camped six miles north of
Kondoa Irangi.   The enemy was found to be holding
a position about two miles farther on, across the
hills either side of the valley running down to the
town.   A reconnaissance was made by General Van
Deventer the following morning.   The artillery was
brought into action in covered positions against the
enemy in the valley and the positions on the hills to
either flank.

Owing to the heavy rain, movement was very difficult, and it was necessary to put double teams into the guns. One section of No. 2 Battery succeeded in getting to a point from which they could bring a reverse fire to bear on the enemy holding the hills to the west. The result was that the enemy vacated all their advanced positions, and during their retirement were subjected to a heavy and well-directed fire from all the guns of both batteries. Owing to the heavy rain, observation of fire was difficult. A section of No. 2 Battery followed up, but the guns of No. 4 Battery sank axle-deep in the soft ground. The advance of the mounted troops was continued. At 4 p.m. the 3rd South African Horse, which was on the extreme left, was held up by a heavy fire from a strong position on the hills to the east of Kondoa Irangi. A section of the 2nd Battery was brought into action against this position, but the mist, which had alternated with the rain throughout the day, now became so dense that it was impossible to do any effective work with the guns, and the artillery was ordered to return to camp.

At 9 a.m. the following day, the 19th, the 4th Battery was again brought into action against the position east of the town. At the same time the advanced guard moved forward down the valley, supported by the remainder of the guns. The enemy rearguard were then holding a ridge to the south of the town. The opposition was short-lived, and before noon the enemy were observed retiring south along the Dodoma road. General Van Deventer occupied the town at noon.

The operations had been particularly trying throughout. There had been no rations, either for men or animals. The former had subsisted on what meat and meal they could collect, and the horses and mules had had nothing but mealie stalks and grass. The rain had been incessant and it had been rarely possible to do any cooking.

The enemy's losses had not been very heavy, but his force had not been large. He had about fifty killed and wounded, and we took prisoners four whites and thirty Askaris. He had destroyed his wireless station and a large quantity of his stores before he left, but some eighty rifles, a quantity of ammunition, and 800 cattle fell into our hands.

There was not a single casualty among the mounted troops, which spoke volumes for the skill of the commander and for the effective work of our guns.

On April 20th General Van Deventer moved down the Dodoma road with a mounted force and a section of guns. They went on some ten miles, but nothing was to be seen of the enemy, and they returned to Kondoa, where the whole force encamped that night.

Orders were then received from General Headquarters to rest men and horses, but to endeavour to maintain contact with the enemy, and to scout towards the railway, Ssingida, Mkalama, and Handeni. The losses in horses and mules had been heavy. During the operations 140 horses and fifty mules had succumbed. These had to be replaced. There was no possibility of pushing on any farther. A deluge of rain had fallen and was falling. The rivers were in flood, the dongas were rivers, the black cotton and red clay soil had all become swamp. The force was practically cut off from Moschi. The distance from Moschi to Aruscha alone is some sixty miles, and the road was quite impassable for wheeled traffic. Fortunately there was a month's supplies accumulated at Longido, and that saved the situation.

It was possible to move by the Longido line via Aruscha to Lol Kissale, and from there on porters had to be employed. General Van Deventer had collected about 7,000. The actual number registered in the area was 15,000, but the Germans had impressed the remainder.

There was no question of starvation. Kondoa Irangi is a very rich district, in which there were plenty of cattle to be found. Meanwhile, supplies were pushed up from Longido. As a result of reconnaissances a new route was found and opened from Sanga to Lol Kissale, which was not only better as regards the physical obstacles, rivers, etc., but was shorter than the old Aruscha route. It, however, took some weeks before the necessary bridging work, etc., on this new route made it fit for use.

Meanwhile, the forces at Kondoa were not idle. Patrols working along the Handeni and Dodoma roads captured depots of supplies and the posts in charge of them. Reconnoitring work was being done in all directions. The troops were suffering considerable hardships. They had no tents and their kits, owing to lack of transport, had been left behind at Himo. They were very short of supplies and their boots were giving out.

By May 1st the 4th South African Horse, the 9th, 11th, and 12th South African Infantry, a howitzer battery, and the East African Machine Gun Company had arrived at Kondoa. The 2nd South African Horse had been sent to co-operate with the 10th Infantry and 28th Mountain Battery against the Mbulu escarpment.

There had been frequent little patrol affairs around Kondoa, in which our troops had generally succeeded in getting the best of it. Eventually, on May 6th,

the enemy was reported to be advancing in strength
from the south. Our patrols on the Saranda road
were ordered to fall back before them to the west of
the Bubu River. The troops at Kondoa were now in
occupation of a defensive position on a front of about
five miles.

On May 7th the enemy were reported to be within
six miles of the camp and our patrols were in touch
with their advanced guard.

On May 9th the enemy occupied all the high ground
to the south-east of Kondoa, having driven back
our piquets. At about four p.m. they opened fire
at long range with a naval 4·1-inch gun. At dusk
they were observed descending the hills to the north
of the Dodoma road. At about 8 p.m. they made
a determined attack, supported by machine-gun fire,
on our centre. They got close to our line, but did
not succeed in gaining a footing in the position. At
about 10.30 p.m., having gradually worked a force
round to the east, they made a strong attack on our
left flank, but were driven back. Meanwhile, they
kept up a continuous gun fire with their 4·1-inch and
field guns on the village. At 11 p.m. the 12th South
African Infantry moved down the valley running to
the south-west and threatened the enemy's left flank.
The fighting went on till about half past two, when
the enemy withdrew. He had made four determined
onslaughts, all of which had been beaten back. Firing
had ceased by a little after 3 a.m.

Our casualties were less than fifty. The enemy
left over sixty dead on the ground, and many cart-
loads of killed and wounded had been taken away.
We captured a few Askaris.

The effect of the defeat was that from this time
on, the fighting at Kondoa, so far as the enemy was

concerned, was confined to long-range artillery work. As was afterwards learned, Von Lettow, the German commander, had been present. The German losses had exceeded 150, among them several well-known officers. When they retired they left a considerable quantity of equipment on the ground and ammunition (dated 1915, which had been brought in by the blockade runners). They had tried their usual ruses, shouting " Don't fire ! This is ' A ' company," etc. When they made their first big onslaught their war-cry had been " Deutschland über Alles."

The 11th South African Infantry had borne the brunt of the attack, supported by the 12th South African Infantry. The heavy fire at short range had lasted about eight hours.

After this attack our forces set to work to strengthen their defences, which had previously been none too formidable. The Commander-in-Chief decided to re-inforce General Van Deventer and sent up two battalions, the 7th and 8th, of the 2nd South African Infantry Brigade, belonging to the 3rd Division, and the 1st South African battery. Later he was still further reinforced by the 10th 4-inch Battery and a section of the 38th Howitzer Brigade. These reinforcements reached Kondoa during the last week of May. There was daily artillery bombardment, and the German 4·1-inch guns had been able to out-range any guns that we had there till the 4-inch battery arrived. From this time onwards there was constant outpost and patrol work, but the enemy did not attempt another serious attack and our guns could more than hold their own.

On May 18th a report was received that the 10th South African Infantry with the 28th Battery had occupied Mbulu. The casualties had been very light. These troops were then ordered forward to Kondoa, and a squadron was left at Mbulu with orders to patrol towards Mkalama, Ssingida, and south of the escarpment.

An advanced depot was ordered to be formed at Ufiume. The rains were getting lighter, and the roads were consequently improving. The new road from Moschi to Lol Kissale, which was now working, considerably shortened the distance.

CHAPTER VIII

DOWN THE PANGANI

WHILE the troops under General Van Deventer had been engaged in the advance to Kondoa Irangi, the remainder of the forces had been resting in the positions taken up at the end of March and holding the line of the Ruwu River.

The rains had burst about the middle of April and were particularly heavy in the Kilimanjaro area. At Moschi there was no less than twenty-seven inches recorded during the month of April, most of which fell during the latter half of the month. The rivers were in flood, and what were dry nullahs became roaring torrents which swept away the temporary bridges on which our road transport depended.

Fortunately by the end of April the railway extension was nearing the Kahe line, and it had been possible to dump supplies at Taveta and other points along the route for the feeding of the troops west of the Lumi. Any form of wheeled transport was as a rule out of the question, and supplies could only be carried to the camps by means of porters. The mud and the greasy, slippery surface of the roads made their rate of movement very slow, and they could only manage the lightest loads. When there was a lull in the rains it was of course possible to use mule wagons.

The distance from Taveta to Kahe was over twenty

miles, a great part of it through what had become swamp. Every day the low-lying country became more water-logged. The rails disappeared under water over long stretches. Thousands of labourers were constantly employed building them up with brushwood and reeds. Notwithstanding their immense difficulties, the railway engineers succeeded in keeping the trains running and conveying the necessary supplies. The journey between Taveta and New Moschi, twenty miles of which, from Taveta to Kahe, was over the new line, took as much as ten hours to accomplish, but the trains got through. Owing to the rapidity of our advance the enemy had not had time to do much damage to the existing line from New Moschi to Kahe, and this section was good going in all weathers.

About the middle of May the rains were becoming appreciably lighter and there was every probability that active operations could be resumed in the near future. The situation was then as follows : The 1st Division (less the 2nd East African Brigade, at New Moschi) was at Mbuyuni ; the 2nd South African Infantry Brigade was about Himo, but two battalions had left to join the 2nd Division at Kondoa ; the 2nd Division, with some batteries of the 3rd Division and of the Army artillery, at Kondoa, under General Van Deventer, and the two battalions of South Africans which were *en route* to join him. In the Lake district was a force consisting of the 98th Indian Infantry, the 4th King's African Rifles, the Baganda Rifles and Nandi Scouts, about 2,000 rifles in all, under Brigadier-General Sir Charles Crewe ; the Belgian forces were advancing through the Ruanda district from the north of Lake Kiwu and the line of the Russisi, driving before them a force under

Wintgens, and had occupied Kigali on May 6th. Brigadier-General Northey was on the Nyassaland border making preparations to advance.

The enemy had transferred a large portion of his force, which had been assembled in the Pare Mountains, to oppose the advance by Kondoa Irangi. After his attack early in May he had remained facing our extended position about Kondoa. In the Pare Mountains and back along the Tanga line, it was estimated that the enemy's forces did not exceed 2,000, with guns.

The next step was to clear the Usambara line to the sea, and so remove all risk of interference with our communications by the Uganda Railway and the Voi-Maktau line, with a view to an advance to the Central Railway.

The average distance from the Usambara to the Central line is about 200 miles. The two most important centres as road junctions in this tract of country are, Kondoa Irangi, already in our hands, and Handeni, opposite Korogwe, near the coast. The German line of communications between the Usambara-Pare theatre and the Central line ran through Handeni to Mombo, at the foot of the mountains just below Wilhelmstal. Mombo and Handeni were connected by a tram line. Kondoa Irangi and Handeni might be considered the strategic centres of this vast tract of country.

In considering the future plan of operations our object must be kept in view. It is always the same, to seek out and defeat the enemy's forces in the field and, to achieve this, to bring him to battle. If his object is not so much to fight as to delay, it is necessary to threaten the vulnerable points which he will consider it essential to defend.

In the East African campaign the problem was
rendered difficult owing to the vastness of the country
and the comparative smallness of the forces engaged.
As before pointed out, the enemy was extremely
mobile, and his supply problems were made easy by
the fact that his troops were natives of the country,
and could find a certain amount of such food as
they were accustomed to in every native village they
entered, while our troops were dependent on supplies
which had to be brought for the most part oversea,
and then along hundreds of miles of communications.
So far we had succeeded in protecting the railway
lines on which we depended. They were our most
vulnerable point, and their security must always be
our first consideration.

When the advance began, transport would be our
great difficulty. Once we crossed the Ruwu (or
Pangani), we could not count on a railway. We
could be certain that the enemy would take care
to destroy his lines of rail before we reached them,
that their repair would take a considerable time,
and even when they were repaired there was the
200 miles of practically primæval forest to be
crossed between the Usambara and the Central line,
for which we must depend on motors, porters, and
animals.

It would be sufficient to think ahead as far as
that Central line, along which lay all the enemy's
principal settlements and present supply depots :
Dar-es-Salaam, Morogoro, Kilossa, Dodoma, Kilimatinde, Tabora, etc. When we were in possession
of that line and the country to the north of it, it
would be time enough to study the problems of the
next phase of the campaign. For the time being
this Central line was of the greatest importance to

him, and the best chance of bringing him to battle was to advance against it.

There were several courses open :

(1) A combined sea and land attack on Tanga.

The necessary shipping could be assembled at Mombasa. Although the sea during the monsoon, in fact till October, was reported to be rough and landing not an easy matter, still it could doubtless have been managed in the sheltered bays which are just to the north of Tanga. It was no longer the problem that confronted us at the beginning of March, when the enemy was all assembled in this theatre, and it was for consideration whether our object would best be achieved by an attack through the Taveta Gap or repeating our previous attempts on Tanga. Not only did we now hold the western end of the line and were in occupation of the Kilimanjaro and Meru areas, but we had a force at Kondoa with some 250 miles of a precarious line of communications between it and Moschi. That force had suffered considerably in men and animals from sickness, largely owing to the privations they had undergone. They had repelled one attack in force with heavy loss to the enemy. It was not likely that the enemy would repeat the experiment, but at the same time it was not desirable to transfer our remaining force, or the bulk of it, out of supporting distance, on a plan by which pressure would be relaxed for a certain time. It was desirable that the pressure should be maintained steadily and certainly, not reduced for however short a time. Also the enemy would be able to retire into the mountains from Tanga, and the great point was to clear them and render our line of communications safe before advancing to the Central line. The occupation of Tanga itself was no asset at this stage.

It is to be noted that the enemy could always transfer troops from a point on the Central line to the northern theatre in from a fortnight to three weeks, and that one of the few good roads in German East Africa was that from Handeni to Kondoa. This distance could be covered in about twelve days. To obviate the enemy's advantage of interior lines it was essential that the next blow should be delivered rapidly and that the pressure should be felt at once. An attack on Tanga obviously did not meet these requirements.

(2) A move by sea and direct attack on Dar-es-Salaam.

In the campaign in German South-west Africa the policy of taking a port and then advancing inland, making use of the railway as the line of supply, had been adopted. Merely looking at the map, it was a plan of operations which would naturally suggest itself. We had undisputed command of the sea, and, as said above, there would probably be no difficulty about the necessary shipping for the transfer of the force. There were, however, very strong reasons against this plan of action. In the first place, the climate along the coast of German East Africa is particularly deadly, as we learned from our experiences in the previous year, when an advance was made from Mombasa against Tanga by land. There was no chance of capturing Dar-es-Salaam by a *coup de main*. There is no sheltered landing-place in the vicinity where a landing could be safely carried out at this season of the year. Doubtless a landing could have been effected on the open beach at Bagamoyo and a base established there, but the enemy had expended much time and energy on the defences of Dar-es-Salaam, and it would have been a matter of laying siege to the town. Dar-es-Salaam is surrounded by swamps, and just after the rains the country would have been one huge swamp. The enemy could very quickly have concentrated a sufficient force for the manning of the defences (the outer line of which ran along the inner line of the swamps) and offered a protracted resistance, during which our forces would have been reduced to one-half by fever. This would have taken much time, and meanwhile the enemy would have been free for such operations as he chose against the Kondoa force and the Uganda Railway.

(3) The third alternative was an advance down the valley of the Pangani. The possibility of attacking the enemy in the mountains would be a difficult and very costly undertaking, and to attempt to advance by the road and railway, against the lines of defence which the enemy had prepared at intervals along the route, were courses which it is not necessary to consider. The enemy expected an advance down this valley, and his idea was that the advance would be by the road and railway, and it was against this that he had prepared. The Pangani flows at about twenty miles' distance from the mountains, and the intervening country is covered by dense bush, with only an occasional track leading through to the river. The enemy obviously counted on the troops in the mountains offering sufficient resistance to enable him to transfer troops to reinforce him, should they be required, from other theatres.

General Smuts's plan was to cause the enemy to evacuate the Pare Mountains, and to occupy Handeni by an advance down the river-bank before the enemy had time to send across reinforcements. The conception was so bold that it is not surprising that it had not entered into the enemy's calculations. The Pangani, a swift-flowing, deep river, would be an impassable obstacle on the right flank of the advance, which would be hemmed in by the dense bush on the other flank, while the troops would have to cut and make the road through the bush and across the nullahs as they went along. If the plan was to be a success, it was essential that it should be executed rapidly.

During the previous weeks scouts had been reconnoitring the country through which it was proposed to move, and the Commander-in-Chief was in possession of trustworthy and detailed reports. The enemy were known to be occupying camps at Schigatini and other places in the mountains, and strong defensive positions had been prepared, at Njata and Loami Hills, and at Kissangire and Lembeni (near the stations), which extended across the road and railway and connected with the western slopes of the Pares. The Ngulu Gap, between the Northern and Middle Pare Ranges, was fortified, and doubtless the enemy considered his position a safe one.

General Smuts's plan was to advance in three columns. The main body was to move down the left bank of the Pangani; a small column, consisting of the King's African Rifles Mounted Infantry Company, the 3rd King's African Rifles, and a section of the 27th Mountain Battery, under Lieutenant-Colonel T. O. Fitzgerald, was to advance direct from Mbuyuni to the Ngulu Gap; while a third column, consisting of the 6th and 7th Field Batteries, 40th Pathans, 129th Baluchis, and 2nd Kashmir Rifles, under Brigadier-General Hannyngton, the commander of the 2nd East African Infantry Brigade, was to follow the railway line. The advance of Fitzgerald's column

and the main body along the Pangani were relied
on to cause the enemy to evacuate his positions across
the railway, which barred the road along the northern
Pares.   If he did not go, he would find himself cut
off.   Colonel Fitzgerald was to join General Hannyngton at the Same Gap between the Middle and South
Pares.

The main body and Hannyngton's column were
concentrated in the vicinity of Kahe Kwa Ruwu on
May 21st. Colonel Fitzgerald's column had of
necessity to start earlier and left Mbuyuni for the
Ngulu Gap on the 18th. General Headquarters
moved from Moschi to Kahe station on the 22nd.

Our troops had been holding the line of the river
since the fighting at the end of March.   A mile below
the station was the wreckage of the railway-bridge
over the Pangani, which the enemy had blown up
on the morning of March 21st; but a new bridge
had been constructed by the engineers one hundred
yards higher up the river, which was connected with
the old line half a mile back, and was ready for traffic.

A quantity of supplies had been accumulated at
" Store," near Kahe Kwa Ruwu, which were shortly
to be moved to the south bank of the river.   Everything was in readiness for the forward move.

That afternoon General Smuts assembled the
Generals for the last time to ensure that everyone
thoroughly understood what was expected of him.
As soon as it was dark, General Hannyngton's column,
consisting of the 40th Pathans, 129th Baluchis, the
Kashmiris, and Nos. 6 and 7 Batteries, started. (It
must be remembered that in these latitudes there is
no twilight. Day ceases and night begins at about
6 p.m. all the year round.) Before he started the
King's African Rifles Mounted Infantry, who had

been scouting ahead, reported that Njata Hill and
Kissengire had been evacuated by the enemy. By
11 p.m. they were occupied by our troops.

The main body, consisting of General Sheppard's
1st East African Brigade, the balance of the 2nd
East African Brigade, the 27th Mountain Battery
(less one section), and the 5th South African Battery,
with the 5th and 6th South African Infantry, the
134th Howitzer Battery, and the 8th Battery, under
Brigadier-General Beves, as Force Reserve, crossed
the Ruwu bridge at 4 a.m. on the 23rd. With this
column was General Headquarters and the Headquarters of the 1st Division. The column halted
that night about three miles south-west of Baumann
Hill.

The march was resumed the following day, the
24th, at 4 a.m., and after a comparatively short
march, a halt was made in line with the " Rapids,"
in order to give time to the 1st East African Brigade,
which was doing the pioneering, to cut the way
through the bush, which had become very dense.
There were also a series of sandy nullahs to be dealt
with, necessitating a corduroy of brushwood before
it would be possible for any motor transport to get
over them, and this would take some time. The
transport, except that of the South African Infantry,
which was equipped with mule wagons, was mainly
motor-lorries, and sandy tracts were their worst
obstacle.

The route along the Pangani was full of interest,
and in parts was not so bad as might have been
expected. The thick bush and the low hills with
nullahs between, running down to the water edge,
gave heavy work to the troops road-making. There
were occasional open spaces, bare but for scattered

patches of reeds, which had evidently been under water when the river was in flood, but now, though the rains had but just ceased, had a hard-baked surface, which was good going, though the crust broke with a very little traffic and became deep sand, which would be almost impassable in a few days. The only sign of life was the spoor of big game, lion, rhinoceros, hippopotamus and every kind of deer and the snakes, of which a number were accounted for in the different camps.

In the distance, to the east, were the Pare Mountains ; far away now, to the north, was snow-capped Kilimanjaro ; to the west the escarpment of the Massai Steppe.   At night all was still, except for the occasional roar of a lion, and so far there was no sign of the enemy.   He had vacated his forward positions and was doubtless aware of our whereabouts.

We had halted early in the day, and the 1st East African Brigade were toiling without ceasing, making a road in front of us.   One of the armoured cars of Colonel Sir John Willoughby's battery had been pushed on, and its lights used to enable the road-makers to continue their work through the night.

Meanwhile, the central column had continued their advance, and meeting with no opposition had occupied Lembeni, which, as was anticipated, had been evacuated.   They had been in constant touch with enemy patrols, which always retired before them. On the 25th the main column advanced to Marago Opumi, halting for a few hours *en route* at Ruwu Lager, and the following day arrived in the vicinity of Old Le Sara.   In the afternoon an enemy post was located by scouts on the river bank.   They were rounded up by a party of 17th Bengal Cavalry, whose leader, a be-spectacled ex-senior-wrangler

Indian civilian, Lieutenant Ibbertson, proudly marched his capture back to camp, one German and six Askaris with their rifles.

On the 25th General Hannyngton had occupied Same station and on the following day joined hands with Fitzgerald's column at Mandi Hill, about ten miles west of the station. The enemy had now evidently vacated the Northern and Middle Pare Ranges.

On the 27th an early start was made. The Commander-in-Chief had a way of going ahead of the troops and reconnoitring for himself, which caused much anxiety to his Staff, who were unable to keep him back. His first days of soldiering had been passed as a scout and he had great difficulty in restraining himself. On this occasion he was ahead of all the troops, except a few mounted men, and had made his way to the top of a kopje, from which he was spying the country to the front, when some thirty of the enemy were discovered making their way towards the kopje through the bush. It was afterwards learned that this patrol had been run into by our mounted men, and had broken back through the thick bush. General Smuts and his party made a rapid retirement down the rear slope of the hill, their garments suffering from the thorn bush, and got away just in time.

That day the march took the column to in line with Old Schurlul, and the following day to Mhesa. The Pangani now took a turn towards the mountains.

Hannyngton's column, which, having been joined by Fitzgerald, was now to move as one column, was to proceed by Zeri Zeri round the eastern and southern sides of the South Pares, through the Gonya Gap, which would bring them on to the railway about Mkomazi and turn any position which the enemy might possibly elect to hold in the comparatively narrow defile between the mountains and the river, through which the main column had to pass to reach Buiko.

On the 29th General Smuts advanced to Mabirioni and the enemy commenced shelling our leading troops from the direction of Mikocheni, when they were about five or six miles away from the railway. As we reached this point two trains were seen making their way in a southerly direction, while periodical explosions told of the demolition of bridges and culverts. Unfortunately we had no guns which could make the range, and the thick trackless bush absolutely prevented any rapid forward move of such guns as we had.

General Smuts with his Staff rode forward and took up a position under cover of the Mabirioni spur, the enemy's shell passing harmlessly over their heads. The enemy had a 4·1-inch naval gun in action, with which he steadily shelled the route by which our transport was advancing from a long range, and two or three small guns of 6 cm. with which he fired on our leading troops. The track was narrow and the transport was held up during the day. The troops bivouacked where they were, under cover of the outpost line, short of food till the transport reached them, which it did under cover of darkness.

Meanwhile, our reconnoitring patrols were busy, and in the evening brought in information that the enemy was holding an entrenched position about Mikocheni, beyond the bend of the river and extending from the river to the mountains, which rose to a height of about 3,000 feet above the plain.

On the following morning, the 30th, the force

moved forward to attack. The 2nd Rhodesians, under Colonel Capel, with the 29th Punjabis in support, were to move by the river bank against the front of the position, while General Sheppard's brigade with the mountain guns and the 5th South African Battery were to take a northern route to the mountains and, moving across the foot-hills, to turn the enemy's position from the east.

The progress of the 1st East African Brigade through the thick bush was necessarily slow. The going was so bad that the 5th Battery could not get on and had to turn back. Sheppard sent on a double company of the Baluchis with a section of the mountain guns to scale the heights and make their way south along the crest, and they reached the crest. A good climb !

The remainder of the force on reaching the foot-hills turned south.

Meanwhile, the Rhodesians pushed in without waiting the development of the turning movement, drove the enemy out of their front-line trenches, and occupied them.

The bend taken by the river here is very sharp. After running due east for some miles it suddenly turns due south. The enemy's position was just round the bend and facing almost north. The Rhodesian advance along the first stretch was covered by the thick undergrowth and high trees along the river bank, and was evidently unperceived by the enemy, who were probably giving all their attention to Sheppard's movements.

At about 4 p.m. the mountain guns came into action from a position on one of the mountain spurs against a hostile column which they had observed advancing, but their position was in view of the enemy, who at once turned their guns on to them. The mountain gunners were not long changing their position, and in a very short time had silenced the hostile guns and caused the advancing column to turn back.

The enemy had meanwhile made one counter-attack against the trenches which the Rhodesians were occupying, but the Rhodesians had the support of the 29th, and had no difficulty in driving them back. Their expected reinforcements not arriving, about nightfall the enemy retired.

The troops halted where they were for the night, and next morning the enemy had gone. During the night frequent explosions were heard in the direction of Buiko.

On the 31st the advance was continued, and Buiko station occupied. Just in rear of the enemy's recently evacuated Mikocheni position was discovered a newly-built, substantial pile bridge over the Pangani. The enemy had removed the roadway, but the bridge was otherwise intact.

On the way into Buiko we passed one overturned train with its engine, which had been badly damaged. The wreckage had been shifted clear of the rails, and there was little doubt that this had been the work of one of our airmen, who, after a flight some days previously, stated that he felt sure he had hit a train.

Meanwhile, Hannyngton's column had been making its way through the mountains, and on the 29th had occupied Gonya. From that point on it had been impossible to continue to use the road. The enemy had broken it up thoroughly and barred progress every few yards by felled trees, so that General Hannyngton decided to continue his advance by the left bank of the Mkomazi River. He arrived at

Mkomazi station on June 1st. During the 31st an enemy rearguard had opened fire from the station on the far bank on our scouts, and that evening they shelled our camp at Buiko with their 4·1-inch gun, without doing much damage.

It was now absolutely necessary to make a halt. Since they left the Kilimanjaro area the troops, who had most of them spent a certain amount of time in the swamps of the Ruwu before starting, had covered 130 miles under a hot sun. They had had to work hard road-making, in addition to the extra fatigues of the engagement on the 30th. The column which had come through the mountains had had an equally trying time.

Supplies were running very short. Many of the motor-lorries had broken down owing to the bad roads on both routes. It had been necessary to dump ammunition from motor-vehicles which were being used in ammunition columns, and hand them over to supplies. Every motor-vehicle with the force was now requisitioned and rushed back to bring up food.

It was essential that the railway, which the enemy had methodically put out of action, should be repaired by the earliest possible date. The sleepers were of iron, and the chairs were of a peculiar pattern. Over long stretches the sleepers had been removed, and for miles the chairs had entirely disappeared. Except over the last few miles all culverts and bridges had been destroyed. At Buiko station, the principal railway-centre between New Moschi and Tanga, the workshops, water-tanks, all points, etc., had been blown up. The explosions of the previous night had prepared us for this.

It would evidently be some time before the railway would be working again.

II

The few inhabitants left at Buiko, which is only a railway settlement, were the Hindoo traders.

General Smuts was in possession of information which led him to anticipate that the enemy's retirement would be towards Handeni and not down the Usambara. He decided that he would adhere to his original plan, and that Handeni should be his next objective. Instructions were accordingly given for the repair of the " German Bridge " at Mikocheni, and the construction of pontoon bridges at Buiko. Preparations were to be made for the continuation of the advance, by the right bank by the main column, while Hannyngton was to push on down the Usambara towards Mombo.

On June 2nd General Smuts motored back to Moschi and on to Kondoa Irangi to see exactly how matters stood there with General Van Deventer's force, and to explain personally his plans for the future operations.

The German missionaries at Moschi had predicted that it would take us two years to turn their countrymen out of the Pares and Usambara. We had taken less than two weeks to accomplish the first part of the task, so there was every reason to be optimistic.

CHAPTER IX

ADVANCE TO THE NGURU MOUNTAINS

THE halt at Buiko was only to enable the necessary preparations for the further advance to be made. There were no supplies with the force. The troops were on less than half rations till such time as the motor-transport convoy, which had been rushed back to the Kahe depot, should return. It was evident that it would be some time before the railway would be in working order, and it was impossible to wait for it, without sacrificing the advantages we had gained by our rapid advance. It was determined to form a temporary depot at " German Bridge," [1] and make a road to connect it with the railway at Makanja. It was hoped by this means to be able to carry on the supply of the force till the railway was ready to do the work. The making of this road was entrusted to the artillery, and after a preliminary reconnaissance the route was divided into sections, which were allotted to artillery officers, who were to carry out the work with native labour, to be provided by the chiefs of the neighbouring hill tribes. This road was completed by June 6th.

The necessary work on " German Bridge " was soon completed, and the equipment and materials having been hurried forward, the crossings at Buiko, consisting of a Berton boat-bridge, a light raft, and a heavy pontoon raft, were constructed by the Faridkot sappers and miners.

[1] The name given to the bridge built by the enemy at Mikocheni.

On June 3rd the 29th Punjabis had been pushed across the river to make the road on the far side between " German Bridge " and Buiko and on to Mkalamo.

On the 5th the 25th Royal Fusiliers (Driscoll's Scouts) and the 1st Division Ammunition Column passed to the right bank by the light bridge and raft, and the following day Sheppard's Brigade followed them. The troops that were over proceeded to a camping-ground in the vicinity of " Palms." The name " Palms " was given to the camping-ground because the spot in question was marked " Palms " on the large-scale German map. The German surveyor had evidently been there. There was a break in the everlasting bush and a big palm grove along the river-bank, while a number of clumps of palms were scattered about in the parklike pasture which extended for some distance back from the river.

These open spaces by the river edge made delightful camping-grounds. We had been very fortunate throughout our march down the Pangani in finding such open spots for our halts. Sometimes the surface was sandy or baked marshland, but at others it would be covered with short grass and formed an ideal site for a camp. It was then hard to realise that it was neither a private park nor grazing pasture, but country in its natural state, untouched by the hand of man, though useless for the purposes for which it seemed perfectly suited, as no cattle could live there, unless they had a fly-resisting hide, like the rhinoceros or hippopotamus.

The troops were settling down when, in the afternoon, a report was received from the 29th Punjabis, who were now beyond Makayo, that the enemy was advancing against them in force. General Sheppard

at once moved forward with all the troops available
to reinforce the Punjabis, but the enemy force proved
to be only a strong patrol.

A certain quantity of supplies had now been brought
forward, but the rapidity of movement of the convoy
had told on the lorries and still more were reported
out of action. Workshop lorries had been sent on to
" German Bridge " to carry out repairs, which till
this time had been dependent on the workshop of the
134th battery. There was a shortage of spare parts,
and it would be some time before many of them would
be fit for the road again.

On the 8th the column was across the river and
moved by " Palms " to an open space about opposite
to Mheza, where they encamped. The march was
resumed the following day. Scouts had located the
enemy in an entrenched position about a mile to the
north-west of Mkalamo, and the leading brigade
attacked, at the same time sending a detachment to
try to get round the enemy left flank and cut his
line of retreat. The bush was exceptionally dense,
and it was due to this rather than to the opposition
met with that this attempt failed. The 1st East
African Brigade attacked at about 5 p.m. and the
action continued till dark. During the night the
enemy retired. He had suffered severely and left
many dead on the ground. His position had been
skilfully chosen behind a prolonged natural clearing.
His right almost reached the river and his left was
covered by the thickest bush and undergrowth.

We suffered some fifty casualties, among them
Lieutenants Myers and Porter of the 130th Baluchis
were killed, and Lieutenant Cousins was wounded.
The troops encamped in the bush.

A section of the 27th Mountain and the 5th South

African Batteries had been with Sheppard's Brigade, but the bush was so dense that it was impossible to make use of them.

When the position was subsequently visited, the cunning in its selection was fully realised. The bush on their left flank was a veritable tangle, through which it was absolutely necessary to cut a way with the " panga " (native knife). There were the usual bush trees, but the ground beneath them was not only thick with thorn and the usual undergrowth, but in this locality the trailing vines and creepers flourished abnormally, and formed an interminable obstacle, worse than a barbed-wire entanglement.

The enemy had had his machine guns distributed along the position in the usual way. For emplacements the ground was hollowed out under trees, behind big roots, selected as growing in the right direction for his purpose, while the position of the guns was hidden by the hanging creepers from the branches overhead. The intensity of his fire was evidenced by the heaps of empty cartridge cases which were piled up in every emplacement.

Earlier in the day the enemy had opened fire with his artillery from the far bank of the river. Doubtless this was in the hope of delaying our advance while the preparations of the Mkalamo position were completed. He had anticipated that our force would continue its advance down the left bank, and had been surprised by our sudden transfer to the right bank. As reported by our patrols, he had been prepared to oppose us from a position between the Mafi Hill and the river.

The force occupied Mkalamo on the 10th, and that afternoon Sheppard's Brigade was pushed on towards Luchomo.

The trolly-line bridge at Mkalamo was intact, as was most of the stretch of line along the river-bank to Luchomo. There were a number of trollies at Mkalamo, many of them damaged, but the Germans had a workshop there and it would not be a difficult business repairing them.

The 17th Cavalry had a sharp scrap with a hostile patrol on approaching Luchomo, in which Lieutenant Knowles, an Indian civilian serving with them, was killed.

On the 12th the Headquarters moved on to Luchomo and Sheppard pushed on to Funda River, where he encamped. The river-bed was found to be dry and it was necessary to send out water from Luchomo. The tract of country from the Pangani to Handeni, something over thirty miles, was known to be waterless, and patrols were sent out to try to locate water-holes.

Meanwhile, General Hannyngton's column had been advancing down the railway. On the 8th he had occupied Mazinde station.

On approaching Mombo the following day, the advanced guard was fired on from Mombo Hill, which, together with the bush south of the railway, was held by the enemy. The main body of the infantry was halted while the mountain guns were brought into action. They opened fire on a hostile machine gun, which had been located on Mombo Hill. The enemy abandoned the gun and retreated up the hill under effective shell fire. The infantry then advanced and occupied the hill, while the 10-prs. and No. 6 Battery shelled the line of bush, with the result that the enemy retired. Our casualties were slight. As soon as Mombo was occupied, the German civil administrator came down and reported that Wilhelmstal had been evacuated and was open to us. The Germans had left some hundreds of women and children there, presumably hoping that General Smuts would adopt the rôle of foster-father and look after them.

As a result of the reconnaissances towards Handeni, General Smuts received information that by digging in the river-bed about Mbagui, some twenty-two miles south of Luchomo, we could obtain sufficient water for the force. Two water-holes had also been located at Gitu, about ten miles north-west of Handeni. General Sheppard was then pushed on ahead, and the main body moved to Mbagui, which was reached on the 15th.

At Mbagui deep holes were dug in the river-bed, and the promised water was found. It was hardly one's idea of water, being very muddy and of a deep chocolate colour; however, it was liquid. Canvas troughs were set up for the animals and the water pumped into them from the holes. It could be used by the men after boiling, and was all right for cooking and for tea, of which there was fortunately an issue. It was only a one-night halt. The enemy was found to be holding a strong position covering Handeni and Nderema. (The latter is about two miles west of Handeni, and was the terminus of the trolly-line.)

General Smuts then decided on another turning movement. The main body was to march by Gitu to Ssangeni, on the Mssangassi River, seventeen miles west of Handeni. To cover the movement and to protect the line of communications from the south-east, General Sheppard, who was now at Kilimanjaro, about five miles north of Handeni, was to move south-west to Nguguini when the force moved to Gitu.

On the 16th the column set out for Gitu, where

two holes were found, each about three square yards
in area, containing some green and very unwholesome-
looking water.   All troops had started with full water-
bottles, and again it was only a one-night halt.   To
get from Mbagui to Gitu, it had been necessary to
leave the track and strike across country over what
proved to be an up-and-down journey, with some
bad drifts, necessitating much bush-cutting and road-
making.

The leading troops had just arrived at Gitu when
firing was heard about a mile back along the road
we had come.   Just as the 8th Battery was moving
down a rather steep descent, through a comparatively
open bit of country, they were fired on from the
bush, about 1,000 yards away to a flank.   The horse
of the officer commanding the escort was shot under
him and a man and a mule wounded.   Some of the
escort, who were on this flank, at once galloped to the
spot whence the firing had come.   The enemy made
off into the bush, leaving behind a helio and a theo-
dolite and a quantity of kit.   It was evidently an
enemy signalling party.   Presumably they had been
moving through the bush, had suddenly observed our
troops within rifle range, and had not seen the escort
close to them.   General Smuts with the Headquarters
Staff had passed a short time before, and two battalions
were already in Gitu.

That night the enemy shelled Sheppard's camp
with their naval guns without doing much damage.

The following morning, the 17th, the force moved
to Ssangeni.   Camp was pitched in the midst of
mealie plantations, in open ground, and there was
plenty of water in the river.   The enemy's line of
retreat was now threatened, and he was bound to
move.   His line of communications with the Central

railway line ran due south from Handeni, skirting the eastern slopes of the Nguru Mountains.

On the morning of the 18th General Beves with the 6th South African Infantry and the 5th South African Battery, and Colonel Byron with the 5th South African Infantry, moved off from Ssangeni across country, to endeavour to intercept the enemy's retreat, while Sheppard closed in on Handeni. General Beves with the 6th Battalion got across the road and ambushed what was the enemy's rear party, killing about thirty Askaris, while Colonel Byron with the 5th, some miles farther to the west, attacked the enemy rearguard towards nightfall and killed a certain number, taking some German and Askari prisoners and a quantity of stores. The enemy made off into the bush, and Colonel Byron dug in and bivouacked where he was.

The following day General Sheppard occupied Handeni and Nderema.

General Hannyngton had meanwhile been pushing on from Mombo down the railway-line. On the 13th one of his mounted patrols had been ambushed a short distance north of Mauri, which was held by an enemy detachment. Mauri was occupied on the 14th without opposition, the enemy having retired. That evening the 3rd King's African Rifles were detached, with the object of seizing the wagon-bridge, just short of Korogwe, before the enemy should have destroyed it. They crossed the river by a native foot-bridge and, making their way down the river-bank, succeeded in driving off the enemy post which was watching it, and captured the bridge intact early on the morning of the 16th. The main body moved on Korogwe by the north bank. The enemy were holding the Zuganotto rubber plantation and

Fundi Hill, close to the town, and opened fire on our advanced guard; but on the mountain guns coming into action, they retired and Korogwe was occupied.

The Western Usambara district, including the railway as far as Korogwe, was now in our hands. Wilhelmstal, the principal town of the district, is one of the most important European settlements in German East Africa. Five thousand feet above the sea, it had been the summer seat of the Government, the Simla of East Africa. The climate is cool and healthy, and it is easily accessible by the excellent motor-road which connects it with Mombo. There is a good hotel and a number of European houses, which are well built. It is more or less surrounded by plantations, coffee, rubber, etc., and there is plenty of open country in the hills around, where, far above the " fly " level, cattle flourish.

Korogwe is where the road from the Tanga and East Usambara districts branches off to Handeni and the Central line.

In Handeni we had occupied the second strategic centre and the starting-point for the advance of the eastern column to the Central line. As far as roads were concerned, now that we had occupied Handeni, the enemy force about Kondoa was cut off from the northern theatre. The trolly-line was in our hands, and when put in working order, which should not take long, would be a useful asset as long as we were dependent on our northern line of communications. The Germans had used porters to run the trucks along the line. We had the trucks, and though many of them were damaged, the parts were there, and the German workshops at Mombo and Mkalamo were in our hands.

General Smuts decided to leave the Eastern

Usambara and Tanga for the present, and ordered Hannyngton's force to move up to Handeni and join the main body.   They arrived at Handeni on June 20th.

There was a strong probability that the small force in the East Usambara district would retire to the south and try to join their main forces when they found themselves isolated and cut off by our forward move.

It was all-important to continue what had practically become the pursuit and to give the enemy no breathing-time, but it seemed that our advance would be held up by lack of supplies, and that we could not make another move forward and add to the length of our communications.   There had been no addition to our transport; in fact, it had been diminished by the breakdown of many of our motor-vehicles and the collapse of a certain number of our mule- and ox-wagons.

The officers of the Supply and Transport were to be seen going about with long faces, and doubtless they had represented to the Commander-in-Chief that any further advance was out of the question. General Smuts's wonderful driving power had not yet been realised, and those who had to deal with him were soon to discover his inability to recognise difficulties, however great, except as obstacles to be overcome.

To push on a big force, already feeling the pinch of short rations, farther away from the source of supply, to shoulder the responsibility of taking his army yet another hundred miles in spite of all that his expert advisers could urge against such a step, was proof of a General of no ordinary calibre.

Such had been the situation when we arrived at

Buiko, but the army had continued to advance. The situation arose in a more aggravated form when we reached Handeni. Again General Smuts's orders were to push on.

Rations had been short now for many days, and conditions were not going to improve. No white flour had been issued for some time. There was, of course, no bread. The rations consisted of hard, very hard biscuit, which had to be soaked before it could be broken, eked out with mealies and mealie flour. It was soon discovered that the mealies, even when cooked, brought on a form of dysentery, and it was some days before it was realised that this was obviated by soaking the mealies over-night and getting off the husks. The bad effects were then done away with and the mealies were very good food. The only meat to be had now was the fly-stricken trek ox. This had to be eaten at once, as in that climate it was impossible to keep meat even for a day. It was terribly tough food.

On one or two occasions there was an issue of bread. The loaf was a welcome sight, but alas! when it was cut, it was found to be green inside and absolutely inedible.

The Indian troops who did not eat meat were even worse off. With nothing but flour, and mealie flour at that, often no " ghi " to help matters, they had a worse time than other units. One could not help wondering if we were really better or worse off than our comrades at Kut. In one way we were far better off. We were hunting our enemy. The moral effect on troops of the knowledge that they are getting the best of it, that their enemy cannot stand up to them, is marvellous. They will put up with any amount of physical hardship without a murmur.

On the 20th the main body moved to Pongwe. That afternoon the 5th South Africans, under Colonel Byron, were sent forward to harass the enemy's retirement and occupy Kangata, which was some eight miles distant. They moved off, some 500 strong, their numbers having been considerably reduced by sickness. Two miles north of Kangata village an enemy piquet was encountered, which was driven back and the advance continued. Word was then brought by Belfield's Scouts, a few of whom were moving ahead of the column, that there was an enemy force in the vicinity, and not very far ahead.

The main body had closed up somewhat on the advanced guard during the encounter with the enemy piquet, and just as they had cleared the next ridge, a heavy fire was opened on them from the bottom of the long slope which lay before them. At the same time machine guns opened from their right rear. The battalion at once extended, and there was heavy firing, which continued till night fell. Colonel Byron held his ground and encamped where he was. By morning the enemy had gone. The battalion lost seventeen killed, including one officer, and seventy-five wounded.

The same day a column, consisting of the 17th Cavalry, a section of the 27th Battery, two armoured cars and the Kashmiri Rifles, under Lieutenant-Colonel Lyall, left Handeni by the direct road for Kangata. They halted that night at Mjimbo and arrived at Kangata the following afternoon.

On the 21st General Smuts with his Staff proceeded beyond Kangata reconnoitring, and in the afternoon he ordered forward the remainder of the force. It was dark before the spot selected for the camp was reached. It was on high ground just off the

road. All that could be seen was that the trees
were not too close together and there was no bush
undergrowth, but the ground was covered with
high elephant-grass. The only thing to do was to
lie down and sleep wherever you happened to be and
wait for daylight. The village of Kangata was a
mile away on a bare knoll, but there is one spot to
be always avoided in East Africa, and that is the
vicinity of a native village. There are always red
ticks, the cause of an objectionable intermittent
fever, and there are certainly " chiggas." There were
few, officers or men, who did not suffer from " chiggas"
while in East Africa. There was a case of one officer
who had forty extracted at a sitting from one foot.

On the 22nd the whole force, with the exception
of General Hannyngton's column, was assembled at
Kangata.

Pongwe and Kangata had both been enemy depots,
and the store huts and stores, to which they had set
fire, were still smouldering when we arrived.

Information was now received that the enemy had
retired to the Lukigura River, where he was taking
up a position. General Smuts decided to push on at
once. General Hoskins was put in command of a
column, consisting of the East African Mounted
Rifles, the 27th Battery (less one section), the 25th
Royal Fusiliers, 2nd Kashmiris, 2nd Loyal North
Lancashires Machine Gun Company, and the 5th
and 6th South African Infantry, with instructions to
march via Kwa Negero, some miles higher up the
river, and to get behind the enemy's position, which
was reported to be in the vicinity of the Lukigura
bridge. The remainder of the force was to advance
direct on the position. General Hoskins started
through the bush at about 4 p.m., and at the same

time General Sheppard set out for Kilima Mssinga, where he was to pass the night.

Sheppard started on at dawn the following day, the 24th, and at about three miles beyond Mssinga his advanced scouts found the enemy in an entrenched position to either side of the road. One of Sir John Willoughby's armoured cars, which was with the vanguard, was hit by a pom-pom in the radiator, but he succeeded in getting it turned round and under cover. The advanced guard deployed, and the 5th and 8th Batteries took up positions behind the crest in rear. The orders were not to push in, as it was all-important that Hoskins's column should get behind the enemy position before they were forced to retire. Hoskins's advance had evidently been delayed, and a message was sent by General Headquarters that the attack would be made from this side as soon as fire was opened on the far bank.

Hoskins's force had halted at midnight, and after three hours' rest had continued the advance, crossed the Lukigura at Kwa Negero, which proved to be considerably farther away than the map and the native guide had led us to believe, and was now pushing on towards the rear of the enemy position.

At a little before noon heavy firing started on the south bank, and Sheppard pushed on. The enemy was found to have crept away through the high grass and crossed the river.

When Hoskins's advanced guard, consisting of Kashmiri Rifles, was approaching the low hills covering the Lukigura bridge from the west, they found the enemy on the nearest bridge. Being reinforced by the remainder of the Kashmiri Battalion, they pushed on and took this ridge. The enemy were then found to be holding a strongly entrenched position

on the next ridge. General Hoskins at once sent up
two of the Loyal North Lancashire machine guns,
and at the same time put in the 25th Royal Fusiliers
on the left flank of the Kashmiris. The 130th
Baluchis from Sheppard's column were then making
their way across the marshy bottom and through the
river to join in the attack. The 17th Cavalry, the
armoured cars, and the 29th Punjabis had been sent
forward by the main road by Sheppard, to try to
get across the enemy's line of retreat.

It was most difficult country. The slopes were
thickly wooded, and the whole area was covered
with grass, six to eight feet high, in addition to which
the enemy had obstructed tracks with felled trees.

The heavy fighting was taking place around the
high ground to the west of the bridge, in the middle
of which was a native kraal. At about 1.30 p.m.
General Hoskins ordered the 6th South Africans to
advance round the enemy's left flank to the north-
west of the spur. At 2 p.m. he received word from
the frontal attack that their advanced guard had
reached the bridge and was pushing along the road
in rear of the position. He then ordered the assault.
The 25th Royal Fusiliers and the Kashmiris at once
rushed in and took the position at the point of
the bayonet. The advance of the South Africans
was unfortunately impeded by the high grass and
dense undergrowth, and they did not get round in
time to get at the enemy as he retired. He got away
through the grass. Some small parties came under
the fire of the 29th Punjabis and the armoured cars,
but the bulk of the force escaped. At about 5 p.m.
firing ceased. The guns had not been able to assist.
Friend and foe were too closely mixed up for them to
open fire. It had been an infantry fight.

12

The enemy's losses were three whites and thirty-four Askaris killed and a large number wounded, and fourteen whites and a number of Askari prisoners. A pom-pom, three machine guns, and a quantity of ammunition fell into our hands. Our casualties were very light. Although every endeavour had been made to prevent the enemy getting away, he succeeded in escaping. The dash of the 25th Royal Fusiliers (familiarly known as " the Old and Bold ") and the Kashmiris in the assault of the enemy's main position had been beyond praise.

We now occupied the line of the Lukigura River, with the heights of the Nguru Mountains towering just ahead of us. General Hoskins's force camped on the south bank, and the remainder of the force with General Headquarters on the north bank. Soon after dark the enemy opened fire, at a range of at least 10,000 yards, with a naval 4·1-inch and an 88-cm. gun on the two camps, the locality of which, being the only open spaces, he probably conjectured. His shell burst short of the camp on the north bank, but the prisoners, who had doubtless heard wonderful tales of the effect of their artillery, were terrified. There were a few casualties in the camp on the south bank. The gun positions were subsequently identified by the empty cartridge cases. They had been firing from the south bank of the Msiha River, about 12,000 yards away.

A spot on the high ground at Kwa Derema, where the enemy had made his last stand and the heaviest fighting had taken place, was selected as the cemetery for those who had fallen. A row of crosses was set up by their comrades and a stout timber fence was built around them.

After a few days' rest the 1st East African Brigade

and General Headquarters moved forward to a camp
on the Msiha, in the vicinity of Makindu, eight miles
farther to the south.

The force had covered about 250 miles since May
22nd, and this was June 24th. Throughout the
march the troops had had to cut their way through
the bush, bridge rivers and nullahs, and make the
tracks passable for motor traffic, on which they
depended for their food. At the outset, though
eager for the advance, a large proportion were full of
fever, contracted in the marshes of the Ruwu or in
the fighting of the previous year, and the exceptional
exertions and hardships told on them.

Since leaving the Pangani, there had been a shortage
of water, and the rations issued had at times been
far short of what they were entitled to. The result
was that the fighting strength had been reduced by
a half by sickness. The enemy had been met and
fought, but on every occasion had succeeded in
wriggling away from his position, avoiding decisive
action by rapid retirement. He had fought a series
of well-executed rearguard actions.

It was absolutely necessary to halt now to get up
supplies and to evacuate sick. Every vehicle with
the force was requisitioned and employed without
ceasing on supply work. There were roughly one
hundred miles of rough sandy track, bristling with
tree stumps, between the camp and " German Bridge "
and another hundred miles from " German Bridge "
to the Kahe depot. The railway, which was being
repaired, would take over the transport as far as it
reached, and the trolly-line would be of great assistance over the stretch it covered, as soon as it was
in working order. Meanwhile, it was impossible to
further extend our line of communications. The

transport at our disposal, which included the whole of the artillery and regimental transport, would be barely able to supply the force where it was, under existing conditions.

We were now within sight of the hills about Morogoro and within eighty miles of the Central line. Our next move was to be in co-operation with the Kondoa Irangi force, and they were not ready to advance. General Smuts had every reason to be well satisfied with the performances of his force during the past month.

CHAPTER X

On June 28th General Sheppard moved forward to Makindu, on the southern bank of the Msiha, to cover the construction of the bridge over the river which had been burnt and blown up by the retiring enemy. He took with him a couple of battalions and the 27th Battery. He was followed by General Head-quarters and the Headquarters of the 1st Division after a few days, and gradually the whole of the 1st Division was brought forward, except General Han-nyngton's column, which was back at Handeni.

Major-General Brits, with the 2nd Mounted Brigade under Brigadier-General Enslin, had arrived in the country, and they were on their way forward with the artillery of the 3rd Division, which they picked up at Mbuyuni.

Owing to our enforced inaction the enemy began to be troublesome. His activities took the form of sniping patrols and mine-laying along our line of communications, cutting our telegraph lines, etc. Several cars had been held up recently between Lukigura and Msiha. On one day General Hoskins's car had been hit and put out of action by rifle shots, and his A.D.C., Captain Macmullen, was killed. The enemy bolted or might easily have secured the remainder of the party, including General Hoskins, as there was no escort. On another occasion, Mahsud

Effendi, an excellent native officer of the King's African
Rifles, was badly wounded, Major McCalmont and
Captain Shakespear, who were with him, fortunately
escaping.   Behind Lukigura motor-ambulances and
supply carts had been blown up by mines, and the
signallers were kept constantly employed all along
the route repairing telegraph and telephone wires.
The sniping was difficult to deal with.   The bush
and high grass came down to the edge of the road on
both sides, and any number of enemy might be concealed within a yard or two of the traffic.   It was impossible to picket the whole road.   A careful look-out
was kept for mines, and there was constant patrolling.
That was all that could be done till the enemy had
been cleared out or it was possible to resume our
advance and keep him occupied in other ways.

The detachment which had fallen back along the
railway before Hannyngton had remained in the
vicinity of the Pangani, and had been particularly
troublesome on the road between Korogwe and
Handeni, and had even ventured to make an attack
on our post at the bridge at Korogwe, which was
beaten back.

General Smuts determined to clear the country
to our rear, between our line of advance and the coast.
While we were advancing on Handeni, the 5th Indian
Infantry, which belonged to the line-of-communication
troops, had moved south and occupied Mwakijembe, -
near the German border, a few miles from the coast.
The enemy had held this spot for a long time and
used it as a starting-point for their raids against the
Uganda Railway.   It was held by a company, which
retired in the direction of Tanga when the 5th
advanced.

Instructions were now issued for the occupation

of Tanga. Arrangements were made by Brigadier-General Edwards, the Inspector-General of Communications, to land a force, under command of Colonel C. U. Price, at Kwale Bay, about eight miles north of Tanga, the navy co-operating in a combined land and sea attack on Tanga. Colonel Price met with but slight opposition, and arrived at Tanga on July 7th, our ships appearing in the harbour at the same time. The enemy retired, and Tanga was occupied without opposition. Nearly two years had elapsed since we made our original landing at Tanga, which had ended so disastrously.

The enemy force at Tanga did not, however, retire south, as it was anticipated he would do, but continued to hang about in the neighbouring hills and cause trouble.

Orders were then issued for a systematic advance against the different guerilla bands, which was what they practically were, being each about two or three companies strong.

General Hannyngton, who had arrived with his column at Lukigura on July 10th, was ordered to move back to Handeni and move down the old caravan road towards Pangani, with a view to intercepting the enemy's retreat. Brigadier-General Edwards was ordered to send the 57th Rifles from Korogwe to Muheza and they were to send a detachment to clear Amani on the left of their advance, the 5th Indian Infantry was to move to Muheza from Tanga, and a detachment under Lieutenant-Colonel C. U. Wilkinson, consisting of the Jhind Imperial Service troops and some sappers and miners, was to move from Korogwe on Segera Hill, about twelve miles down the right bank of the Pangani, which was reported to be the headquarters of one band.

At dawn on July 15th Colonel Wilkinson surprised the force at Segera, and they retreated in the direction of Hale, pursued by our troops, leaving a Hotchkiss gun and a quantity of ammunition in our hands. Muheza was occupied on the 20th. The detachment which had been sent to Amani captured twenty-five whites, who surrendered without opposition.

General Hannyngton arrived at Mumbwe, about half-way between Handeni and Pangani, on the morning of the 20th, and received information that an enemy force was then at Ngambo Kidoto, having just passed south across the road. At noon a column was sent under Major Money, consisting of two mountain guns, 400 rifles, and nine Maxims, to Ngambo, which was eight miles distant. On arriving within sight of the village, late in the afternoon, parties of enemy could be seen in the vicinity of the village. The guns were ordered into action and opened fire on good targets, the column having meanwhile deployed for attack. The enemy did not return the fire and disappeared. Our scouts entered the village about 10.30 p.m. to find it deserted. A captured Askari reported the enemy to be 350 strong, with four machine guns. The detachment returned to Mumbwe the following morning, owing to lack of water at Ngambo.

The enemy force, which was under the command of Major Boemken, broke up into two parties, one of which retired towards Mkwadja on the coast, but the greater part by a track towards Rugusi and Manga (which is about forty miles south-east of Handeni), *en route* for Mandera, on the Wami River.

General Hannyngton was then ordered to send Lieutenant-Colonel W. J. Mitchell with the 40th Pathans to pursue the enemy towards Manga and to return to Lukigura with his brigade, bringing the 57th Rifles in place of the 129th Baluchis, who were much reduced in strength by malaria.

Pangani was occupied by the navy on the 23rd, after a preliminary bombardment the previous evening.

The enemy detachments were now all moving south and our troops were close on their heels. A detachment of the Cape Corps, which had been employed safeguarding the road from Handeni to Lukigura, with headquarters at Kangata, was sent to Manga to co-operate with Mitchell's detachment. The two forces arrived there simultaneously. The enemy, who were at Manga, were attacked and retired south towards Mandera. The remainder of the Cape Corps was brought on to Lukigura. On August 1st the navy occupied Sadani, the next town down the coast, and a detachment of the British West India Regiment was landed there to co-operate with Colonel Mitchell's column, which was following the enemy to Mandera. The West Indians moved south and then west, clearing the lower Wami, and, having joined hands with the Pathans, the whole column moved south-east towards Bagamoyo.

The enemy had now a considerable force opposed to us in the Nguru Mountains, amounting to some twenty companies. The position occupied by their main body was about eight miles south of the Msiha camp and extended from the lower slopes of the Kanga Mountain, across the road, till it rested on the swamps of the Lukigura. They were strongly entrenched, and their front was covered with every sort of obstacle. The road south from our camp was obstructed every few yards with felled trees and was doubtless mined.

There were detachments in the mountains to the

west of us, about Mahasi and Hesapo, which were
a threat to our communications, and hostile posts
had been located at Mssente and Mssangeni to the
east. Our patrols were active reconnoitring routes
to the south-east and through the mountains for
our advance.

The enemy had persistently shelled our camp with
his naval 4·1-inch and 88-cm. guns from the time of
our arrival. He opened fire at all hours of the day
and night, using a high-explosive shell with time fuse,
and allowed us about fifty rounds a day. At first
the fire was not very effective, but having established
an observing station in the hills above us, the bursts
became unpleasantly accurate. The position of the
guns was located by the flash of discharge and the
time of flight of the shell, but it was unfortunately
impossible to reply to them. The only guns we
possessed which could fire at the range were the 4-inch
naval guns, and they were at Mbuyuni. The transport
could not be spared to bring them up.

The troops very soon prepared themselves the
necessary dugouts, and the camp was like a huge
rabbit-warren. As soon as firing commenced, all
went to ground. During the period of our halt at
Msiha there were about seventy casualties in personnel
and a certain number among the animals. The
enemy generally sent over some shell to the river-
bank at the time that the animals went to water.
There were few in camp who had not had splinters
very close to them, and the lucky escapes were
marvellous. General Smuts was in the habit of
remaining in his " banda," and it was not till he had
had several splinters very close to him that he could
be induced to realise that the safe place was the
dugout that had been prepared for him.

We had one form of retaliation, and that was the bombing by our airmen. They had established an aerodrome in the vicinity of Mbagui, a long way back, but the nearest suitable piece of ground. It was with great satisfaction that they were seen to pass over and the explosion of their bombs in the enemy camp was eagerly listened for. There was hardly a day that the enemy was not visited. As we saw later, he had dug very deep underground shelters. The noise of the aeroplane engines is heard from a long distance, and doubtless he had plenty of time to reach them as a rule. However, we know that he hated our bombs, and it was a consolation to know that we were hitting back.

While at Msiha the force was visited by General Botha, who came up during the parliamentary recess. He went round the camps and inspected all the South African troops. On his return he was able to give the account of an eye-witness of how things were going in German East and of the hardships the South African forces were cheerfully undergoing.

Towards the end of July the prospects of an early move seemed to be brighter. The 3rd Division was at Kwa Derema, the camp north of the Lukigura, Hannyngton's column was on its way back there from Handeni, and there was a certain accumulation of supplies. The Kondoa force had already started forward.

The effect of the advance of our column to the Lukigura at the end of June had been at once felt at Kondoa Irangi. After their unsuccessful attack on May 9th/10th the enemy had taken up a line facing our position. General Van Deventer had continually increased his front, to which the enemy had replied by a corresponding extension of his line.

The strength of the 2nd Division had been greatly reduced by sickness, due to the hardships and exposure during their original advance and the rainy season, and to the shortage of supplies. The state of the roads in rear had made it most difficult to get anything forward to them. About the middle of June there were some 1,200 sick in hospital, and they were short of 1,600 horses and mules. Towards the end of May and at the beginning of June reinforcements and fresh units arrived. Among them were the South African Motor-cyclist Corps, from 200 to 300 strong, the 4th Light Armoured Car Battery, 1st South African Field Battery, the 10th Heavy Battery of 4-inch guns, the 11th Section of 5-inch Howitzers, and the 7th and 8th Battalions of South African Infantry, belonging to the 3rd Division. An aerodrome had been set up at Kondoa and there were two aeroplanes.

The enemy kept up an intermittent bombardment on our camps and positions, paying particular attention to the aerodrome, so that it was eventually moved to another spot, about twelve miles north of Kondoa, where the machines were safe from enemy gun fire. Our casualties were not heavy. The gunners were very active, and the enemy was reported to have suffered heavily from our shell fire. The enemy's artillery consisted of two naval 4·1-inch, one 88-cm., and four guns of lighter natures, so we had a very satisfactory preponderance. On June 24th explosions were heard and fires seen behind the enemy's position, and on the following day the infantry were pushed forward against the enemy positions supported by the fire of the guns. The positions were found to be only lightly held, except at one or two points, against which the infantry advanced, and the enemy retired. By nightfall the whole of his line was occupied by our troops. The 1st South African Mounted Brigade supported by the 3rd South African Infantry Brigade were sent to try to cut off the enemy rearguard, but, owing to the very broken nature of the country and the exhaustion of the troops, the enemy succeeded in getting away. Among the empty cartridge cases found on the position were a number of 4·1-inch marked " Nov. 1915," which had evidently been brought out by the blockade runners.

On the following day the enemy rearguard retired to Chambala, the main body being reported to have retired on Dodoma. General Van Deventer had now to await the accumulation of sufficient supplies before he could advance. General Smuts's instructions were that the main body should move towards Dodoma, a small column towards Kilimatinde, and a detachment to clear the right flank to Ssingida. The main body was then to move east on Mpapua, and so reduce the distance between the 2nd Division and the main column, with a view to the probable necessity of close co-operation later on when dealing with the enemy's concentrated forces.

On July 7th the 9th South African Horse joined the 2nd Division. The Saranda (Kilimatinde) column, consisting of a squadron of South African Horse, a section of the 28th Mountain Battery and the 9th South African Infantry moved off under command of Colonel Kirkpatrick, on July 14th, for Kwa Mtoro, which was occupied on the 20th. On the 26th they reached Kaia ; and on the 27th, just as the advanced guard was approaching Mpondi, a heavy fire was opened on them with machine guns and rifles. The country was very dense bush, and the enemy were in position barring the road. The mountain guns were

at once brought into action, and the 9th South
Africans pushed straight in, under cover of a well-
directed gun fire. They carried the position, and
Mpondi was occupied late in the afternoon. They
had eight killed and nine wounded. Considering it
was a direct frontal attack on a prepared position,
they got off very lightly. On July 30th this column
occupied Saranda and Kilimatinde without further
opposition.

On July 26th the Ssingida detachment, consisting of
a squadron of the 4th South African Horse, a section
1st South African Battery, the 8th South African
Infantry, and a wireless installation, left Kondoa under
Colonel A. J. Taylor. On July 31st Mgari was
reached and a small fort on the escarpment was
surrounded, and the garrison of fourteen Askaris
surrendered. On August 2nd Ssingida was occupied.
Colonel Taylor received instructions to leave a post
in charge and to proceed to Kilimatinde, which he
reached on August 11th.

Meanwhile the main column had set out and
Chambala was reached on the 18th and Aneti on
the 19th. The country was found to be very dry,
and there was great difficulty about water. Reports
were received that the enemy were in occupation of
entrenched positions covering the water-holes at
Tissa Kwa Meda and Tschenene. General Van
Deventer then decided to divide his force into two
columns : the Mounted Brigade with the South
African Field Artillery Brigade was to move by Tissa
Kwa Meda and Njangalo, and strike the railway at
Kikombo, under command of Brigadier-General Manie
Botha, while the remainder of the force was to move
by Tschenene and Meia Meia to Dodoma, by the
direct road.

General Manie Botha occupied Tissa Kwa Meda on the 22nd, after a sharp engagement. General Botha was then recalled to South Africa on urgent private business, and the brigade was taken over by Colonel Nussey, who had been Chief Staff Officer to General Van Deventer. Naju was occupied on the 26th and Membe on the 27th. On the 28th the enemy was found to be holding a strong position at Njangalo. They were attacked and driven out, leaving a machine gun and 1,500 head of cattle in our hands. Kikombo, on the railway, was occupied on July 30th.

On July 25th General Berrangé, who was in command of the other column, found the enemy in occupation of a strongly entrenched position at Tschenene. The enemy was driven out and the position occupied, much credit being given to the work of the armoured cars at close range. On the 27th Meia Meia was occupied, and a hostile mounted detachment captured, without any loss to our troops. On the 29th General Berrangé occupied Dodoma.

Colonel Taylor's column, which had come down from Ssingida, remained at Kilimatinde, relieving the column under Colonel Kirkpatrick, which marched down *via* Dodoma to rejoin the division, which it overtook at Mpapua.

General Van Deventer then concentrated the division at Njangalo, where they were assembled on August 9th. The railway from Kilimatinde to Kikombo was in our hands, but the enemy had already blown up all the bridges and culverts, although he had not carried out the same detailed destruction as on the Usambara line.

CHAPTER XI

THE OCCUPATION OF MOROGORO

THE time had now arrived for the resumption of operations by the main column. The situation had been materially altered by the advance of the Kondoa force to the railway. Although it had been impossible to keep up an effective pressure with the two columns, the enemy had not succeeded in making use of his interior lines. The threat of an immediate advance by the eastern column along the Nguru Mountains against Morogoro had at once caused him to withdraw the bulk of his force from Kondoa to oppose it, and this had enabled Van Deventer to advance and occupy 100 miles of the Central Railway with comparatively little opposition. Had the enemy known that the eastern column could not possibly continue its advance for some weeks, he doubtless would not have rushed his forces across in such feverish haste to oppose it.

The enemy forces in what may be called the central theatre were now cut off by the 2nd Division from the forces in the Lake area, and from his position Van Deventer threatened the flank of any retirement towards Iringa.

In the Lake District our forces had advanced from the Kagera and had occupied Mwanza at the southern end of Lake Victoria. The enemy had retired, pursued by our troops, leaving a 4·1-inch naval gun

and some useful ships in our hands. We had thus
obtained undisputed control of the lake. The Belgians had continued their advance through Ruanda.
They had occupied Mariahilf on July 24th, and were
now advancing in two columns from Mariahilf and
Bujombe on St. Michael.

Another column had occupied Gitega and
Usambara, and moving south down the eastern side
of Lake Tanganyika had occupied Kigoma, Ujiji,
and Rutchugi during the last days of July. Tabora,
the most important German centre in the west,
was now threatened by the Belgians from the north
and west and by our Lake force under General
Crewe.

Earlier there had been some doubt as to the
direction which would be taken by the German forces
if we succeeded in driving them back to the Central
line. They could retire towards Tabora or to the
Morogoro—Dar-es-Salaam section.

The latter left them the south-eastern portion of
the protectorate with the extensive Mahenge Plateau
as a concentration area and a coast-line with several
good harbours. (After the successful feats of the
Rubens and the *Maria*, they might still cherish hopes
of receiving further reinforcements and supplies by
sea.) They might also hope to retain possession of
Iringa. The Uluguru Mountains could be looked
upon as a useful zone of manœuvre for further retirement, and the Rufiji River beyond as a formidable
obstacle to the forces attacking them. Also it was
natural that they should hold on as long as possible
to Dar-es-Salaam, the capital of the colony. There
was not only the moral effect of its capture to be
considered, but it was also their central depot, and
there and at Morogoro they carried on the manu-

13

facture of such warlike stores as they could produce
with the resources at their disposal.

From Tabora, on the other hand, there were two
routes by which they could retire—to the north, to
the rich cattle district of Ruanda, or to the south
towards the Rhodesian and Nyassaland borders.

While the Lake detachment and the Belgians had
been pushing in from the north and north-west,
Brigadier-General Northey had made headway from
the south and had reached Malangali, which he had
captured after a successful engagement, in which
the enemy had lost heavily in men and material.
He was now about eighty miles south-west of Iringa.
Tabora no longer held out any possibilities, and with
the advance of Van Deventer's force and the occupation of a big section of the Central Railway, all doubt
as to the enemy's subsequent movements was of
course at an end.   The main forces were cut off from
the western territory.

In planning their strategy, the enemy had always
carefully considered climatic conditions and their
effect on the health of their own and our forces.

Any long halt in an unhealthy district meant a
heavy reduction in personnel, varying with the season
of the year, but always considerable.   An advance
through bad " fly " areas meant a still heavier toll
on our animals, and having themselves impressed
every able-bodied man in their own service, the
Germans knew that our transport must be mechanical
and animal, and that we could not possibly procure
a big army of porters.   These points had been and
still were important factors.

The Germans had " fly " maps of the whole country,
on which were marked the bad districts as far as
they knew them from their peace-time explorations.

We had copies of these maps and were consequently equally aware of the recognised bad areas ; but though we had the initiative, it did not mean that we could determine our lines of advance—our movements were of course dependent on those of the enemy. We might defeat him and drive him from position to position, but the direction of his retirement and the area he selected for his next stand still remained more or less in his hands.

At the outset, on the northern front he had been about Kilimanjaro, and the Pare and Usambara Mountains, living in the hills, in a pleasant and very healthy district. When driven from Kilimanjaro and Meru, he had spent the rainy season in the Pare Mountains.

These points had naturally been recognised by our Commander-in-Chief, and his first thought had been to ensure healthy sites for the various camps during the rains, but it was necessary always to keep some troops, and the numbers were reduced to the smallest compatible with the work to be done, in the low-lying ground along the banks of the Ruwu and Pangani. When we advanced to Buiko and Handeni, the rains were over and the health conditions favourable, but the reduction of our strength due to sickness by the time we reached Lukigura had been enormous.

As before pointed out, this was due partly to exposure during the rains to the feverish swamps along the rivers, but that was not the main cause. A large portion of our force had been in East Africa since 1914 and the beginning of 1915, and during that period they had been posted at unhealthy spots along the railway, had taken part in excursions in the Lake district, the shores of which are notoriously unhealthy, and along the coast, which is pestilential and when they were called upon to undergo the fatigue and exertions of the long and trying marches of the advance and to live for considerable periods on very reduced rations, they succumbed.

From the Usambara the Germans had gone back to the Nguru Mountains. Here again they were living under the best of conditions, while we were in the foot-hills; but during this period we were not too unfavourably placed, and it was the healthy season of the year.

South of the Central line the healthier areas are the Mahenge Plateau, the Iringa district, and the Uluguru Mountains, and in a lesser degree the Mtumbi Hills south of the Rufiji River. The rest of the country is low-lying, swampy, with many rivers and always unhealthy, but particularly in the rainy season, except under most favourable conditions, which cannot be provided when campaigning.

There were only two courses open to the enemy: he might stand and fight, which would mean a decision one way or the other, as far as he was concerned, or he might continue to retire, holding us up on every possible occasion, causing us as much loss as possible.

He was immediately covering Morogoro, an important centre and one-time seat of Government. He would keep us out of it as long as possible.

The present situation was as follows: The Nguru Mountains cover an area of forty to fifty miles from north to south, and twenty to twenty-five miles from east to west. At the north-eastern end, for about fifteen miles from north to south, there is an additional block of hills about ten miles across from east to west, ending with Mount Kanga on the south. This excrescence is divided from the main block by the valley of the Mdjonga River, with Mahasi at the northern and Mhonda and Turiani at the southern end, on the western and eastern banks respectively.

Two streams run through the main block of mountains in a south-easterly direction, joining this valley at about Matomondo and Mhonda.

The enemy's main body was, as already explained, in position on the lower eastern slopes of Kanga. He held Mahasi and had posts down the Mdjonga Valley. There were, according to the reports of scouts and from natives, three routes through the mountains : the eastern route down the Mdjonga Valley; five miles farther west the line of the stream joining the Mdjonga at Matomondo; and on the extreme west the valley of a stream which, after running due north for fifteen miles, turned south-east and joined the Mdjonga about Mhonda.

The enemy's position at Kanga was flanked and protected by his detachments in the Mdjonga Valley on the west and the nature of the country to the east.

The road south on leaving the Msiha skirted the hills till south of Kanga Mountain, when, after crossing the Russongo, it turned a little south-west, till it reached Turiani, situated on the banks of the River Mdjonga. After crossing the river it ran in a southerly direction, skirting the hills till at the south-eastern extremity it branched off, one road leading due south to Morogoro, crossing the Wami River at Dakawa, and the other running along south of the mountains as far as Kidete at the western end, when it turned south and joined the railway at Kimamba.

From the information received it would be possible to move transport and guns by the eastern (Mdjonga Valley) and the western routes through the mountains.

General Smuts's plan of operations was accordingly

as follows : General Sheppard's brigade was to advance from Msiha camp and make what would be practically a holding attack on the main Kanga position at Ruhungu, eventually co-operating with the column advancing down the Mdjonga Valley.

The 2nd Brigade under General Hannyngton and the Divisional Reserve with the 1st Division Headquarters were to enter the mountains at Mahasi and advance down the Mdjonga Valley on Matomondo and Turiani.

The 3rd Division, under General Brits, was to move along the north of the mountains by the Valley of the Lukigura and advance by the western valley on Mhonda, where they would be in rear of the enemy forces at Ruhungu and farther up the Mdjonga Valley.

On August 5th the 3rd Division, 2nd Mounted Brigade, and 2nd South African Infantry Brigade (less two battalions), started, and the following day Hannyngton's brigade set out for Mahasi.

On the 7th Sheppard's force set out before daylight from Msiha Camp. In addition to the infantry the artillery with his force consisted of the 6th and 134th Batteries, both motor drawn, the 5th South African Battery, and a battery of armoured cars.

General Sheppard ordered that the 29th Punjabis should clear the road towards Ruhungu as rapidly as possible, and he proceeded to cut a road through the bush to the east of the road, taking with him the remainder of the infantry and the 5th Battery.

The enemy was not aware of the move of this column, and continued to shell the camp from Kanga at intervals during the day. By evening Sheppard had arrived opposite the enemy position, and was about one to one and a half miles east of the road.

He found the enemy in a strong position in front of him, and the ground between him and the enemy, and to the east of the enemy position, marshy swamp, while to the west and up the mountain slopes was dense bush.   The 29th Punjabis had meanwhile cleared the road for some miles.   (One bullock-cart had been blown up by a mine, but no lives lost. Several other mines had been discovered and removed.) Meanwhile, the Mounted Brigade under Brigadier-General Enslin had been pushing forward on the western flank and had, after a great march through the centre of the mountains, reached the gap above Mhonda that night, and the following day were at the Mission Station at Mhonda, so far without encountering any opposition.   General Sheppard decided to move back to the Msiha Camp and endeavour to work round the enemy's position by a more easterly route along the right bank of the Lukigura.   He accordingly moved his force back to Msiha on the 8th, and starting that night encamped on the 9th on the Lukigura River, due east of the German position.   On the 10th he moved in a south-westerly direction and camped on the Rukwenyi.

Meanwhile, Hannyngton had advanced to within one and a half miles of Matomondo, where an enemy force was located in position.   Reports from both him and Enslin were that the mountain routes could not possibly take any kind of wheeled transport along them, in fact in many places it was difficult going for the men on foot.

General Beves, with the South African Infantry, had arrived at Pembe just beyond Kimbe.   He had been held up by water difficulties and his supplies had not been able to get forward.   The road had proved to be very difficult, one precipitous hill after

another, on which it had been necessary to put men
with drag ropes and extra mule teams on every
vehicle.   In addition to steep gradients, much of the
surface had been heavy sand.   On the evening of
the 7th some of the artillery and transport had
reached Kimbe water-holes, where the infantry were
halted.   This column had covered only twenty miles
from Lukigura Camp.   Till they arrived at Kimbe,
they had had no water since leaving Lukigura and
men and horses were exhausted.   On the 8th the
leading units reached Pembe and the infantry were
three miles beyond.   It was realised that it would
be impossible to get the vehicles along, and all
wheeled transport was ordered back to the Lukigura,
where they were to follow the main road behind
Sheppard's column.

Getting the guns and loaded transport back was
an equally difficult business, and it was not till
the 11th that they arrived at Lukigura.   General
Smuts then ordered Beves's infantry down the
Mdjonga track in support of Hannyngton, who was
facing the enemy position at Matomondo.

On the morning of the 10th patrols of the 3rd
King's African Rifles and of the 57th Rifles worked
up to and were in touch with the enemy, and the
latter succeeded in capturing a maxim.   The enemy
were shortly afterwards reported to be working
round towards our left, and General Beves, who had
arrived with the South African Infantry, was sent
up the hills to that flank to counteract this move
and work against the enemy's right, the 2nd East
African Brigade moving against the front and the
enemy's left.

The ground was very difficult, and the advance up
the hill-slopes correspondingly slow.   Firing along

the front became heavy, and the Mountain Battery, the only artillery with the force, was brought into action. At about 5 p.m. the East Africans pushed in in front and the 5th South Africans from the left flank, supported by the fire of the guns. Fighting went on till dark. During the night the enemy retired.

The following day the column, consisting of both Hannyngton's and Beves's brigades, under the command of Major-General Brits, continued to advance. The enemy suffered heavily in the two days' fighting. We had about sixty killed and wounded.

On the same day, the 11th, General Sheppard, having moved west, reached the main road at the Russongo River crossing, to find that the enemy had already passed in response to the pressure exerted further on by the 2nd Mounted Brigade.

The 25th Royal Fusiliers, who had been patrolling along the main road towards Ruhungu, arrived on the 10th at the Msilika River, and the following day had advanced to the Ruhungu position.

The 2nd Mounted Brigade had arrived at Mhonda on the 8th and pushed forward detachments to the hills to the north of Turiani. They were thus athwart the enemy line of retreat, and were engaged by enemy troops from Turiani, who were subsequently supported by the force retiring from Ruhungu.

General Enslin was forced to retire before superior force to the position which he had occupied up the valley, in the vicinity of the Mission Station. The enemy opened fire on him with their artillery with some effect, but did not attack. Enslin not having any guns, could not reply.

On August 12th Headquarters moved to the Russongo, and on the following day reached Turiani, where the force moving down the Mdjonga had joined hands with the Mounted Brigade.

General Sheppard with the 1st East African Brigade was ordered on the 12th from the Russongo to seize the crossing in the vicinity of Kipera, where the Bagamoyo road crosses the Wami River.

It was advisable to deny it to the enemy, and our force there would be in position to operate against the enemy's flank, should he elect to contest our passage of the Wami, where it was crossed by the Morogoro road. General Sheppard arrived at Kipera on the afternoon of the 13th, a small enemy post retiring on his approach, and secured the bridge intact.

On the same day the Mounted Brigade under Enslin was pushed forward by the left, on Ngulu Kwa Boga, with instructions to move in on Kwedi-hombo and Mwomero (where the Kidete and Morogoro roads branch), on the Mkindu River. On the 14th, the 17th Cavalry and 130th Baluchis from Sheppard's force and a section of the 27th Battery were sent to his support.

The 2nd East African Brigade and the South African Infantry were at the same time pushed forward along the direct road. They encountered a hostile rearguard that afternoon, just north of the Mkindu River, which was forced back, and the following day Kwedihombo was occupied without opposition.

The enemy had burned the bridge at Turiani, and the troops of the Divisional Reserve and the artillery were hard at work at the construction of a low-level bridge. Across the river from Turiani the road became particularly difficult. For some three miles it led through a papyrus swamp, and it would be a difficult task to keep the causeway in order for the traffic which it would have to bear. Within the next few miles beyond that there were numerous streams, the bridges over which had been destroyed by the enemy, and all of them had to be reconstructed.

On the 15th orders were issued for Hannyngton's brigade to move to Mwomero to clear up the situation on that route. The remainder of the force was to pursue the enemy along the Dakawa road, in the direction of Morogoro, and Sheppard was ordered to move up the right bank of the Wami towards Dakawa to co-operate in an attack on the crossing.

On the 16th Hannyngton arrived at Mwomero unopposed. From the information received, it was learned that the enemy's main body had retired along the Morogoro road, while a few companies had taken the Kidete road for Kimamba and Kilossa.

The remainder of the force advanced on Dakawa.

The column halted at 9.30 a.m. about four miles short of the river, while patrols went forward to ascertain the enemy's dispositions. They were found to be holding an entrenched position on the far bank with advanced posts on the near side of the river.

At about 2 p.m. the force advanced, the 130th Baluchis to the right and South Africans to the left of the road, followed by the 6th South African Horse, the Mounted Brigade, less the 6th South Africans, operating independently on the right or western flank.

The leading troops came under fire at about 4.30 p.m., and the mountain guns were brought into action at about 400 yards north-west of Dakawa village, the infantry firing-line gradually pushing on towards the river, till they occupied a line which was in places not more than 200 yards from the German trenches on the far side of the river. Firing was kept up till nightfall.

At this time General Sheppard's force had reached a spot about eight miles north-east of Dakawa, where they had encamped. They had encountered slight opposition throughout their march from hostile patrols, which had fallen back before them.

That night, orders were issued for Sheppard to attack as early as possible on the 17th, and the 3rd South African Battery and 13th Battery (a section of 5-inch howitzers) were ordered forward from Turiani.

At an early hour of the 17th the action recommenced at Dakawa. Our infantry had somewhat improved their cover, which on the previous evening had been merely such cover from view as could be obtained from the brushwood.

The mountain guns came into action in their previous position to the west of the road, and were soon reinforced by the 3rd South African Battery, which took up a position east of the road, at a range of 1,600 yards. About 2 p.m. the 13th Battery arrived and took position west of the road at a range of about 2,500 yards from the far bank. Three or four machine guns were located by the different battery officers forward with the infantry firing-lines. The mountain guns smashed up one, and the South African Battery silenced two of them.

The Commander-in-Chief arrived at the scene of action in the early forenoon. The fire was kept up by infantry and guns with varying intensity throughout the day.

Meanwhile, Sheppard had been advancing from the east. He found the enemy holding an entrenched

line about two miles east of Dakawa, to cover his
right flank and line of retreat. Sheppard's advanced
guard consisted of the 29th Punjabis, who, reinforced
by the Rhodesians, attacked, supported by the fire
of the 5th South African Battery.

At about 3 p.m. the Punjabis were relieved by the
2nd Kashmiris. A little later the enemy's fire
slackened and, scouting forward, the Kashmiris found
the enemy's position vacated. The 130th Baluchis
had been transferred to the 3rd Division, and General
Sheppard had not more than 500 rifles at his disposal.
He camped where he was for the night. His casualties
had mounted to over eighty, among them six British
officers.

On the Dakawa front, Enslin, with the Mounted
Brigade, had been sent by the Commander-in-Chief
to cross the river higher up to the west, and work
round to the rear of the enemy's position. The Wami
is a river with steep banks, which are covered as a
rule with high grass and lined with big trees. There
was plenty of water in the river, which was flowing
fast. Enslin eventually managed to get across, but
the advance was held up by the denseness of the
undergrowth. Farther south the country was more
open and the grass but knee-high. The enemy,
finding his line of retirement threatened, retired.
The next morning our infantry were across the river
and Sheppard closed in to the position the enemy had
vacated.

Their position had been well entrenched. In
parts there were two tiers of trench or pits, one near
the river-bank, and one on the higher ground beyond.
The trenches were deep and well concealed. There
had been a substantial wagon-bridge and a suspension
boat-bridge, both of which had been entirely destroyed

by the enemy.   On the north bank the enemy had
cleared a field of fire for about 150 yards from the
river edge.

Our guns, directed by the officers with the infantry
firing-line, did good work in knocking out and silencing
the enemy machine guns, and the enemy had suffered
considerable losses in personnel.   Our total casualties
in the two days amounted to about 120.

The Gold Coast Regiment, which had arrived at
Turiani, was now ordered up to Dakawa.

The work on the road from Turiani to Kwedihombo
had been very heavy.   There was first of all the
digging out of the ramps to the low-level bridge which
we constructed at Turiani, and as the banks at the
crossing were over twenty feet high and very steep,
this meant much labour.   Then there were the miles
of causeway through the swamp, which not only had
to be constructed in the first instance, but required
continued labour and material to be kept passable.
This was the more difficult, as for two or three miles
there were no trees or timber, and for every vehicle
which passed a fresh surface of reeds from the swamp
had to be provided.   The road kept to the west of
the swamp for about a mile before reaching the
Mwuhe River, which, after flowing for some hundreds
of yards just west of the road, turned east into the
swamp.   This was one of the worst spots on the
road.   The Germans had had a causeway on piles
for 200 yards before reaching the bridge over the
river.   They had burned the bridge and the pile
causeway, and both had to be replaced, with no
material handy.   There was no possibility of a
deviation across the river, as the far bank was a
precipitous cliff.   The engineers, however, got to
work, and had soon made it practicable for the time

being. The guns of the 3rd South African Battery and, still more difficult, the howitzers of the 13th Battery, which were motor drawn, were got through in the early hours of August 17th.

On the 18th the force encamped about Dakawa close to the river. On the 19th Hannyngton's brigade was ordered to rejoin the force, the Cape Corps, which had been brought forward to Mwomera, being sent down the Kidete road. The bridges over the series of small rivers between the Mwuhe and Kwedihombo were plain sailing and offered no especial difficulties. In the road work and bridge-building it had to be remembered that this would be our line of communications for some time to come.

The advanced depot was at Handeni, and the lines of communication were not concerned with transport beyond that point. A small supply of ammunition had with great difficulty been assembled at Lukigura, and the problem was to get it forward within reach of the fighting troops. The whole of the vehicles of the Divisional Ammunition Column had been taken over by the Supply and Transport months previously. With great difficulty sufficient transport for the 15th Battery of 4-inch guns had been recovered, and they had arrived at Msiha Camp on August 11th, in time for the advance. The Commander-in-Chief considered it possible that the enemy would stand and fight before Morogoro, and if so they would be required to answer to his long-range naval guns. It was now necessary to produce the transport to bring forward ammunition, as it was wanted. However, by denuding batteries as opportunity offered, the difficulty was overcome and a safe margin of reserve was gradually brought forward as far as Turiani.

It was now necessary to get it forward to the

Wami.   The force would be moving forward as soon
as the bridge could be built.   For the time being
all troops were employed assisting in the preparation
of the necessary material and getting it where it was
required by the engineers.   The hills of Morogoro were
clearly to be seen barely twenty miles ahead of us.

Meanwhile, General Van Deventer had been press-
ing on down the Central railway.   He had concentrated his force at Njangalo, with the exception of
the detachment under Colonel Taylor at Kilimatinde,
by August 9th.

On the 10th the 3rd South African Infantry Brigade,
with the 28th Mountain and 2nd South African
Batteries and the 12th Howitzers, followed later by
the Mounted Brigade with the 4th South African
Battery, advanced south-east on Tschunjo.   On the
11th the enemy had been located holding a strong
position in the hills covering the water.

The advance had been through difficult country
practically waterless.

On arriving opposite the position, from which the
enemy opened fire with 7-pounders and machine
guns, he was at once attacked.   The 10th South
African Infantry with the mountain guns worked
round his flank.   From the front the 2nd Battery
engaged the guns, which were speedily silenced.
Fighting went on through the darkness.   By midnight the enemy was driven out of his position, and
when day broke was found to have retired.   The
advance was continued at once, the Mounted Brigade
leading, and the enemy was next found occupying
the high ground south-west of Mpapua.   Their
7-pounders opened fire on the Mounted Brigade,
which brought the 4th South African Battery into
action.

Meanwhile, the 10th and 11th South African Infantry arrived with No. 2 Battery and a section of the mountain guns. The mounted troops were withdrawn and sent round the flanks, while the infantry attacked from the north, covered by the fire of the artillery. The enemy retired and succeeded in escaping the mounted troops, which were prevented by the difficult nature of the country from getting across their line of retreat.

Our casualties in the two days' fighting were: officers, 2 killed, 2 wounded; men, 4 killed and 33 wounded.

The advance was continued by the 3rd South African Infantry Brigade with the 2nd, 12th, and 28th Batteries, and on August 15th the enemy were found holding the heights about Kidete station. Their position, along a semicircle of hills, was a strong one, and they had an 88-cm. gun in action and one 7-pounder. The latter was located and silenced early in the day by the mountain guns. The 88-cm. gun was located by the artillery forward observing officers and the fire of the 2nd and 12th Batteries was turned on it. It soon ceased fire. Meanwhile, one 13-pounder was got into a position enfilading the enemy left flank. The 10th South African Infantry advanced against the enemy's centre and right, covered by the fire of the mountain guns, and took the enemy's advanced positions, but the attack was not pressed home against the main position. The infantry had marched twenty miles before coming into action and were suffering greatly for want of water. The enemy retired during the night, and trains were heard running from Kidete station. On the 16th the force camped at Kidete.

The advance was continued on the 18th, and on

14

the 19th the enemy were found in position again, holding a narrow pass leading to the Msagara station. They were again forced to evacuate their position by a turning movement over the hills by the infantry. They got away through the dense bush, pursued by the fire of the artillery.

On the 20th they were located in a position covering the exit from a narrow valley, four miles north-west of Kilossa.

Before dawn on the 21st the 3rd South African Infantry Brigade and the guns of the 2nd and 12th Batteries were in position at the exit of the valley.

At dawn the 1st and 2nd South African Horse, dismounted, with the 10th South African Infantry, climbed the heights to the left and right respectively. The enemy opened fire with a 4·1-inch and 88-cm. guns from long range. They were not located, but their observation post was discovered and shelled, and their fire became very erratic. The enemy was driven back from ridge to ridge and eventually retired during the night. Our force occupied Kilossa and Kimamba the following day, August 22nd. Throughout these operations the enemy had fought delaying rearguard actions. On every occasion he had advanced posts in ambush, in front of his prepared position, on which they fell back when compelled to do so. His naval guns were used for long-range fire, but their effect was not great.

The arduous work performed by the infantry in particular, who covered long distances, not only in the actual marches, but in the turning movements, which were the feature of the attacks, could not be too highly praised. The advance had been to some extent through a waterless tract of country and the troops had been on short rations throughout the period, so that they had undergone exceptional hardships.

The minimum distance covered by any unit from the time they left Kondoa Irangi until they reached Kilossa was 220 miles.

The performance of the animals was extraordinary. The South African batteries and much of the transport of this force were mule-drawn. As with the eastern column, the motor-lorries with ammunition columns and other units had been taken over by Supplies, while at Kondoa, and ox- and mule-wagons were handed over to replace them just as the march commenced. Both animals and vehicles were in sorry condition, and it reflected great credit on those concerned that they should have succeeded in getting them along. The animals had received practically no grain since they arrived at Kondoa Irangi in the middle of April. It was wonderful that they lasted as long as they did. The wastage in animals was naturally very heavy. The march had been through a very bad " fly " country and there was but little chance of any of them surviving more than a few weeks.

While at Kilossa information was received that the enemy had retired to Uleia, about twenty miles south of Kilossa.

By the evening of August 21st the bridge over the Wami River was completed. While halted at Dakawa, scouts and patrols had been busily employed. There was no doubt that the enemy had retired the whole of his force on Morogoro. As before pointed out, should he not stand and fight at Morogoro, it seemed probable that his next move would be in the direction of Mahenge, and he could proceed by either the east or west of the Uluguru Mountains.

Covering the Ngerengere River and Morogoro from the north is a line of hills, which extended some ten miles either side, to east and west of the Dakawa road. A direct advance over the plain against this line would enable the enemy to at all events hold up our force, and we should have been in difficulties for water. The enemy would have been able to retire south, by the east or west of the mountains, when he judged desirable.

To overcome these difficulties, and if possible to prevent the enemy's escape, General Smuts adopted the following plan of operations : Brigadier-General Enslin with the 2nd Mounted Brigade and the 3rd South African Battery was sent off across country on the 21st to strike the Central railway at Mkata, some fifteen to twenty miles west of Morogoro, with a view to barring the enemy's way to the road to the west of the mountains. On the 23rd the main body was to move in a south-easterly direction, turning the line of hills above referred to, and approach Morogoro by the Valley of the Ngerengere, and thus, if possible, bar the route by the east. This route necessitated a two days' march without water. From the time the force left the Wami there would be no water till the Ngerengere was reached. The enemy was of course aware of this fact, and doubtless considered that it would effectively prevent any advance by this flank, which could be considered secure.

In order to reduce as much as possible the time that the force would be without water, having crossed the river, the column first marched some nine miles down the right bank, where a halt was made for a couple of hours in the middle of the day.

The march was resumed soon after 2 p.m., the troops moving in two parallel columns. The country was open bush and short grass for a considerable distance, and it was good going. About a mile to the left of the line of advance the thick bush commenced again.

The force eventually encamped for the night about six miles south of the river, just under cover of the thick bush on the left. No fires were allowed.

A little before daybreak on the 24th our slumbers were suddenly disturbed by the reports of two or three rifle shots. This was of course contrary to all orders, but within a few minutes a report explaining the circumstances was received. Three rhinoceros had charged into one of the South African camps. Two of them had been accounted for, and the third had bolted.

At dawn the march was resumed. Darkness was just coming on when the leading troops reached the Ngerengere River about Msungulu. Men and animals were very exhausted. The sun seemed to have been exceptionally hot during these two days and the water in bottles and carts had soon been exhausted. The columns were feeling their way along in the pitch darkness, proceeding to their different camps and then making their way to the water, till after midnight.

Colonel Brink, Chief Staff Officer to General Brits, had been sent on the previous evening, with a mounted detachment, to seize Mkogwa Hill, about four miles south-east of Msungulu, and a report was received that he had occupied the hill.

The force halted on the 25th, patrols being sent out to south and west. The enemy had concentrated all his forces to cover Morogoro from the north in the direction of Dakawa, with the exception of a small force he had detached towards the west, presumably to oppose Enslin's Mounted Brigade, and gain time for a transfer of his forces to that point, should it be found that our main columns followed the Mounted Brigade.

On the following day, the 26th, General Hannyngton's brigade moved across to Mikesse and occupied the station, the remainder of the force moving west to Mohale on the Ngerengere. A detachment of South African mounted troops, with the 2nd Rhodesians and 130th Baluchis, were pushed on and occupied Morogoro, which was found to have been evacuated.

The enemy, on learning of the presence of our troops on the east, had hurriedly retired to escape envelopment at Morogoro. One enemy column moved by the Kiroka Pass, east of the mountains; another force was located in the mountains due south of Morogoro. With the latter, it was afterwards learned, were von Lettow, the German Commander-in-Chief, and the Governor, Dr. Schnee.

On August 27th General Smuts, with the Headquarters Staff, rode into Morogoro. On all sides were evidences of the precipitate haste with which the enemy had retired. The store-houses at the station were still burning. At the goods station the platforms were deep in coffee, which they had not had time to destroy, and which hundreds of native women were now carrying off in baskets and sacks for their own use.

The station buildings had been considerably damaged and most of the engine shops and workshops had been burned. On the engine turn-table were the remains of an 88-cm. which had been mounted there, evidently for use against our aircraft. It could of course have been turned to fire in any direction. The gun had been blown up, and some charges had been used to damage the turn-table. Near the oil store the ground was under oil, which had been turned out of the barrels. The saw mills, near the station, had been blown up. As far as could be seen, every bridge and culvert along the line had been demolished and the points about the station blown up, but the rails themselves, chairs, etc., were there. They had not had time to attend to details. Preparations for these demolitions had probably been made all along the line, and when it became necessary, one last train went down, and as each point was reached, stopped for the firing of the charge.

Many of the inhabitants had bolted off into the hills or bush on the day before our troops marched in. They returned a few days later when they found that civilians did not suffer at our hands. There were still a large number of families, women and children, living in the different bungalows, who preferred to risk our treatment to the certain dis-comforts and dangers of the bush. There was also quite a colony of alien traders, Greeks for the most part, and the usual Hindoo traders in the bazaar.

We found a number of Indians in the vicinity of the station. They had been brought over by the Germans to do the railway work, drive the engines, etc. They received good pay prior to the war, and were over on a three years' agreement. On both the Central and Usambara the working of the railway was apparently in the hands of Indians. Most of them came from the Punjab and a large number from Lahore itself. They were delighted at our arrival, or at all events professed to be.

Morogoro is not a big settlement. There was one

cluster of bungalows and a couple of hotels near the station, and another with a third hotel on the river banks, on either side the bridge, which was left intact.   Here were the police-station with the police-barracks, hospital, market-place, etc.

All the natives were compelled to live on the west side of the river.   There were a few European shops on the east side, but the native bazaar, banyas' shops, and market-place were all on the west side.   About a mile from the town, some 200 or 300 feet above it, was the old Government house, latterly the Secretariat, a fine, imposing building, and round about it were the bungalows and compounds of the administrative staff.   Just below was the jail and the barracks of the detachment of Askaris, quartered here in peace-time.   Between them and the town, to either side of the road, were the public gardens and Government farm.

The roads were wide, well kept, and all lined with trees, some streets all mangoes, others " gold mohur " or coco-nut palms.

The bungalows of the Europeans were well built and designed.   As a rule they were of stone, provided with good wide verandahs and comfortably cool.

Far up the mountain-side was a big Protestant mission-house, and about two miles east of the town the Catholic mission buildings and church.   Dotted about on the lower slopes were a few bungalows of Europeans, who preferred the cooler climate to the advantages of the society of near neighbours.

We found one Englishwoman, a missionary who had been interned by the Germans and kept working as a nurse in their hospitals.   This lady had been left behind, and was overjoyed to find herself once more in British hands.

The German sick and wounded who were too bad
to move were left in the hospitals, and nuns from
the convent and German ladies, who had been
nursing, were left with some doctors in charge of
them. One or two of our wounded prisoners, among
them Captain Buller of the 57th Regiment, who had
been ambushed and wounded in the fighting near
Matomondo and brought back by the Germans to
Morogoro, had been sent down by the last train to
Dar-es-Salaam. Some of the German nuns and
ladies continued to nurse in the hospitals after the
German sick were finally evacuated.

In most of the compounds, close to the bungalows,
were deep underground shelters for protection against
aeroplane bombs. Our airmen had paid frequent
visits to Morogoro lately, and our arrival was probably welcomed by a large proportion of the civilians
even of German nationality.

Lieutenant-Colonel Capel of the Rhodesians was
installed as Post Commandant, and bungalows were
soon allotted as offices and dwellings to the Headquarters Staff, which moved in to Morogoro on the
29th. Nos. 15 and 134 Batteries, the 4 and 5·4-inch,
had arrived there the previous day. The setting in
order of Morogoro occupied some time. It was
necessary to see whom we had in our midst. There
were Germans over age, convalescent, etc., and their
cases had to be dealt with. Stores of all kinds
were taken over, discriminating between what was
Government and what was private property.

There were plantations for some miles along either
side of the railway, chiefly rubber, sisal, and cotton,
belonging to Europeans. The first named, which cover
large areas, were said not to have paid very well of
late, but the sisal and cotton had been satisfactory.

In the mountains, a mile or two from the town, were mica works, but these had been shut down during the war. In the plantations the houses and go-downs were as a rule good stone structures, and the planters had evidently been prospering.

A planter, who represented himself to be an Alsatian, had a sugar estate a few miles east of Morogoro. He made very good rum and some brandy. He had planted vines and was satisfied that they were going to do well. The soil is very fertile and, judging by the plantations, public gardens, etc., will grow anything. " Fly " was everywhere, and it was necessary to keep cattle some 3,000 feet up in the mountains in order to be safe. Morogoro has a rainfall of about forty-five inches, the wet months in normal years being from the beginning of December till the beginning of May, and during that time it is unhealthy. The town is picturesquely situated about 1,600 feet above sea-level, just at the base of the northern slopes of the Uluguru Mountains, which tower up some 6,000 feet immediately to the south of the settlement, while to the north and west is a semicircle of lower hills, so that it lies more or less in a basin, open only to the east, whence every evening there is a strong wind, which brings clouds of dust through the town.

Such was the new seat of Headquarters. The first question was that of food. Everything had to come from Handeni by the track which we had followed, except for the last stage, which was of course now the direct road from Dakawa. In addition to the forces, the population of Morogoro had to be fed, enemy women and children. They could not be allowed to starve. There was not a big population to start with, but with the advent of Headquarters it would

increase by leaps and bounds. All the open spaces
were soon to be covered with big camps, comprising
hospitals, ordnance and supply depots, engineer
and motor transport stores and shops, porter camps,
etc.   Gangs of natives were busily employed putting
up " bandas " and mud houses. The Secretariat
buildings became a hospital and other buildings in
the town were also given over to the Medical Department.   The public gardens and Government farm
were placed under Captain Brown, of the Heavy
Armoured Car Battery, who supervised the collection
of all vegetables and their subsequent distribution.
A market was started and the natives were encouraged
to bring their produce, but it did not amount to
much.

For the time being Morogoro was entirely dependent
for the transport of its supplies on the heavy batteries
and ammunition column. All other transport was
working with the advancing columns. It was an
anxious time. The line from Handeni was long and
dependent on the weather. The effect of heavy
rain would be very serious both on the bridges which
we had built and on the miles of swamp through
which the road passed. All mechanical transport
would at once be held up, so it was a matter of getting
as much forward as possible before rain came. However, we had come a long way and every confidence
was placed in the man at the wheel.

CHAPTER XII

On August 26th the 2nd Infantry Brigade under Brigadier-General Hannyngton had been sent straight across from the Ngerengere to Mkesse station, twenty miles east of Morogoro. The 1st East African Brigade had been employed making the road to Mohale and then on to Morogoro. On the 27th strong patrols were sent by General Sheppard to Kingolwira, to occupy the " nek " and report on the possibility of moving the brigade across by the Kiroka Pass, on the eastern slopes of the Uluguru Mountains.

On the following day, the 28th, the 1st East African Brigade moved to the Kiroka Pass, the 2nd Brigade having advanced to the Mssambissi River, and the Force Reserve to Kwembheai on the Ngerengere.

Although the units had reached the Ngerengere on the 24th, it was not till the evening of the 25th that all the transport had arrived. In addition to the sufferings due to the long marches across the waterless tract between the Wami and the Ngerengere Rivers, they had had further difficulties due to numerous and extensive bush fires. One of these, about a mile in length, had overtaken a column, and in spite of every endeavour to arrest it and get everything clear, several vehicles had been sacrificed, or rather lost. It would naturally take a little time to recover from what they had gone through.

Again the driving power, the strength of will, and boldness which characterised the Commander-in-Chief were to be manifested. The whole of the advance from Msiha had been very trying to all concerned. Troops not actually marching had been constantly employed throughout the time in road-making and bridge-building; they had had most exhausting experiences over the worst of roads to start with, and then marches over waterless country. Supplies were at a low ebb and man and beast were worn out. The outlook as regards the upkeep of supplies was not too promising, as the mechanical transport had reached its extreme radius of action. In spite of these conditions, General Smuts decided to continue the advance, as there appeared some hope of bringing about a general surrender.

On the western flank General Van Deventer had occupied Kilossa and Kimamba on August 22nd, after a long and trying march through the defiles of the Usagara Mountains, during which his forces had been in constant touch with the enemy, fighting a series of actions and turning them out of one position after another. The enemy had then been located at Uleia, where they were reported to have been reinforced by troops from the Kissaki direction, part of the force which had been opposing General Northey's advance. General Smuts wired ordering General Van Deventer to continue his advance to Uleia.

Brigadier-General Enslin had arrived at Mlali on the western slopes of the Uluguru Mountains on August 23rd, and had engaged an enemy force moving from Morogoro that evening. On the 24th a position had been taken up on the northern bank

of the Mlali River flanking the enemy's line of advance.
The enemy opened fire with a naval 4·1-inch and an
88-cm. gun.   They were engaged and silenced by the
3rd South African Battery.   Desultory fighting went
on all day, and during the night the enemy retired
into the Uluguru Mountains.   They left the guns
which they had blown up behind them and a quantity
of ammunition.   Meanwhile, the 1st Mounted Brigade
had been ordered forward to reinforce General Enslin.
This brigade with the 4th South African Battery left
Kilossa at 4 p.m. on the 24th, under Brigadier-
General Nussey, and moving by the Mkatta Bridge
and crossing the railway, joined Enslin's force at
Mlali at 8.30 p.m. on August 25th—a forced march
of fifty miles.   When the condition of the animals
is taken into account and the nature of the country
crossed, it stands out as a very fine performance.
Men and horses were weary and exhausted.

The 2nd East African Brigade was advancing along
a good road, the best that was found in German
East Africa, which led from Mkesse station, through
the foot-hills, down to the bridge over the Ruwu River.
The Uluguru Mountains are a massive range, with
peaks rising to some 9,000 feet.   They are not more
than twenty-five miles in width from east to west,
but the foot-hills extend for miles away to the
east and frequently rise to a couple of thousand
feet.   The road wound its way through and round
these foot-hills.   The country is naturally thickly
wooded, but is far more populated and had consequently been more opened up than any part through
which we had previously passed since leaving the
Kilimanjaro area.   For some distance south of the
railway were big farms and plantations, evidently
the property of Europeans, while the native villages

were numerous and all around them considerable
tracts had been cleared and cultivated.

On the 28th, when advancing from the Mssambissi
River, the advanced guard of the 2nd Brigade had
just crossed the Makamo River when the enemy
guns opened. The column at once halted and the
troops took cover in the various nullahs to right and
left of the road. After a rapid reconnaissance,
General Hannyngton decided to seize a long ridge
some 2,500 yards south of the river. The 3rd King's
African Rifles were sent to make a wide turning movement to the eastern flank, while the guns of the 27th
Mountain Battery took up positions on the knolls
just north of the river. The infantry reached the
eastern end of the ridge by 2 p.m., and covered by
the fire of the guns, which, by the aid of their forward
observing officers and the artillery flags carried by
the infantry, were able to keep their shell just in front
of them throughout the advance, gradually fought
their way along the ridge and drove the enemy to
the far end. At nightfall the enemy retired. The
enemy had two howitzers, one gun of 4·1-inch action
and one field gun in action.

On the 29th there was heavy rain. The 2nd East
African Brigade pushed on to Pugu and reconnaissances were made as far as Mkuyuni. The 1st
East African Brigade moved to the camp on the
Mssambissi, at the road crossing, patrolling as far
as Kindle. With them was General Hoskins and
Divisional Headquarters. The Divisional Reserve
reached Kikundi. On the 29th the 29th Punjabis
were sent to Tununguo, and the 57th Rifles had
occupied Mkuyumi and the heights overlooking
the Ruwu River. The same day a strong patrol of
the Gold Coast Regiment had encountered two hostile

companies on the Manga River, and attacked and driven them off with heavy loss. The detachment of 130th Baluchis and the 2nd Rhodesians, who had been at Morogoro, rejoined the 1st Brigade on August 27th and September 1st respectively. The advance was continued, there being daily scrapping with the enemy. On September 2nd the 2nd East African Brigade occupied Matombo Mission on the far side of the Ruwu, the remainder of the force and Headquarters being on the banks of the Ruwu.

The Ruwu is the principal water-course on the eastern side of the Uluguru and at the crossing-place was some forty to fifty yards wide, flowing here through a regular ravine between high hills. The road from the north gradually descends for some miles through the densest and at the same time most beautiful of tropical forests. Every kind of tree fern, aloes, palm, and creeper luxuriate beneath the shade of the bigger trees. The beauty of the road is added to by the natural rockeries, any height up to one hundred feet, covered with beautiful ferns, through which the road winds. When the river is reached, it is seen flowing some 150 feet or more below, the road, cut out of the hillside, gradually winding down to the level of the water, descending by artificial embankments over small plateaux, which exist on both banks where the bridge has been located.

After crossing the bridge there was a steep ascent to the little plateau on the far side. This was bounded by a mountain of rock, rising perpendicularly for hundreds of feet and apparently barring further progress. The river flowed round the base of it. The Germans had constructed a gallery round it, partly on piles and partly by blasting a way through the rock.

When they retired they had of course destroyed the
bridge and blown up the gallery, so that it was impossible to get any transport along till the engineers
had rebuilt it. It was a matter of much blasting as
well as bridge-building, and an urgent demand went
into Morogoro for all the blasting material there was
available. General Sheppard, who was originally
an engineer officer, was put on the work with his
brigade. The bridge over the river had to be rebuilt
and then the gallery reconstructed. The latter
demanded the skilled engineer. In parts the new
roadway was on platforms on piles, in some places
passages had to be blown through the rock, in others
connecting bridges had to be built. The gallery
was some 200 yards in length, and as it wound round
the rock, it was not possible to see far ahead. With
a very narrow roadway only one vehicle could move
along at a time. If one met another half-way it
would be a matter of one or other backing out,
possibly for a considerable distance, so it was necessary
to have a telephone at each end to regulate the traffic.
Even when clear, with a drop of some forty feet to
the river below on the one side and the perpendicular
or overhanging cliff on the other, it was not an inviting
bit of road. By the afternoon of September 5th it
was possible to get guns along. It was subsequently
in constant use, with loaded lorries crossing daily,
and there was never an accident, which says much
for the excellence of the work carried out under
difficult conditions. The enemy had abandoned his
4·1-inch gun when he reached this defile, and we
found it in the bush on the north side of the river.

Meanwhile, on September 4th, the Magali Ridge
had been occupied by the 25th Royal Fusiliers, without opposition, while the Gold Coast Regiment had

15

advanced as far as Kikarunga, which they reported to be strongly held.   That afternoon the 1st Division received orders from the Commander-in-Chief not to relax pressure so as to ensure that the enemy should not be able to throw the weight of his whole force against the 3rd Division, on the other side of the mountain, at this time approaching Kissaki and having no artillery with it.   The operations of this force will be described later.

On September 5th the Gold Coast Regiment drew in closer to the Kikarunga slopes, while the 57th, moving down the main road, got in touch with the enemy at the eastern end of the spur and at once brought its pressure to bear.   A section of the 27th Battery and the 3rd King's African Rifles were sent to co-operate on the right of the Gold Coast men, and the 29th Punjabis were pushed on to Tununguo. The enemy kept up a heavy artillery fire from Kikarunga throughout the day.   The fighting went on all through the 6th, and our 5th and 7th Batteries were brought into action in support.   By dark that evening the Gold Coast and 3rd King's African Rifles were in occupation of the position, and the enemy retired, having suffered heavily.

The advance was continued on the 7th, the 3rd King's African Rifles reaching the hills above Kissanga, the 29th Punjabis the Tununguo mission, and the 2nd East African Brigade camping at Bukubuku.

South of the Ruwu the road was of a different character.   As far as the river it had been an excellent, well-built road, but south of the river it required a lot of work in places before it would be capable of bearing the loads that would have to pass over it, and the 1st Brigade was at once got to work.

Bukubuku is just short of what was subsequently

known as " Sheppard's Pass." The pass consisted
of a footpath, cut out of the side of the mountains,
and winding round the face of the hills, which were
very precipitous, to the plains some 2,000 feet below.
On this side the Uluguru Mountains terminate
abruptly.

This road was practicable for men and animals,
and for most of the way for very light vehicles, but
it was necessary to drive with great caution. There
were two steep descents, which necessitated gangs
of porters with ropes for every vehicle that came
along. At more than one spot on the descent remains
of smashed vehicles could be seen at the bottom of
the khud. The usually careful enemy had tried to
go too fast and some of his transport had come to
grief. Among the wreckage was a lorry of about
two tons. This had probably been brought from
Morogoro, as we had seen no signs of it previously.
(One lorry and a car were found at Morogoro, which
the enemy had hidden in the bush near the river-
bank and abandoned.) Looking down from " the
Pass " over the plains below reminded one of the
view from a hill-station in India, except that here,
as far as the eye could see, the plain appeared to be
covered with forest, the visible surface being the tree-
tops. Here and there an exceptionally tall palm,
towering above the neighbouring trees, broke the
monotony of the dull green surface.

On September 8th the Gold Coast Regiment and
3rd King's African Rifles reached Wakami, the 29th
Punjabis were at Mssonge, and the 2nd Brigade had
descended the Pass and crossed the Mwuha River.

General Sheppard with his troops remained working on the road above " the Pass " and on the descent.
The latter had to be widened and, to do away with the

necessity for man-handling at the steeper spot, a
deviation of about half a mile of new road had to be
cut ; and at the other, which was much shorter, a
lot of digging was necessary to make the gradient
possible. This all meant a great amount of work.
When completed, there were very few spots on the
descent where lorries could pass one another comfortably and safely. As at the " gallery," there had to
be telephones at either end to control traffic.

On the 9th the King's African Rifles were brought
in from Wakami, and reinforced by the 130th
Baluchis, the 2nd Brigade advanced and occupied
Tulo unopposed. On their way from Wakami, the
King's African Rifles surprised and dispersed an
enemy company (the 22nd Field), killing a number
and taking prisoners two whites and twenty Askaris,
besides capturing a quantity of ammunition and
equipment.

The advance was continued the following day, the
10th. Just as the advanced guard was approaching
Nkessa's village, on the Dunthumi River, they found
the enemy occupying an entrenched position across
the road, near the river-bank. General Hannyngton
decided at once that a hill, Kitovo, just about a mile
to the north of the road, was the key to the position.
At 10.30 a.m. the 57th with the machine guns of
the 129th Baluchis (which had come on when the
rest of the regiment was left behind) and a section
of the 27th Battery were sent forward to occupy
this hill, the general idea being to hold the enemy
in front and turn his left flank. The 57th succeeded
in taking the hill, after some opposition, the enemy
retiring to the western and south-western slopes.
The mountain guns were got up into action near
the summit and were destined to be very useful.

They very quickly silenced the enemy guns which had opened fire from a position on the far bank of the river, in which they could be seen from the hill-top. Unfortunately Captain Haskard, who was in command of this section, was severely wounded at this juncture. This officer had been in command of the section of mountain guns which accompanied General Hannyngton during his advance down the Pare and Usambara Mountains, and had distinguished himself on many occasions. His place was taken by Lieutenant Davies. The guns kept up their fire on the enemy camp, which was distinctly visible till dark.

Meanwhile, the 3rd King's African Rifles were sent to support the 57th and work round their outer, or northern, flank. The 3rd Kashmiris were working down the main road, with the machine guns of the Loyal North Lancashires, their advance being covered by the fire of the remainder of the 27th Battery, from a position just north of the road at a range of about 1,700 yards. The 5th South Africans came into action a little later to the south of the road, at about 3,000 yards from the enemy's main position.

The following morning the 57th and the 3rd King's African Rifles, leaving a double company, which was subsequently reinforced by three of the Loyal North Lancashire machine guns, to hold the hill, started off in a south-westerly direction in order to envelop the enemy's left flank. The Kashmiris continued to make way towards the river, the fire of the enemy's machine guns, which was troublesome at times, being kept under by the fire of our mountain guns.

The 57th, after a short time, wheeled to their left and occupied the next lower ridge, to the south of

Kitoho, the King's African Rifles continuing the turning move, but they were unable to make much progress, as, owing to the thick trees, it was almost impossible for the artillery to give them any direct support.   At 2 p.m. the enemy launched a counter-attack against Kitoho.   It was not very strongly held, and the guns could not fire at the short ranges from their position.   However, the gunners assisted the infantry and used rifles.   The enemy's counter-attack was beaten off.   At 4 p.m. the detachment on Kitoho was reinforced by two companies of the Gold Coast Regiment.

The enemy now brought two 4·1-inch howitzers into action at very long range, which our guns could not make.   A little later a strong counter-attack was made by the enemy against the right flank of the King's African Rifles, which was repulsed.   From Kitoho the preparations for this counter-attack had been observed, and the guns below, which were in communications with Kitoho, as well as those on the hill, were directed on the enemy columns with good effect.   Troops remained where they were, and fighting was resumed the next morning, the 12th.

During the night the 29th Punjabis, who had been sent up by General Hoskins to reinforce the 2nd Brigade, joined General Hannyngton, and were put in to support the Gold Coast Regiment on our left. The enemy were found to have retired from the lower spurs of Kitoho, under cover of darkness, and the 57th started to work down a nullah to the west of these hills towards the river.   Meanwhile, the King's African Rifles, with a section of the mountain guns and two companies of the Gold Coast, by whom they had been reinforced, were pushing forward, and by 1 p.m. had occupied a position which commanded the village and the German camp. On our left the Gold Coast Regiment advanced into the village, and were forced to withdraw again ; but the enemy's position was becoming untenable, and about 3 p.m. parties were seen to be retiring in a south-westerly direction. Our left and centre were ordered forward and followed up, supported by the machine guns of the Loyal North Lancashires and the fire of the 13-pounders and mountain guns, which did great execution on some of the enemy columns which were observed going along the road. The enemy abandoned an 88-cm. gun, the limber of which had been smashed up by a direct hit from the guns on Kitoho Hill.

The fighting had been going on for three days, and the troops were worn out. The country was very difficult : in the low ground swamp and very high grass alternated, while the hills, which were the out-lying foot-hills of the Uluguru, were steep and stiff climbing. During the whole time the heat had been intense, and it had been difficult to obtain water for men and animals. The enemy had been in possession of the river-line, and it had been necessary to send back to a marsh some miles in rear. We were now in possession of the river and there was no longer any difficulty about water.

At the top of " Sheppard's Pass " the temperature was not too high, but in the plain below, which is really the low-lying Rufiji Valley, no breeze found its way through the forest and dense jungle to mitigate the fierce rays of the sun directly overhead, and it was very trying for man and beast.

The following day, the 13th, patrols of the Gold Coast Regiment found an enemy force occupying a village, a short distance beyond the river. They attacked, and the Gold Coast and 3rd Kashmiris, who were sent up in support, finally drove them out towards evening.

Our force remained where they were for the next three days. Nothing more was seen of the enemy, who had retired to the Mgata River.

While the 1st Division had been fighting their way down the Uluguru Mountains, the other columns had been busily engaged. It will be remembered that on the coast-line Bagamoyo had been occupied on August 15th. General Smuts had then instructed Brigadier-General Edwards, the Inspector-General of Communications, to advance on Dar-es-Salaam. He organised his available force (L. of C. troops), in two columns, of which one was directed to proceed straight to the Ruwu railway-bridge, in the hope of saving it from destruction, the other was moved along the coast. Unfortunately, it was too late and the bridge over the Ruwu was found to have been destroyed. This column encountered a small enemy force a short distance to the south-west of Ruwu station, about forty miles west of Dar-es-Salaam, which they attacked and defeated with heavy loss, the enemy retreating towards the south. They then turned east towards Dar-es-Salaam.

The column moving along the coast, on arrival at Mssassani Bay, extended to the west of the town, along the Mssimbusi River. At the same time the Fleet, which was co-operating, appeared. Dar-es-Salaam surrendered on September 3rd, and our troops moved in on the 4th. It was afterwards learned that the enemy garrison had moved out some days previously, and had retired in a southerly direction towards Maneromango. Before their departure they had blown up a 6-inch gun, and the railway-station and all works in the harbour, which they thought might be of use to us, had been hopelessly destroyed. The floating dock and the ships in the harbour they had sunk. One ship, the *Feldmarschall*, was subsequently floated, and there were still hopes of the *König*, which was ashore, half under water at the narrow entrance of the harbour.

General Smuts now arranged that the navy should occupy and land military garrisons at the remaining harbours down the coast. Accordingly Kilwa Kivinge and Kilwa Kissiwani were taken on the 7th, Mikindani on the 13th, Sudi Bay on the 15th, and Lindi on the 16th. The whole coast-line, except the Rufiji Delta, was now in our hands.

In Dar-es-Salaam we possessed a good base for future operations, but before it would be of any practical use it was necessary that the railway connecting it with the theatre in which we were working should be repaired. The road had practically ceased to exist. The railway would be a big problem. All the very numerous bridges down the line had been destroyed, and there was no rolling stock remaining.

The Ruwu was the worst obstacle. During the rains the water rises till it is some two miles across. The Germans had run the line over this on a series of embankments, connected by bridges. The Ruwu bridges alone had a total length of over 400 yards. They would take a considerable time to rebuild. Another bad spot was the crossing of the Ngerengere. The viaduct there was one hundred yards long. The chasm was deep and the enemy had run a quantity of their rolling stock into it. Engines, cars, and trucks were piled up at the bottom, a heap of destruction. To make doubly sure, they had removed similar

parts of every locomotive so that under no circumstances could one be used to repair another, should
we ever attempt to get them up.

There were in addition numerous smaller bridges,
all demolished. Altogether the Pioneer Corps restored
about sixty bridges between the coast and Kilossa.
The railway would take a long time, and there was
much to be done in the harbour to make it possible
to deal with all the traffic which would have to be
dealt with. From the beginning of September to
the end of December continuous work at high pressure
was necessary to equip the harbour and restore the
railway from the coast to Dodoma.

To return to the operations in the Uluguru Mountains. After the encounter at Mlali, the enemy retired
into the mountains to the vicinity of the Mgeta
Mission. They were followed by the men of the
Mounted Brigades. General Nussey, with the 1st
Brigade, pushed straight towards the mission, which
is about ten miles south-east of Mlali, the men leaving
their horses and proceeding on foot. Enslin, with
the 2nd Brigade, worked in farther to the west, with
the intention of getting across the enemy's line of
retreat. He cleared a hostile detachment from the
Hombossa Mountain, just south of west of Mgeta.

General Smuts now arrived on the scene. He at
once ordered General Nussey to follow the enemy
by a footpath, shown on the map as running about
due south from Mgeta. Enslin was recalled and
sent by the track shown to run down the west of
the mountains, by the Mssongossi River, and Mahalaka, towards Kissaki, which lies in the foot-hills at
the south-western extremity of the Uluguru Range.
General Beves was ordered to proceed with his
brigade (less the two battalions with the 2nd Division)

and the artillery of the 3rd Division from Morogoro
and follow and join Enslin, the whole being under
Major-General Brits, who would thus, in addition to
Nussey's brigade, have his division complete, less
two battalions.

General Beves accordingly started from Morogoro,
but the going was very bad, and the artillery made
very slow progress. General Brits found that the
track became worse and worse the farther he went.
He first sent orders that all motor-drawn vehicles
should return to Morogoro. The track was crossed
by a series of nullahs running west from the mountains, and these nullahs became more frequent and
more impassable the farther he advanced. They
were deep with precipitous sides, and finally impossible for any wheeled vehicle. On arrival at the
Mssongossi River he decided to send all vehicles
back. This meant that his guns and transport would
have to follow the 1st Division and make their way
round the eastern and southern sides of the mountains
before they could rejoin him at Kissaki, and the
troops would meanwhile be without their kits.

It was a critical juncture. By the evidently
unsuspected advance of the main body by the
Ngerengere and their rapid move south by Mkesse
and the Kiroka, the bulk of the enemy forces had
been cut off from possible retirement by the eastern
route down the mountains; while by the arrival of
Enslin's brigade at Mlali, they were similarly prevented from using the western line, such as it was,
and were compelled to retire through the mountains.

Our only information as to the routes leading south
was what could be gathered from the maps, and they
were not always reliable, particularly as to roads.

From the cross-questioning of prisoners and letters

which had fallen into our hands, it appeared that the enemy, if forced to retire from the Central line, would make his next stand about Kissaki. As the columns pushed on through the mountains, however, large quantities of ammunition, particularly heavy gun ammunition, fell into our hands, and it became evident that it had been his intention to hold us up and contest the passage of the Uluguru Mountains, which would have been a very troublesome business for us. This plan had been frustrated fortunately by the rapidity and surprise of our advance east and west, and by the rush of the Mounted Brigades into the heart of the mountains.

The bulk of the enemy's forces, with von Lettow and Schnee, the Governor, were now retiring through the mountains to Kissaki. A detachment had moved across south-east and joined the force, endeavouring to bar the advance of the 1st Division. General Smuts's intention was to push on with all speed and bring the enemy to battle about Kissaki. If this could be done, there was a possibility of delivering a knock-out blow and practically ending the campaign.

General Brits was connected with Headquarters by telephone, and there was a telegraph wire from Morogoro to Mlali, to which point General Nussey could send his messengers. Both columns had wireless sets for inter-communication.

On reaching Mahalaka General Brits turned south-east by the elephant track, the same by which Burton and Speke had moved in the opposite direction when making their journey into the interior in 1857. By September 5th he was approaching Kissaki. The country was found to be covered with dense bush and thick grass, eight to ten feet high. He found that Kissaki was strongly held. So far he had had no

word from General Nussey and could not get into
communication with him.   He decided to attack on
the 7th under any circumstances.

His plan of attack was for General Beves to advance
with the infantry by a footpath, which ran close along
by the Mgeta River, directly to Kissaki, while General
Enslin made a détour to the west and approached
Kissaki from the south and south-west.

General Beves advanced accordingly until he
found himself held up by a line of German trenches,
running at right angles to his line of advance, at some
little distance from Kissaki.   He saw that by working
along the river-bank, if it were possible, he would
be able to enfilade this line.   A party accordingly
moved forward and succeeded in reaching a position
whence they could fire down the German line, and
the enemy at once retired.   The advance was continued till our troops found themselves faced by a
strong line of entrenchment directly covering Kissaki.
General Beves then dug in.   The Mounted Brigade
was meanwhile making its way round and came out
to the south-west and south as directed.   Due south
of Kissaki they found a very extensive rubber plantation.   In the course of their attack, they were suddenly counter-attacked on their right flank by a strong
enemy force from the direction of the hills a little to
the south of Kissaki.   Enslin was entirely cut off
from Beves and had been seeking in vain to establish
communication.   There was dense bush between
them, and no possibility of effective co-operation.
Finding himself between two fires and unable to
make headway, Enslin decided in the afternoon that
it was better to retire his force, which he accordingly
did.

General Brits then sent orders to Beves to retire

his force on to the Headquarters camp, which was
done as soon as it was dark.   The 3rd Division now
entrenched themselves on the lower slopes of Little
Whigu Hill, about four miles north-west of Kissaki.

Meanwhile, General Nussey, having left two detachments, one of 300 men at Mgeta and one of 100 at
a point a little farther to the north, in order to bar
the possible return of the enemy, whose movements
through the mountains at this time were a little
obscure, started off down the footpath from Mgeta.
(These detachments consisted of men whose horses
had succumbed.)   The route soon proved to be
impossible, and Nussey struck off farther to the west,
to a track running closer to the Mgeta River.   The
going was very bad.   The set of wireless came to
grief and could not be used, which accounted for the
breakdown of communications with General Brits.

Knowing nothing of what had been going on,
Nussey's column approached Kissaki from the north
on the morning of the 8th, when they came in contact
with the enemy.   They at once extended and an
action developed, which went on all through the day.
The firing could be heard from the 3rd Division
camp, but the dense bush which intervened prevented
any assistance being given to them.   It was not till
evening that General Brits's scouts reached General
Nussey, with instructions to withdraw to Little
Whigu and join the 3rd Division.   The 1st Mounted
Brigade had suffered some fifty casualties.   Though
heavily outnumbered, they had held their ground,
and when darkness fell the enemy withdrew.

The results of the fighting around Kissaki were
very unfortunate.   It had been the intention of
General Smuts to be present and direct operations.
He endeavoured to get out by car, but was held up

half-way down the mountains, and could go no farther. Having no horses, he was forced to turn back. His plan had been to make a simultaneous attack with the infantry and the two mounted brigades. Had this plan been put into execution, the results might have been very different and far-reaching. The troops fought at a great disadvantage, as, having no artillery with them, there was no gun fire to support the dismounted troopers and infantry. The attacks had been piecemeal. On the 7th, Beves's infantry and Enslin's brigade failed to gain touch and there was no co-operation between them, while Nussey's brigade was not there at all, and when it did arrive, made an attack single-handed. The enemy was in considerable strength. As was afterwards learned, his actual numbers had been between 3,000 and 4,000, and he was fighting in strongly entrenched positions, which he had previously prepared. In addition he had a good knowledge of the ground over which he was fighting. It is not surprising that he succeeded in beating back the isolated attacks which were levelled against him. Till that time he had been beaten and driven off the field on every occasion that he had fought us, and now for the first time he saw our troops retire. The inevitable result was that his morale was considerably raised.

General Smuts did not receive the news of Nussey's fight and subsequent withdrawal till the 9th. The whole force was then assembled in the position below Little Whigu. He immediately sent instructions to General Brits to push round by the south of Kissaki. General Brits decided that this was impossible and suggested that he should move by the north, which he considered feasible. General Enslin was accordingly moved by the north and occupied Dakawa, east of Kissaki, on the Tulo road, on the 15th. As previously related, Hannyngton's brigade had already occupied the line of the Dunthumi, nine miles more to the east along the same road.

The enemy, finding his line of retreat to the Rufiji thus threatened, evacuated Kissaki on the 14th, and we moved in on September 15th.

We found a large number of sick he had left behind in hospital, among them no less than seventy-two whites. All stores and supplies had been carried off or destroyed.

The enemy now retired to the south of the Mgeta River, and we were in undisputed possession of the Uluguru Mountains. The troops were very exhausted by the hardships they had undergone on very reduced rations. The force about Kissaki was cut off by a sudden downpour of rain in the mountains, and for a fortnight they were living largely on the meat of hippopotami they shot in the Mgeta River, and " matama " or native millet. Large numbers went down with malaria in the pestilential Mgeta Valley, and the improvised hospitals were crowded. All that was humanly possible was done, and the work of the doctors, under Colonels Moffatt (a grandson of the great missionary), Müller, and de Vos was above all praise and was subsequently duly recognised by the Commander-in-Chief. This force was for a time practically isolated by the rains, and it was not for some time after the occupation of Kissaki that it was possible to run ambulances and regular transport down " Sheppard's Pass." Consequently it was impossible to get food and medical comforts forward to them, or for them to evacuate their sick.

When the enemy vacated Kissaki, our troops were

holding a line from Kissaki on the west to Tulo on the east. There was no possibility of continuing the attack. Our troops were thoroughly exhausted, their numbers greatly reduced by sickness, in addition to which the supply difficulties were immense.

The columns had pushed on nearly a hundred miles beyond their original destination on the Central Railway line, where there had been no halt or opportunity for accumulating stores for the advance. The fighting front was being fed from a railhead at Korogwe on the Tanga Railway. Everything had to be brought up some 300 miles, over winding tracks through bush and swamp. Over 600 animal-drawn vehicles had been added to the transport since the beginning of June, but the animals themselves were dying by hundreds. Owing to horse-sickness and " fly " the life of a mule or an ox was not as a rule more than six weeks. It was very difficult to make good the wastage. The animals when they arrived had to be broken, and this took over a month as a rule.

As regards motor transport, a large proportion of the lorries were out of action, and spare parts were not forthcoming to keep the vehicles on the road, apart from absolute breakdowns. The only increase of mechanical transport since we left Moschi had been 300 " Ford " box lorries and a few Reos. The box lorries were organised as what was known as the " Chigga " (jigger) convoy. They did not arrive till well into August in Africa, and it was the end of September before they reached the Central line. Although the rains were not due for some time, there were several spells of wet weather, with heavy rainfall, and these always meant all traffic being held up for some days. Not only were the roads impassable, but bridges were washed away and had

16

to be rebuilt, the embankments along the hillsides sank and had to be bolstered up before anything could pass. The Supply and Transport branches had some anxious times.

Although it was not possible to advance, it was necessary to clear up the situation. The 2nd Mounted Brigade, which was now at Dakawa, was joined by the 3rd South African Battery, under Captain Gordon Grey, on September 17th. This battery had gone back from the western side, and passing through Morogoro, had come down the eastern side. On this date General Enslin, with his units greatly reduced in numbers, carried out a reconnaissance in a south-easterly direction, across the Mgeta River, supported by the fire of the guns. The enemy were encountered about half a mile south of the river, holding an entrenched position. The dismounted South Africans took a line facing them and dug themselves in. Firing went on for some three hours. The following day the enemy made a half-hearted attack on their line, which was easily beaten off. Meanwhile, the 5th and 6th South African Infantry Regiments came across from Kissaki, under General Beves, and prolonged the right of the Mounted Brigade.

Orders were now issued to the 1st Division to send a battalion across the river and feel for and threaten the enemy's right, which had been located near Mssogera, about three miles south-east of Nkessas, with a view to holding the enemy on this flank while the 3rd Division operated on the western end of the line. The 2nd East African Brigade was ordered to carry this out. The 57th were detailed to contain the enemy in front, while the 3rd King's African Rifles crossed the river some two miles lower down and

worked against their right flank, the Gold Coast
Regiment moving abreast of them and supporting
them from the left bank, with the 5th South African
Battery in readiness to support the infantry movements.

At 2 a.m. on the 19th the King's African Rifles
crossed by a ford and advanced about a mile, driving
back enemy patrols, and found the enemy in a
strongly entrenched position. They were engaged
throughout the day, the enemy being supported by
howitzers. At about 5.30 p.m. the enemy counter-
attacked. The infantry, materially assisted by the
fire of No. 5 Battery, had no difficulty in repelling
them. The King's African Rifles were ordered to dig
in where they were, while the Gold Coast Regiment
took position at the ford by which they had crossed.
The enemy remained in their trenches.

At the other end of the line there had been a
vigorous fire fight. The enemy's position was found
to be strongly held.

Orders were now issued for the 3rd Division to
move back into reserve and the 1st Division to take
over the line they were holding. The 1st East
African Brigade was accordingly ordered down from
the " Summit " (of the Pass), and during the next few
days these movements were carried out.

The dispositions then were : at Kissaki, the 17th
Cavalry and the 25th Royal Fusiliers ; at Dunthumi
(Kkessas), 1st East African Brigade Headquarters,
2nd Rhodesians, 29th Punjabis, 130th Baluchis,
2nd and 3rd Kashmiris, and the 5th, 6th, and 7th
Batteries ; at Tulo, 2nd East African Brigade Head-
quarters, 3rd King's African Rifles, and the Gold Coast
Regiment ; at the Summit, the 27th Mountain
Battery and the 57th Regiment.

The 3rd Division moved back to Morogoro in order to recuperate and to be redistributed in a fresh organisation which the Commander-in-Chief had planned for the next advance.

From now till the end of December the situation remained practically unchanged on this front. When the 1st East African Brigade took over the line from the Dunthumi to Kissaki, General Sheppard made some modifications in the previous dispositions, as his force was only about half the strength of the forces which had been holding this section. He withdrew to the north of the Mgeta, where he would have a shorter line, and being on higher ground the conditions would be more healthy.

As an index to the conditions existing, in the vicinity of Dakawa alone, no less than 500 carcases were burned by the troops taking over this sector.

At this time the enemy had eighteen companies between the Mgeta and the Rufiji. Their patrols were becoming active and pushing across the Mgeta in strength. The road from the Dunthumi to Kissaki, running parallel and close to the enemy's front, was a very vulnerable line of communications. The enemy started sniping and mine-laying on a large scale. By means of vigorous and aggressive patrolling on our part and constant observation for and immediate attack of hostile patrols, his activities were soon put a stop to.

The enemy was given no rest. By the orders of the General Officer Commanding the batteries were always in action, there was constant artillery observation from dawn till dark, and any target was at once taken on by the guns. The enemy's positions were accurately located, partly by reconnaissance, partly by information obtained from prisoners and deserters, of whom there were a large number constantly coming in. One feature of the fighting was the firing of the grass and aggressive raids under cover of the smoke. An aerodrome had been established at Tulo, and there was constant combined work of guns and aeroplanes. The aeroplane would drop incendiary bombs on the grass between the lines when the wind was in the right direction, and the guns lying in wait turned on the enemy when they came forward to extinguish the fires. This procedure was attended by some very good results.

There was a certain satisfaction about the situation on the Mgeta to be derived from the realisation of the fact that the enemy were in the pestilential swamps of the Rufiji and Mgeta Valleys, while the bulk of our force was, if not in the hills, at all events on higher ground for so long as it was necessary to halt.

Simultaneously with the advance down the Uluguru Mountains the 2nd Division had moved south from Kilossa towards the Great Ruaha River.

On August 28th a force consisting of the 10th and 11th South African Infantry, with the 2nd South African Battery, having been preceded by the 1st South African Horse, left Kilossa for Uleia, under command of Lieutenant-Colonel Burne. They were followed on the 31st by the 12th South African Infantry and the 28th Mountain Battery, under command of Lieutenant-Colonel L. Davies, R.G.A. The country was found to be very difficult and the roads very bad. From the time they started they were in constant touch with the enemy, but he avoided action during the first few days. As soon as our troops deployed he retired. On September 3rd, however, he took up a position on a ridge near Kikumi. The infantry advanced, covered by the fire of the South African Battery, while the 1st South African Horse worked round his right flank. Fighting went on throughout the day, and in the evening the enemy retired to a parallel ridge a short distance to his rear. We again attacked on the 4th and again he retired, having suffered considerably from our fire.

The road by which Colonel Burne's column was advancing now disappeared entirely, and there was nothing ahead of him but a narrow path through a deep gorge. The battery was held up and the personnel of battery and ammunition column spent the next week road-making, advancing a mile or two a day on the road they made.

On the 4th a third column left Kilossa, consisting of the 9th South African Infantry, with No. 12 Howitzer Battery (two 5-inch). On the 6th Colonel Davies's column joined Colonel Burne at Kikumi. The two columns now advanced by parallel routes, Lieutenant-Colonel Burne, who was given a section of the 28th Battery, taking the eastern route. The enemy fought rearguard actions each day, being gradually forced back, till on the 10th the two columns joined hands again at Kidodi. The going had been bad and a few mules had fallen down precipices, but the guns were all still in action.

On September 11th No. 2 Battery rejoined the column. The enemy had taken up a position on the Great Ruaha River between Kidodi and Kidatu. They had a 4·1-inch gun in action on the far side of the river, with which they shelled at our camps Kidodi at long range.

Our force could go no farther, as the supply difficulties were becoming insuperable. During the whole
advance from Kilossa they had been on short rations,
and any rains in that swampy area would mean their
practical isolation. The effect of these privations,
continuous trekking over bad country, and the labours
of road- and drift-making had been very disastrous.
Strongly worded reports went in from the medical
officers to Headquarters. For the time being the
forces remained where they were, facing each other,
neither side making any move.

In other theatres, too, progress had been very satisfactory. Brigadier-General Northey had pushed forward one column, which had occupied Lupembe on
August 19th, and another which occupied Iringa on
the 29th. These two columns were now converging
on Mahenge, the northern was on the Ulanga River,
to the north-west, and the southern to the south-west
of Mahenge, on the Ruhudje River. In the south
he had occupied Ssongea, about eighty miles east of
Wiedhafen, on Lake Nyassa.

In the Lake region the progress of the Belgian forces
and our Lake detachment had been continued.
General Smuts had arranged with General Tombeur,
the Belgian Commander, that Colonel Molitor's
Ruanda column and Brigadier-General Sir Charles
Crewe's columns based on Mwanza, and Colonel
Olsen's column based on Ujiji, should converge on
Tabora. The ships on Lake Tanganyika had occupied
several ports on the eastern coast, and one Belgian
battalion was disembarked at Karema to advance on
Tabora *via* Sikonge.

Colonel Olsen's column left Ujiji early in August,
and on the 14th crossed the Mlagarassi, defeating the
enemy force opposing it, another column crossed

at the same time some thirty miles farther to the south. A halt for some days was then necessary to collect supplies.

Meanwhile, the main German force, which had retired from Mwanza, had taken up and entrenched positions about the Kahama and Tindo Hills, to bar the advance by the two routes from Mwanza to Tabora. Colonel Molitor's column was at St. Michael on the western and General Crewe's column at Iwingo on the eastern road, both being delayed by difficulties of supply and transport.

Finding Tabora threatened from the west by the advance of Colonel Olsen's column, the German force at Kahama was suddenly withdrawn about the end of August. General Tombeur ordered Colonel Molitor to press forward at once. He sent on two battalions and a battery on September 1st, the remainder of the brigade following later. The enemy rearguard was dislodged from the Kahama position and they retired, leaving a 4·1-inch gun behind, which they had put out of action.

Colonel Olsen was meanwhile pushing eastwards along and to either side of the railway, the Karema battalion coming by Ulwila towards Sikonge. Colonel Olsen's force was in constant touch with the enemy, driving them before them, till on the 12th they came to the strong position, which the enemy had prepared in the Lulanguru Hills. The Belgians at once attacked and succeeded in taking the advanced posts that day. During the night German reinforcements arrived by rail and on the 13th they counter-attacked. There was heavy fighting all day. The same day Colonel Molitor had occupied the two hills at Itanga, about eight miles north of Tabora. On hearing this, the Germans withdrew part of their force from Olsen's front during the night by rail and, reinforcing the northern command, succeeded in retaking the Itanga position the following day, after a hard fight. This was the enemy's last effort. They had been seeking to cover their retirement from Tabora, which was commenced on September 11th. The enemy rearguards were gradually dislodged from their positions, and on September 19th the Belgians entered Tabora.

The enemy retired in two columns : one under General Wahle, by the railway, the other, under Major Wintgens, by Sikonge towards Itunda. General Crewe moved his column up and occupied Igalulu on the railway, to the east of Tabora, a few days later.

These two columns made their way in a south-easterly direction and arrived on the Great Ruaha River, to the north and west of Iringa, about the middle of October, when our patrols gained touch with them.

The enemy losses in and about Tabora amounted to fifty whites killed and 120 prisoners, 300 Askaris killed and wounded. They left four guns, two of them 4·1-inch, and three machine guns behind them. They destroyed a quantity of stores and ammunition.

The Belgian forces now remained in occupation of the Ujiji-Tabora line.

On the southern frontier at this time the Portuguese had entered German territory and were holding certain points on the north bank of the Rowuma.

The situation was now as follows : the enemy forces were in the area bounded on the north by the Rufiji, Mgeta, and Great Ruaha, and on the west by the Ruhudje and Ulanga, while the coast-line on the east was in our hands.   Outside this area there were only the detachments making their way down from Tabora to join up with their main forces, and a small detachment between Dar-es-Salaam and the Rufiji. On the south the Portuguese held the line of the Rowuma and their detachments held posts to the north of it.

HANDENI to the MGETA

Sketch 2.

Scale 1:1,000,000

10 5 0 10 20 Miles

Routes followed by columns are shown ———

To avoid excessive length
the country north of Kangata
is shown as an inset, on the
same scale as the rest of the map.

CHAPTER XIII

REORGANISATION—A NEW BASE FORMED

Such was the situation towards the end of October, 1916. The campaign had entered upon a new phase and the plan for the future operations had now to be considered. Again a dominating factor was the rainfall. How much time was available before the rains would burst ? Although there is rain in December and January in this part of the country, which might be expected to hold up movement for a few days at a time, the real heavy rains, which would bring operations to a standstill, do not commence, as a rule, till about the beginning of March.

There was much to be done before our forces would be ready to move. The parade states of the white troops, not only the South Africans of the 2nd and 3rd Divisions, but the 25th Royal Fusiliers, the batteries of artillery manned by white men, and the motor-transport drivers, showed but a comparatively small percentage of effectives. On the strength of the reports of the medical officers the Commander-in-Chief authorised the assembly of medical boards to report on the fitness or otherwise of all white troops for further service in the country. The area before us was notoriously more unhealthy than any through which we had previously passed. It was obviously useless to take men who were constantly down with malaria into this country; they would only prove an encumbrance. The result of the medical examinations was that some 12,000 white troops were sent to South Africa as unfit to stand the hardships of further campaigning in this region, till they had regained their normal strength by a period of rest with good food in a healthy climate.

The Loyal North Lancashires were just returning from the Cape, where they had been sent some months previously, at full strength. The usual drafts of reinforcements were arriving from home, but no ordinary drafts would make good the enormous wastage which the force had suffered. General Smuts had, however, formed additional battalions of King's African Rifles. Some of these had already been brought forward, and others were near the end of their training and would soon be ready. There was also the Nigerian Brigade, commanded by Brigadier F. H. B. Cunliffe, which was expected to arrive in the country early in December, and two batteries of Kashmir Imperial Service Mountain Artillery were coming from India. When these reinforcements arrived, General Smuts considered that he would have an adequate force at his disposal to resume operations.

Transport was another question. The condition of the animals was deplorable, but meanwhile the work of the transport had been considerably reduced by the restoration of the railway-line from Dar-es-Salaam to Dodoma. It was not till the beginning of January, 1917, that trains could run, but the divisional engineers had carried out repairs to the bridges which enabled them to sustain a light load and a number of motor tractors, Napiers and Reos, had been converted into rail tractors. These tractors, of which there were some thirty-five, ran from Dar-

es-Salaam to Dodoma, dragging loaded trailers behind them. A tractor would carry about five tons
and the trailer an additional ten tons of supplies.
There was only one break of bulk, at the Ngerengere,
in the whole 300 miles. The repair of the line for
regular traffic was doubtless somewhat delayed by
this duplication of repair work, but that was comparatively unimportant. The depot at Mkesse for
the troops on the Mgeta and Morogoro, Kilossa, and
Dodoma were supplied with foodstuffs, and it was
possible to do away with the long trek through the
bush from the railhead at Korogwe. The improvised
rail tractors on railway trolley-wheels worked excellently.

At the beginning of November the distribution
of the enemy's forces, according to our information,
was as follows : On the Mgeta front, sixteen companies ; about Kissangire and Lower Rufiji, six
companies ; Kilwa district, six companies ; Kidatu-
Iringa district, seven companies ; on the Ruhudje,
in the south-west, 7 companies ; columns from
Tabora, in the west, eight companies ; unplaced,
five companies.

The companies from Tabora were in the vicinity of
Iringa, to the north-west, west, and south-west. The
unplaced companies might be on any of the fronts.

Information had been received that the enemy had,
in addition to his depot at Mahenge, formed depots
at Liwale, about 130 miles south-west of Kilwa, and
an intermediate depot at Madaba, some ninety miles
due south of Kissaki and sixty miles east of Mahenge.
There was a big depot at Utete on the Rufiji, which
was his base for the Kissangire detachment, and
another at Beho Beho supplying his force on the
Mgeta.

His object was to delay our advance as long as possible. When forced to retire, our information was that he would withdraw to Mahenge or, if that were impossible, he would move south and try to cross into Portuguese territory.

Meanwhile, his main force was facing us to the north of the Rufiji. If we attacked him directly, we should force him back on country which he was preparing to defend. To drive him back and cross the Rufiji in face of opposition would be a very lengthy business. Our troops would be detained for a considerable time in the swamps of that river. Once the rains commenced, vast tracts along the banks are under water and quite impassable. It is only about Kibambawe, the crossing south of Kissaki, about Mroka on the northern bank and at Utete on the southern bank, where the hills come to the banks, that the river is approachable during the rains. The Rufiji was a different proposition from any of the rivers we had previously encountered. The average width of the water-way is about a quarter of a mile, and in parts considerably more. A river-steamer was reported to have worked as far inland as Kibambawe, due south of Kissaki, during the rains, and to Mtanza, some eighty miles up from the mouth, in the dry season. Once in our hands, the Rufiji could therefore be used as a line of supply.

The forces opposed to Generals Northey and Van Deventer, on the north-west and west, were based on Mahenge and widely separated from the Rufiji force.

Our immediate objective was the line of the Rufiji, or more correctly, the forces to the north of it, as their defeat was our first object. If, however, they succeeded in evading decisive battle and retired south of the river, it was important that the river-line should be in our hands and that we should not have to contest the passage. It was also desirable that we should prevent their retirement farther south and separate them from the Mahenge force. From Kibambawe to the coast is over 100 miles, a wide gap to be guarded.

General Smuts's plan was to establish a coastal base to the south, for which Kilwa was selected, and land an adequate force there, which would be ready to work to the north-west or north as required. When this had been accomplished, he proposed to attack the enemy from the north, and at the same time to seize a crossing over the Rufiji, unknown to the enemy, above Kibambawe, and move a force from this to the south-east, to cut the enemy's line of retreat towards Mahenge, and eventually join hands with the Kilwa force and close in on the enemy's rear before he could escape. If the enemy broke through, it was hoped to at all events bring him to action and deal him a heavy blow as he retired. A column based on Dar-es-Salaam was to advance simultaneously against the Kissangire detachment and press on to Utete.

The plan of operations was not simple, but the problem was not easy. The establishment and organisation of the base at Kilwa, the transfer of the force to Kilwa, the arrangements for necessary transport for this force, etc., would demand careful study of the means available and the preparation of an accurate time-table by the Staff.

Simultaneously with these movements Generals Van Deventer and Northey were to co-operate and press in from the north and west, from Iringa and Lupembe to the south respectively. The preliminary steps for the execution of these plans had already been taken.

At the end of September Brigadier-General Hannyngton had been recalled from the Mgeta front to
Morogoro to receive instructions. Incidentally his
journey in had been none too easy. There had just
been two or three days of heavy rain down the east
of the Uluguru, with typical results. On reaching
the Mwuha River, between Tulo and Sheppard's
Pass, what had till that time been an easy ford,
through which it was possible to drive and drag
motor-cars, was a deep river, and he and his party
had to strip and swim. (There was a bridge built
a little later, but at that time there had not yet been
labour available.) It would be some days before the
road would be fit for any wheeled traffic, and consequently they had to trek the whole way in to Morogoro
through the mountains, with porters carrying their
baggage on their heads following them.

General Hannyngton was then placed in command
of a force to be assembled at Kilwa, consisting of :
2nd Loyal North Lancashires (back from the Cape),
40th Pathans, two battalions 2nd King's African
Rifles, a composite battalion of Indian troops from
the lines of communication and the 8th and 14th
(5-inch Howitzer) Batteries, all to be conveyed by
sea, partly from Tanga and the remainder from
Dar-es-Salaam. The infantry brigade was known as
the 3rd East African Brigade. The 8th Battery and
the 2nd King's African Rifles, which latter had
recently come to the front from Nairobi, where they
had been raised and trained, had been sent back to
Tanga from Morogoro in the middle of September.

On arrival at Kilwa, General Hannyngton pushed
out detachments and occupied Njingo, Mtumbei-
Chini, Mitole, Matandu, and Kibata, to cover the work
on the harbour landings, etc., and the road-making

between Kilwa and Kilwa Kisiwani. The latter possesses an excellent, natural, land-locked harbour, the best along the coast. It lies fifteen miles south of Kilwa, which is the headquarters of the district, but has no harbour, ships having to lie a mile out. Kilwa Kisiwani is notoriously unhealthy, and would be used only as a port.

On the transfer of Brigadier-General Hannyngton, Colonel (later Brigadier-General) O'Grady replaced him in command of the 2nd East African Brigade. This brigade now consisted of the 57th Rifles, the Gold Coast Regiment, and the 1st and 2nd Battalions of the 3rd King's African Rifles. The 57th Rifles were at this time about Mssanga, about twelve miles north-east of Kissangire. A small force of line-of-communication troops, consisting of Jhind Imperial Service Infantry and details, had bravely but unsuccessfully attacked the enemy position at Kissangire, without artillery support, on October 9th, and as a result, the 57th, under Major T. J. Willans, D.S.O., who was now in command of this column, had been sent across country from Tulo to reinforce them. The enemy were still about Kissangire and Kissegesse, fifteen miles to the south-east of it, barring the two roads leading from Dar-es-Salaam to the Rufiji.

The situation on the Mgeta front was unchanged.

General Van Deventer's command, on the west, had been reorganised. The 3rd Division had been disbanded. The majority of the personnel had been invalided, and there had been very few horses left in the 2nd Mounted Brigade. The fit men and horses had been transferred to the 1st Mounted Brigade, under Brigadier-General Nussey, and this brigade now consisted of the 1st, 4th, 7th, and 9th Regiments of South African Horse. A large number of the

17

men of this brigade also had been invalided. The reorganisation of the Mounted Brigade had taken place at Morogoro, and they had then marched via Kilossa to Iringa. Of the 2nd South African Infantry Brigade, the 5th South African Infantry had been sent round by the Zambesi and Chinde to Wiedhafen on Lake Nyassa to join General Northey. Its place had been taken by the Cape Corps, and a third unit had been added to Brigadier-General Beves's command, known as " the African Scouts."

The Lake Detachment had ceased to exist. Brigadier-General Sir Charles Crewe had, for reasons of health, to return to South Africa. The 17th Indian Infantry and the 1st Battalion 4th King's African Rifles had been transferred to the 3rd South African Infantry Brigade, which now had five battalions, including the 7th, 8th, and 10th South African Infantry, under command of Brigadier-General Berrange. The remainder of the Lake Detachment had been disbanded. Part of this brigade were holding the line Kikumi, Kissanga, Njukwa Drift, and the remainder, with the rest of the fighting troops of the 2nd Division, were under orders to concentrate at Iringa.

About the middle of October the enemy force from Tabora was approaching Iringa. They were in several parties and numbered in all about 2,000. At this time General Northey's main body was facing the enemy on the Ruhudje, and there were detachments at various points, Lupembe, Malangali, Mgeta Pester (about fifty miles south-east of Iringa), and at Iringa, Colonel Rodgers's being the most northerly detachment.

On October 25th General Van Deventer reported that the main portion of the Tabora force had

broken through on the night of the 22nd / 23rd
and had cut all communication between Northey
and his Iringa detachment. Colonel Rodgers was
consequently placed temporarily under command
of General Van Deventer, and shortly received
instructions to move south. He was relieved at
Iringa by a column, consisting of the 7th South
African Infantry, under Colonel Freeth, the South
African Cyclists, under Lieutenant-Colonel J. M.
Fairweather, D.S.O., and two sections of the 28th
Mountain Battery.

Meanwhile, General Northey was sending his South
African Mounted Rifles Battery with an escort, under
Lieutenant-Colonel Baxendale, to join Colonel
Rodgers. On reaching Ngominji, Baxendale dropped
a post, consisting of two guns and fifty men under
Captain Clarke, S.A.M.R., and proceeded to Iringa.
Having handed over the battery to Colonel Rodgers,
he was returning with the escort to Ngominji, when,
on October 23rd, he was ambushed. Lieutenant-
Colonel Baxendale was killed, thirty-three of his
party were killed, wounded, or missing, and the enemy
secured one machine gun.

The enemy, who were in force, then attacked the
little post at Ngominji. They held out gallantly for
several days, but by the morning of the 29th the
enemy had got up to within a few yards of their
trenches, Captain Clarke had been killed, and the
remainder of the little force, after a good and prolonged effort, surrendered to an enemy twenty times
their strength.

Meanwhile, Colonel Rodgers, who was moving
down towards Ngominji, had reached Mahansi.
Here he was joined on the evening of the 29th by a
detachment, consisting of the 7th South African

Infantry, some 250 strong, a section of the 28th Mountain Battery, and a party of about eighty South African Horse under Colonel Freeth, which had been sent forward to see them safely through this danger-zone. They were too late to relieve Ngominji, but were in time to reinforce Colonel Rodgers' force.

At noon the following day the enemy attacked, and there was hard fighting till nightfall and all through the 31st. The following morning the enemy were found to have retired, and the column set out for Iringa on the evening of November 1st. Our losses had been comparatively light, but the enemy had lost heavily. He moved off to Madibira, about thirty miles west of Mahansi. When he subsequently quitted Madibira, he left behind 150 sick and wounded, who were taken over by us.

During this time there were frequent patrol encounters all along this line between our troops and the Tabora columns.

There was one particularly successful engagement, when on October 25th a small party of the 4th South African Horse, under Captain Walker, encountered an enemy force at a spot about twelve miles north of Iringa, on the Dodoma road. The South Africans attacked and after a sharp little fight the enemy retired. They left behind four Germans and thirty-four Askaris, killed, wounded, and prisoners, and also an officer and eighteen Askaris, who were sick. There was a suspicion that the Germans had been firing into each other, as they largely outnumbered the South Africans. Under any circumstances it was a very creditable performance on the part of our men.

The Mounted Brigade began to arrive at Iringa on November 16th. (Large bodies could not move

on the road at the same time, as there were water
difficulties, the holes only providing enough for a
small party each day.) The brigade had already
lost a large number of its horses. They had left
Morogoro at full strength at the beginning of the
month.

During all this period General Northey's detachments were constantly fighting. Lieutenant-Colonel
Hawthorn, who had been facing the enemy for some
days on the Ruhudje, attacked at dawn on October
30th, and getting in with the bayonet drove them
across the river with considerable loss. Five whites
and thirty-seven Askaris were found dead and buried
by us, and six whites and seventy-six Askaris were
taken prisoners. A quantity of stores and ammunition, a 6-cm. gun and three machine guns were left
in our hands. Lieutenant-Colonel Hawthorn was
then ordered to withdraw to Lupembe.

General Northey received information that General
Wahle with a considerable force was concentrating
about Malangali, where we had a small post of not
more than one hundred men, under Captain Marriott.
Having closely invested the post, the enemy commenced his attack on November 8th. The fighting
was continuous, the enemy making determined
assaults, all of which were repulsed with heavy loss.
General Northey had ordered Lieutenant-Colonel
Murray, who had been fighting under Colonel Hawthorn on the Ruhudje, to proceed with 400 rifles
to the relief of Malangali. The force was rushed
across, partly in motor-cars. Having sent out patrols
from his halting-place and made himself acquainted
with the situation, Colonel Murray started with his
force in the early hours of the 12th and delivered
a surprise attack on the enemy's rear, killing and

taking prisoners a considerable number of whites and Askaris. A machine gun and a quantity of ammunition fell into our hands, besides mules and cattle, the enemy retiring in the direction of Lupembe.

At about the same time the enemy attacked our post at Lupembe, which consisted of about 300 rifles with a proportion of machine guns. Fighting went on during the 12th, 13th, and 14th, the enemy shelling the post and making several attempts to rush it without success. On the 15th Colonel Hawthorn's column was approaching and Colonel Murray was on his way back from Malangali, and the enemy retired, having suffered heavily in whites and Askaris.

It had been reported for some time that there was an enemy force at Madibira, and it was now decided to seek out this force. General Northey was to send Lieutenant-Colonel Murray with his detachment in motor-cars, and General Van Deventer was to co-operate from Iringa.

On the 21st information was received that the enemy had vacated Madibira, had been at Ilembule the previous day and was moving east. Ilembule is about twenty miles north-west of Ubena. Lieutenant-Colonel Murray set out with his mobile force, some 450 rifles with eighteen machine guns, learned that the enemy were still at Ilembule, and by midday on the 24th had established posts all round them. In addition to machine guns the enemy had a 4·1-inch howitzer, which they at once brought into action. Fighting went on till the afternoon of the 26th, when the enemy surrendered. We captured here seven officers, forty-seven other whites, and 250 Askaris, with a 4·1-inch howitzer and three machine guns, under the command of Lieutenant-Colonel Huebener. It was a very satisfactory enterprise.

The number of enemy casualties, killed and prisoners, exclusive of wounded, in the operations around Lupembe and Iringa during the past few weeks, amounted to 129 Europeans and 619 Askaris. Breaking through from Tabora had cost the enemy dear.

On November 25th General Smuts left Morogoro for this front to reconnoitre the country and investigate the existing conditions on the spot, with a view to issuing orders for the future operations. It was known that the effect of the rains on the Valley of the Ruaha, between Dodoma and Iringa, and south of Iringa, in the vicinity of the Ulanga and its tributaries, would be to convert the country into hundreds of square miles of swamp. It was obvious that no forward move could be made beyond the Ruhudje and Ulanga till after the rains, as transport of supplies would be absolutely impossible. The plan of action for the Nyassaland force and 2nd Division had to be dependent on this.

Having completed his investigations, General Smuts decided on the plan of operations for these forces. General Northey based on Lupembe, and Van Deventer based on Iringa, were to drive the enemy beyond the Ruhudje and Ulanga Rivers. A supply depot was to be formed at once south of the Ruaha for the maintenance of a force to observe and contain the enemy till the rains were over and the advance could be resumed. When the general advance commenced, General Van Deventer was to retake Muhanga, which had been occupied by the enemy, and move a strong force thence to Ifakara, an important crossing of the Ulanga, about fifty miles to the east of it, and on to Luwegu, a German post on the road from Madaba to Mahenge, about fifty miles east of Mahenge, where

the Luwegu and Ulanga meet. General Northey
was to advance to the Ruhudje and Mponda. These
combined movements were to commence on December
24th.   We were already holding Ssongea.   The
second half of the 5th South African Infantry had
arrived at Wiedhafen on November 22nd. The
enemy had made an attack on the night of November
14th / 15th on Ssongea which had been repulsed.
It was impossible to add to General Northey's force
in the south, as no more than there were at present
could be supplied by the Nyassa line of communications.   Otherwise, having regard to the strategic
situation, a column could have been very effectively
employed in this south-western portion of the theatre
of operations.   General Northey transferred his headquarters to Lupembe from New Langenburg, and
General Van Deventer moved to Iringa early in
December.

At the end of October General Smuts had proceeded
to Dar-es-Salaam by trolley, and thence to Kilwa
by sea.   He had there investigated the local conditions
and discussed the situation with Brigadier-General
Hannyngton.   On his return, orders were issued for
the transfer of the headquarters and the remainder
of the 1st Division from Tulo to Kilwa.   There was
a reconstitution of the 1st Division, the 3rd East
African Brigade taking the place of the 1st East
African Brigade.   General Sheppard was to remain
on the Mgeta front under the direct orders of the
Commander-in-Chief.

Major-General Hoskins took over command at
Kilwa on November 15th, the move of the division
being completed by the 29th.   Any such move was
necessarily slow, as there was a very limited amount
of shipping available, and the facilities for embarka-

tion and disembarkation at Dar-es-Salaam left much
to be desired. The collecting of the large quantity
of transport and supplies necessary and the shipping
of it to Kilwa was a very big business in itself and
threw a great amount of work on the administrative
branches.

Meanwhile, the enemy had awakened to the situation and the possible results of the presence of a
force in his rear threatening his lines of retreat to
the south.

From information obtained from different sources,
it appeared that the enemy's strength in the Kilwa
area at this time was ten companies, which accounted
for most of those which had been " unplaced "
by the Intelligence Department at the end of
October. Reports were received at the same time
that the enemy proposed shortly to take the offensive against the Kilwa force, and that the detachment at Kibata would be his first objective.

This information proved to be correct, and on
November 7th the enemy attacked. General Hannyngton had received timely warning and they were
easily driven off. If an attack were intended, this
was obviously a preliminary reconnaissance in force,
as the enemy's strength was estimated not to have
exceeded 400 rifles. They withdrew the following
day, the 8th.

No further attempt at attack was made in November, and except for occasional patrol encounters,
in which we took a few prisoners, the remainder of
the month passed quietly. General Smuts's original
intention had been to send a force from Kilwa to
occupy Liwale, but owing to the enemy's activity in
the neighbourhood of Kilwa, this part of the
programme was in abeyance for the time being. A

detachment had, however, been sent down the Liwale road and had occupied Mpotora, about seventy miles south-west of Kilwa, on the 7th, the day of the attack on Kibata. A battalion was also sent to Ngarambi, about forty miles due south of Utete and thirty miles north-west of Kibata. They arrived there on December 2nd, having met with no opposition.

The transport difficulties in the Kilwa area were very great. The tracks leading from Kilwa are all shifting sand alternating with black cotton soil, and so bad that it was with difficulty that even pack-mules could be got along some of them. The different posts were about forty miles distant from Kilwa, and the transport was by A. T. carts (the Indian army two-wheeled transport cart), pack-animals, and carriers. Kilwa is a " fly " area, and the mortality among animals was consequently very high.

Rain was predicted during December and commenced to fall early, continuing intermittently all through the month. The result was much sickness among the troops.

After a day or two of very active patrolling, on December 6th the enemy again attacked our position at Kibata. It was soon evident that this was to be a serious effort and on very different lines from the attack in November. A 4·1-inch gun and a howitzer, besides two or three small field and mountain guns, the bringing forward of which must have required much time and labour, were brought into action and bombarded our positions. The 2nd East African Brigade was holding Kibata, the post and the hills in the immediate vicinity. The enemy at once occupied a series of higher hills to north, east, and north-west. Reinforcements were pushed up by

General Hoskins.   The 2/2nd King's African Rifles,
with a section of the 28th Mountain Battery, which
left Mitole on the afternoon of the 7th, arrived at
Kibata at 2 a.m. on the 9th.   The fighting was
continuous.   The enemy dug themselves in and
endeavoured to extend their lines to the south on
both flanks, with the object of investing our force.
On the night of the 9th/10th the enemy made a
night attack, which was repulsed.   We had only
one section of mountain guns at Kibata at the time,
and the very bad roads combined with heavy rain
made it most difficult to get more artillery forward.
However, the Headquarters and another section of
the 28th Battery arrived on the night of the 13th,
and they were followed later by the 5-inch howitzers
and a naval 12-pr. with its crew which the Fleet
had landed.   The force at Ngarambi had also been
ordered to Kibata.   The enemy now held some
isolated hills due west of our position, which gave
them excellent observation posts commanding Kibata.
On the 15th attacks were made on the two more
southern of these hills, and after heavy fighting they
were both occupied by us.

The more northerly of the two, a bare hill which
gave no cover, was taken by the Gold Coast Regiment, who drove the enemy out of their positions
and held the hill against the subsequent counter-
attacks, losing heavily during the advance and
subsequently, particularly from the 4·1 howitzer,
which steadily bombarded them.

That night the 129th Baluchis advanced at midnight against the ridge immediately north of the
camp, pulled up the stake entanglement which the
enemy had set up, and assaulted the enemy trenches
with bombs, the mountain guns co-operating as soon

as the bombing commenced, having laid out night lines. They effectively kept any reinforcements from reaching the enemy, and in less than half an hour the position was in the hands of the Baluchis.

The enemy had now been driven from all the positions in the immediate vicinity of our lines. They made a half-hearted attempt to retake one of the hills on the west on the 26th, and this was easily beaten off. They made no further infantry attack, and contented themselves with long-range gun fire till they withdrew, and our forces advanced in January.

General Hoskins now felt that he was in a position to prevent any attempt by the enemy to break south through the Matumbi Mountains, and also to co-operate with our forces from Mgeta when the general advance took place.

General Smuts's plan for the Kilwa force was for one brigade to advance north on Mohoro, the old headquarters of the district, and clear the Lower Rufiji, while the other moved west and joined hands with our forces advancing across the Rufiji from the Mgeta.

North of the Rufiji the situation had undergone little change. The enemy detachments were about Kissangire, Mkamba, and Kibesa. After the fight at Kissangire on October 9th, our detachment had entrenched at Maneromango, where they were rein-forced by South African details from Dar-es-Salaam. They had then advanced to Mssanga, about six miles farther to the south, and were joined there by the 57th Rifles from Tulo on October 21st. The enemy detachments, being less than fifty miles from the Central line of rail, were a constant threat to our main line of communications. Patrolling was active and vigorous. The enemy made several attempts to reach the railway, but never succeeded. At the beginning of November a detachment of 300 rifles was sent to occupy Kongo, five miles west of Mssanga, which left 450 rifles with a couple of 12-prs. at Mssanga. Colonel N. H. M. Burne, D.S.O., took over command of this force from Major Willans on November 18th. On December 16th the enemy advanced on Mssanga and, driving in our piquets, succeeded in occupying the greater portion of the ridge to the south, which commanded our camp and the water-supply. The ridge was retaken the same day and the enemy retired the following morning, leaving some dead behind him.

General Smuts instructed the Inspector-General of Communications, Brigadier-General Edwards, under whose orders these troops were, that the Mssanga and Kongo detachments were to advance, and arrangements were to be made for the landing of a separate detachment on the coast to the north of the Rufiji Delta, to co-operate from the east, if possible, when the general advance took place later.

On December 4th news was received that the Portuguese had been forced to evacuate Newala and their posts at Marunga and Majomba and had re-crossed the Rovuma. Some guns, machine guns, ammunition, and stores had fallen into the enemy's hands. There would consequently be no assistance from the southern front when the general advance took place.

CHAPTER XIV

On December 22nd General Headquarters moved forward from Morogoro to the Dunthumi. Much had been done by the engineers and pioneers during the past few weeks to improve the roads. A depot of supplies and ammunition had been gradually built up on the Dunthumi, and when General Headquarters arrived on the 22nd, enough had been collected for thirty days. This had all come by motor from Mkesse by the mountain road to Bukobuko, down by Sheppard's Pass to the plains below, on to Tulo, crossing the Mwuha River and a swamp, which became deep water with very little rain, from Tulo another fourteen miles to the Dunthumi, six miles being through swamp. From the Dunthumi to Dakawa was an additional eight miles, with more swamp, and four miles beyond lay Kissaki, our western post on this section of front.

The work on the roads had been very heavy, and would be incessant. Rain had not been continuous, but during the previous weeks there had been frequent and heavy thunderstorms, and as much as ten inches had fallen on certain sections of the road. Above the Pass the greater part of the road was cut from the side of the hills, the outer portion being supported by stakes driven into the hillside. With rain this washed away, and the road became dangerous even when apparently passable, unless constantly watched. Through the swamps in the plains below, causeways were built and corduroyed, with bridges over the channels where the water lay. When the rain came, much of it would be under water, and there was constant building-up necessary. It was anxious work for Colonel Collins [1] and the Royal Engineer officers under him, who were in charge of this road.

On the Dunthumi the troops were encamped on the ridge, the last of the foothills running from Kitoho to the river, the battlefield of the 2nd East African Brigade in September. General Headquarters camp was at the foot in the middle of the bush, which had been cleared, just above the native village.

Along a bare ridge to the east, just above their camp, were the hospital " bandas." These had recently been shelled by the enemy, but a note had been sent pointing out that this was the hospital, and from that time on they had turned their attention to the old outpost camp to the south of the road. The piquet line ran about 3,000 yards to the south of the road, and the outpost camp had originally been in the bush, about 800 yards behind them, but it was located by the enemy and had been moved to an island in the swamp about 1,000 yards nearer the road, and the new site had not yet been discovered. They still fired on the old spot.

On the way down, the heavy artillery, the 4-inch guns and 5·4-inch howitzers, which had left Morogoro on the 20th were passed in the vicinity of Tulo. They all arrived within the next three days. Three battalions of the Nigerian Brigade were nearing the top of the Pass. They had only landed in the country

---

[1] Since deceased.

a few days previously, just in time. At too frequent
intervals along the whole route were the carcases of
horses, oxen, and mules which had fallen by the way
during the last few days, and here and there a
skeleton, which had been picked clean by the beasts
of prey. On this journey Lieutenant-Colonel Dobbs,
the Assistant Quartermaster-General, who was in a
motor-car, saw a fine leopard gorging himself on the
carcase of a horse a few yards off the road. He
stopped the car and bagged the leopard at about
fifty yards' range. On another occasion the same
officer had the luck to come on three lions, also when
motoring. There were two other officers with him,
and they each got one. What was satisfactory was
that on both occasions it was possible to stop and
secure the skins, which were good ones.

From the top of Kitoho Hill, which was a steep
climb from the camp, a good view was obtained over
the whole country to the south, to and beyond the
Rufiji and to the west, as far as the hills running
south-east from Kissaki to Kibambawe. A good
map of the immediate front had been prepared by
the airmen at Tulo, based on the German map and
supplemented by their own observations and photos
taken from aeroplanes. This showed not only the
bush, courses of rivers and tracks, but also many of
the enemy trenches, except where they were hidden
by the bush and grass.

An officer of the 7th Battery, Lieutenant Foster,
had lived for weeks on the top of the hill, observing
and directing the fire of the 15-prs. in action in the
outpost camp below, on any targets which might
present themselves. He was thoroughly conversant
with every spot in the area and could give the range
from his guns to any point without any reference

to notes. The officers of the newly arrived
batteries were soon with him, and busy identifying
all the points to which names had been given on
their maps. These maps were soon ruled out in
squares by the gunners, and the squares lettered
and numbered, so that they would be able to turn
their fire on to any point required with the least
possible delay in the coming encounter. The course
of the Mgeta could be followed, and with good glasses
the enemy trenches could be distinguished here and
there. During the next day or two the distances to
prominent objects were all verified by accurate
telescopic triangulation by Major Oats and the
officers of the 134th Battery, and copies of the finished
map were distributed to the gunner and infantry
officers who were to be engaged in this area.

On the 23rd there was a heavy fall of rain, which
lasted three to four hours, so that all mechanical
transport, except the light cars, were brought to a
standstill wherever they happened to be. It was
on such occasions that the motor-transport driver
got his chance at the lions and leopards, and if he was
near the front, he also had the excitement of keeping
a look-out for enemy snipers. The ground was just
drying when, on the 25th, Christmas Day, there was
rain which continued for the next forty-eight hours
and absolutely suspended all traffic and caused the
commencement of operations to be postponed.

The enemy on the Mgeta had now been located as
follows : On the west he held a strong entrenched
position covering the junction of the roads leading
from Kissaki and from Dakawa. Facing our main
position on the Dunthumi, there were a series of
lines of trenches in the neighbourhood of the Mgeta
and along the dongas running into the Mgeta. A

18

4·1-inch howitzer had been located approximately close to the track leading to Kiderengwa, at a distance of about 8,000 yards from our camp. Between these two positions he held an intermediate post south of the Mgeta, across the track leading from Kwa Hongo to Kiderengwa.

At Kiderengwa, Beho Beho, Wiransi, and Kibambawe camps and hospitals had been located by our airmen. These were all north of the Rufiji, which was bridged at Kibambawe.

The road from Kissaki and Dakawa, which passed Wiransi, and was joined at Beho Beho by the Nkessas-Kiderengwa road, led to this bridge. General Smuts's plan was to attack, and if possible surround the forces immediately opposing us, and at the same time to secure a crossing of the Rufiji, unknown to the enemy. There were consequently two objectives : the defeat of the enemy's force and the seizing a crossing of the river. The latter was at the present juncture the more important in the eyes of the Commander-in-Chief, as on it depended the carrying-out of his ultimate plan of joining hands with General Hoskins's troops of the 1st Division and cutting off the whole of the enemy Rufiji forces from the Mahenge or western force.

To achieve these ends, the following were the plans and distribution of the forces :—There were to be four different columns : (1) General Beves's Brigade, with the Kashmiri Mountain Battery and the Faridkhot Sappers and Miners, was to make a wide move to the west, proceeding by Kissaki to Kirengwe, ten miles farther to the west, and then turn south and strike the Rufiji below its junction with the Ruaha, cross in Berthon boats and establish himself on the far bank, the bulk of his force crossing by rafts, which were to be constructed as soon as the bridge-head on the opposite bank was completed ; (2) General Sheppard and the 1st East African Brigade, to which were attached the 3rd, 6th, 13th, and 7th (less one section) Batteries, were to proceed from Dakawa to a point east of Kissaki, making a wide turning movement, attack the enemy opposite Dakawa, press on and clear Kwa Hongo, and then close in on the Kiderengwa position. One battalion was to start on the afternoon preceding the general movement, occupy or mask Wiransi from the north on the following day, and, leaving the necessary posts, to move west and establish connection between the 4th column under Colonel Lyall and General Sheppard ; (3) Brigadier-General Cunliffe with the Nigerian Brigade, supported by the Army Artillery, was to attack the Mgeta position from Nkessas, but not to press in till instructions were received to do so, which would be dependent on the progress of the flanking columns ; (4) Lieutenant-Colonel R. A. Lyall, with a column consisting of a battalion of the Nigerian Brigade, with two of their 2·95-inch guns, and the 2nd Kashmiris, from the 1st East African Brigade, was to advance from Tulo to Kiruru, twelve miles east of Nkessas, arriving there the evening before operations commenced, and move on to Tshimbe the following morning and take up a position there to bar the enemy's line of retreat and establish communication with General Sheppard. If the enemy were cut off, General Sheppard would take command of both columns, Colonel Lyall's and his own.

Colonel Lyall's column had started once from Tulo, but was recalled owing to the weather. They had only made a few miles and were then wading in water up to their waists. In the meantime General Cunliffe and his Nigerians arrived on the Dunthumi. From the time of their start from the railway they had been exposed to a series of heavy rainfalls, with the consequence that some 400 of them were on the sick-list, the greater number with pneumonia. Brigadier-General Beves with his brigade had passed through the Dunthumi and Dakawa camps and was at Kissaki on the 31st.

Orders were now issued for the operations to commence on January 1st, New Year's Day. By 5.30 a.m. Beves's leading troops were at Kirengwe, the 130th Baluchis, under Lieutenant-Colonel Dyke, were some miles along the road to Wiransi, and Sheppard was at his starting-point east of Kissaki. The main object of the move of the separate battalion to Waransi was to prevent any information reaching the enemy of Beves's move by Kirengwe. Colonel Lyall had reached Kiruru the previous day, and was on his way to Tshimbe. The Nigerians and the guns to support them were in position.

General Sheppard first came on a small enemy rearguard at the Dakawa position, which was attacked, some captured, and the remainder dispersed. They were completely surprised and were actually at their breakfast. Among the prisoners was a German doctor with five native African wives. He was quite hurt at not being allowed to keep the wives. Many of the German settlers kept a small harem of native women, others had housekeepers from the Fatherland. The morals of the German settler in East Africa were not of a high standard.

The Germans retained their hold over the Askaris to a great extent by keeping their wives and families in rear of them. The wives of the Askaris, apart from any feeling of affection, practically represent their

worldly possessions. They are the equivalent of
so much solid cash or of so many head of cattle,
and as long as they were behind them they had every
inducement to remain with the Germans and not
come over to us. At this time their women were
all collected in different camps to the south of
the river.

General Sheppard had just dealt with this body of
the enemy when he received information that the
130th Baluchis, who were at that time a little north
of Wiransi, were being attacked by three German
companies, the troops which had just vacated the
Dakawa position. He at once hastened to their
support, reporting his action to General Headquarters.
When he arrived, the enemy had already withdrawn.
The enemy had come up behind the Baluchis and
had attacked vigorously. They made four determined assaults on Colonel Dyke's force and then
retired to the east of the road. The fighting was hard
while it lasted and the casualties were heavy. The
Baluchis lost one Indian officer and thirty-six men
killed, and two Indian officers and twenty-four men
wounded.

Meanwhile, the Nigerians, supported by the guns,
advanced against the enemy's advanced line on the
Mgeta, and opened fire with machine guns and later
with rifle grenades. The howitzers prepared the
way and covered their advance, and as the enemy
were observed retiring, which they did after a
very few rounds, the 15-prs. and howitzers followed
them with a heavy fire till they reached the river-
bank. There was one more line of trenches, which
was held by another body, between the advanced
line and the river. This also was cleared, and the
Nigerians were masters of the north bank of the Mgeta

by 1 p.m. They did not press the attack any farther for the time being.

At about 2.30 p.m. information was received that Lyall's column had arrived at Tshimbe. Soon afterwards the Nigerians resumed their advance. The donga and river-bed were searched by the guns, two machine guns which were near the bridge were located and silenced, and the Nigerians crossed the river. It was some eight feet deep and fifteen yards wide at this part, so was an obstacle. The Nigerians had been able to cross by the bridge without enemy interference.

At the same time the 4-inch naval guns, with the assistance of the aeroplanes, had made excellent practice on Kiderengwa at a range of about six miles. Five shell had actually burst in the middle of the market-place. This was discovered later. The enemy were now retiring by the Beho Beho road, where they found themselves confronted by Lyall's force. They opened fire on him with their 4·1-inch howitzer and proceeded to attack, but were driven back by the Nigerian Battalion. A party, led by Lieutenant Gardiner, then charged the howitzer detachment, having crept up close to it, made short work of the enemy near by and captured the gun. Fighting continued till after dark, the enemy making one last attack at 7 p.m. Lyall remained where he was through the night.

Beves's brigade had made progress, and by the evening of the 1st his advanced troops were at Kwa Hobola, about ten miles south of Kirengwe. Sheppard was at Wiransi, which had been occupied by the advanced double company of the Baluchis at about 11 a.m. They had taken a few prisoners and some stores

At dawn on the 2nd the enemy were found to have disappeared from Lyall's front. They had gone through the bush between the Kiderengwa and Wiransi roads towards Beho Beho. The company which had been holding Kwa Hongo had retired by the same route. The Nigerians had moved in and occupied Kiderengwa early on the 2nd, and had joined hands with Lyall's force. The whole of the enemy forces were south of the Wiransi - Kide - rengwa line. The Nigerians were now ordered to withdraw to Nkessas and Dyke and Lyall to move to Beho Beho kwa Mahinda on the morning of the 3rd. Information had been received of the existence of an enemy position on the Tshogowali River south of Beho Beho. General Sheppard was accordingly ordered to take his brigade to the west from Wiransi till he reached the vicinity of Fuga Mountain, and then come down by the southern bank of the Tshogowali. As he approached Beho Beho that afternoon, Lyall's column was held up by an enemy force and an action developed, which terminated with darkness. He had gained touch late in the afternoon with Dyke's force.

Orders were now issued to the 1st Brigade to push on and get astride the Beho Beho-Kibambawe road, behind the enemy, and Lieutenant-Colonel Dyke, with Lyall's force and his own Baluchis, was ordered to attack from the north. If the enemy got away, he was to be followed rapidly and pressed, to prevent any interference with Beves's operations up the river.

At 11 a.m. the following morning, the 4th, a simultaneous attack was delivered by Sheppard from the south-west and Dyke from the north, on Beho Beho Tshogowali. By one p.m. the enemy had again slipped away through the long grass and our two forces joined hands. It was at this fight that Captain F. C. Selous, D.S.O., the well-known big-game hunter, was killed when leading his company. He had been to England during the summer, and had returned with a big draft for his regiment, the 25th Royal Fusiliers. He met his death on his 65th birthday. Notwithstanding his years, he was as active and keen as a youth of twenty.

Meanwhile, General Beves's force had accomplished much on the west. On the night of the 2nd he had reported his arrival at the Mhumbi, about twelve miles from the Rufiji, after a twenty-mile march, and in reply was told to push on.

An advanced party, consisting of Cape Corps, a section of guns, the Faridkhot Sappers, with four Berthon boats, led by a party of scouts under Major Pretorius, D.S.O., the best known of scouts in East Africa, started off at once to try to seize the crossing. They had already had a very tiring day, and now they set out on another twelve miles through the darkness, feeling their way, the porters laden with the Berthon boats, the signallers laying the telephone wire, the machine-gun porters near the head and closely followed by the mules with the mountain guns, all creeping along as quickly and as quietly as they could. They reached the banks of the Rufiji at dawn. They had met with no opposition, but they had done a great march. With every sort of impedimenta they had covered over thirty miles within twenty-four hours. They now hurried to get the boats in the water, and before very long the first troops were across and busy digging themselves in. The rest of Beves's force followed on, and by the following morning the whole of the Cape Corps

were across the river. That day they seized the
post at Mkalinso, on the route to Mahenge from
Kibambawe, taking prisoners five whites and some
Askaris, and later captured two patrols, who,
ignorant of their presence, walked into their lines.
Some useful information was obtained at Mkalinso,
from captured documents, the prisoners, and over
the telephone, which was tapped and listened on
for thirty-six hours before the Germans were aware
of it.

It was learned that the enemy had received orders
to retire east by the north bank of the Rufiji, and
not to make for Kibambawe, but the rapidity of our
movements and the unexpected appearance of Lyall's
column on their east flank had rendered this impossible. It appeared also that the Germans had
been aware of a projected movement by the west
flank, but when they encountered Colonel Dyke with
the Baluchis, they concluded that this was the column
in question and took no further steps to observe
Beves's movements.

General Sheppard with the 1st Brigade reached
Kibambawe on the 5th. The enemy had already
crossed the river, destroying the bridge behind them.
There was no doubt that the enemy were watching
from the other side. Artillery had been sent forward to join Sheppard now that the road was available. It had been impossible for any wheeled
transport to accompany him through the bush. He
was now facing the enemy with a river, 800 yards
wide as it proved, between them.

That night, the 5th / 6th, he got a double company
and two machine guns across in Berthon boats,
unperceived by the enemy, at a spot a little higher up
the river. The crossing was rendered more difficult

by the hippopotami. They went for the boats. It was impossible to fire, as the Germans would have been at once alarmed. The crews of the fragile craft could only do their best to fend them off with their bayonets. Unfortunately a boat or two were upset and some lives lost. The passage of this advanced party was, however, successfully accomplished, and they lay hidden in the grass all the next day unsuspected by the enemy. General Smuts visited Kibambawe on the 6th, to see how matters stood. He ordered the crossing of the troops to be continued as soon as it was dark. By the morning of the 7th the 30th Punjabis were over, and the enemy now became aware of their presence and attacked them vigorously. They had been reinforced and had with them two light guns. It was impossible to reinforce our men by daylight, as the shooting of the enemy guns was too accurate for a boat to make the passage. The 3rd South African Battery of 13-pounders, under Captain Gordon Grey, was able, however, to render good assistance from the north bank, and the Punjabis held their position, though their casualties were heavy. Under cover of darkness more troops were passed over. While the enemy attacked the party on the south bank, they also poured in a fire, which was at times heavy, throughout the day on our camp on the north bank.

Meanwhile, General Beves had entrenched a strong bridge-head at his crossing. A strong patrol had made its way to the German post at Luhembero, five miles south of Kibambawe, on the 4th, and captured six Germans, eighty porters with their loads, and destroyed 500 loads of foodstuffs. On the 6th an enemy force had been located a couple of miles east of Mkalinso. They were attacked and retired, and General Beves kept a strong detachment at Mkalinso.

On January 8th General Smuts proceeded to General Beves's crossing, *via* Kirengwe. He then ordered him to withdraw the Mkalinso detachment and remain concentrated at the bridge-head for the time being. Orders were issued to General Cunliffe to take the Nigerian Brigade to this crossing.

The brigade had, as before explained, been rushed up to take part in the advance, immediately after it had landed. They had been brought back to the Dunthumi camp virtually to complete their mobilisation. They had originally gone into action without all their equipment, short of some of their machine guns and entrenching tools, and without all their little 2·95 guns, of which they made great use. Everything had now arrived and they were ready to take the field.

The result of the operations had been very successful. Colonel Lyall's column had come as a complete surprise to the enemy and upset all their plans for their retirement. The advance of the 1st East African Brigade by the east of the hills had entirely masked the movement farther to the west by General Beves's column. The enemy had been driven back from his positions on the Mgeta with considerable loss, and, most important of all, the crossing of the river had been effected without opposition and we were firmly established on the south bank.

The enemy detachments in the Delta, north of the Lower Rufiji, had evacuated Mkamba on the night of the 8th / 9th and were retiring to the south. Colonel Burne occupied Kibesa, which is six miles farther south-west, on the 10th.

In the Kilwa area the enemy was reported to be retiring, and orders had been issued for the advance

on Mohoro to the north, keeping touch with the
enemy, while General Hannyngton's brigade was
moving to the west and had occupied Ngarambi.
On the western front General Northey had advanced
and, after an attempt to surround the enemy force
at Mfrika, had occupied that place on the 27th, the
enemy having succeeded in escaping towards Mahenge.
They left a rearguard in a position some six miles
east of Mfrika.   This force was attacked by Colonel
Murray.   He took the southern end of their position
and on the 1st was threatening the northern flank.
The enemy retired and took up a position about
fifteen miles east of Lupembe.   The advance was
continued and the enemy retired a part towards
Mahenge, but the main force towards Ifinga.   On
January 16th Murray's column took the bridge over
the Ruhudje at Malawis, six miles north-west of
Ifinga.

Farther south, Colonel Byron with the 5th South
African Infantry had advanced from Ssongea and
captured the post at Njamebenjo with a supply of
stores and cattle on December 20th, and, moving
north, had dispersed an enemy detachment at Gumbiro on January 6th.

On December 25th operations commenced from
Iringa.

On December 19th General Van Deventer had
reported that owing to the heavy rains it had been
impossible to get forward the reserve of supplies
which it had been intended to form at Iringa for the
ensuing operations, and consequently it would be
impossible to feed the whole division during an
advance.   He recommended that he should keep
three battalions only and a squadron of mounted
troops, and retire the rest of his division to the rail-

way.   To this arrangement General Smuts was forced to agree.

On December 25th an enemy force, estimated at 500 rifles, with a proportion of machine guns, was holding a position about three miles to the north of Lukegeta, with advanced posts about the Lukegeta Neck.   General Van Deventer divided his force into three columns.   Our troops had been concentrated at Boma Himbu on the 24th (Dabaga).   On the right, Colonel Hartigan with the 1st, 4th, 7th, and 9th South African Horse (dismounted, as all their horses had succumbed), numbering in all about 500 rifles ; on the left, under Colonel Taylor, the 4th King's African Rifles and a company of the 8th South African Infantry, 750 rifles in all with two machine guns ; in the centre, under Brigadier-General Berrangé, the 7th South African Infantry and the 17th Indian Infantry, with two companies of " Ruga Rugas " or native levies.   With Colonel Taylor's column was a section of the 28th Mountain Battery.   The right and left columns had orders to march by Makungwas and Boma Likininda's respectively to Muhanga.

On the 25th the central column attacked, the 17th Infantry in advance.   The enemy were in position at the top of a glacis-like slope, giving no dead ground, except half-way up, where there was a knoll, behind which the Germans had two machine guns.   The infantry advanced slowly under a heavy fire from the enemy.   By nightfall they were half-way up and had occupied the knoll referred to.   Orders were then given that the frontal attack was not to be pressed home till the flank columns came in, and at the same time orders were sent to them, by aeroplane (the wireless was not working), to close in.

On the 26th the 17th lay in position, having dug

in during the night, and strong patrols were sent out to left and right, while the arrival of the flank columns was awaited. There were no signs of them that night. What by the map had appeared to be ten miles proved to be some twenty-five by the tracks which wound round the hills by circuitous routes and up and down the steepest slopes. The nature of the road may be gathered from the fact that the Mountain Battery section lost seventeen mules on the way, two of horse-sickness, six from debility, and nine from falling down precipices. A large quantity of the supplies was also lost from porters falling down the " khuds."

That night the enemy broke up into small parties and escaped through the bush in the direction of Makungas.

On the morning of the 27th a squadron of the 7th South African Horse, which had been left to hold Makungwas, encountered a portion of them, the Germans by then having more or less reorganised, and fighting went on from early morning till midday, when the enemy continued their retreat in the direction of Mgeta Pesten.

The two flank columns had arrived at Muhanga on the morning of the 26th, having left detachments at Makungwas and Boma Likininda's to prevent the enemy escaping, the idea being that the enemy, when driven from the vicinity of Lukegeta, would fall back on Muhanga, where the flank columns would then be. When they were half-way back to Lukegeta, they received orders to reinforce the detachment at Makungwas. When they arrived there the enemy had gone.

It was then decided to relieve all white troops and send them back to Iringa. The South African In-

fantry with Colonel Taylor's column were replaced
by the 17th Indian Infantry. There was a depot
of about 7,000 Indian rations at Iringa, and this
would suffice for the time being. The white troops
would return to Dodoma, where they could be fed.
The force had been on half-rations all the time.
There had been heavy rain, making every nullah a
river, and the troops were constantly wading through
them breast high. For ten days all mechanical
transport had been at a standstill. The intention
had been to drive the enemy beyond the Ulanga
River, but the impossibility of supply had necessitated
the abandonment of the plan. This enemy force was
now reported to be making for Mahenge, *via* Ifakara.
This finished the offensive movement as far as the
2nd Division was concerned.

The results show the practical impossibility of
surrounding an enemy and fighting him to a standstill in country of this nature. In the south he had
escaped from General Northey at Mfirika, he had
slipped away from General Van Deventer at Lukegeta,
and on the Mgeta he had succeeded in avoiding the
several columns which had worked round him and
had got across the Rufiji.

Colonel Burne continued his advance in the Delta
and had occupied Kissegesse on the 17th and proceeded to Koge. The enemy were reported to be
clearing away towards the south and several companies had already crossed the Rufiji. In the Kilwa
area we had occupied Mohoro on the 16th, and had
found the 4·1-inch naval gun, which the enemy had
been using against Kibata, abandoned.

On the Upper Rufiji General Cunliffe had been
ordered forward to Luhembero, while the 1st East
African Brigade was to co-operate with Beves's

brigade in clearing the enemy from the vicinity of
Kibambawe.   These orders were successfully carried
out, and the enemy was in retreat to the south and
we had occupied Luhembero by the 18th.

The enemy's artillery had been considerably reduced.   Of the heavier natures he had started with :

One 6-inch .	. .	Taken at Dar-es-Salaam, August, 1916.
Ten 4·1-inch	. .	One taken at Kahe, March, 1916.
		One taken at Mwanza, July, 1916.
		One taken at Bagamoyo, August, 1916.
		Two taken in the Uluguru Mountains, August, 1916.
		One taken at Tabora, September, 1916.
		One taken at Kahama, September, 1916.
		One taken at Mohoro, January, 1917.
Four 4·1-inch howitzers .		One taken at Malangali, June, 1916.
		One taken at Tshimbe, January, 1917.
Four 88-cm.	. .	One taken at Sebea, May, 1916.
		Two taken in the Uluguru Mountains, August, 1916.

Consequently he could not have more than two
4·1-inch guns, two 4·1-inch howitzers, and one 88-cm.
gun remaining of the heavier natures.   Two other
guns had been taken at Tabora, the calibre of which
had not been reported.   We had captured, in addition, a number of guns of smaller natures, besides
machine guns.

General Smuts left Dar-es-Salaam on January 20th,
1917, and the situation at that time was as follows :

On the west General Northey had advanced to the
line of the Ruhudje, over which he had driven the
enemy, and held crossings at Mfirika and positions
some miles to the east of that place, the enemy
having retired towards Mahenge, and the vicinity of
Ifinga.   Farther to the south he was in occupation

of Ssongea and Gumbiro. In the north-west our troops held Muhanga, based on Iringa.

The enemy on the Mgeta front had been driven across the Rufiji, and our troops had crossed at Kibambawe and near Mkalinso and occupied Luhembero and Mkindu.

In the Delta the enemy had withdrawn and our forces had advanced and occupied Kissegesse and Koge.

South of the Rufiji, in the Kilwa area, one column under General O'Grady had occupied Mohoro, General Hannyngton had occupied Ngarambi and was moving to Njimbwi-Kiave.

Such was the situation of the various columns.

From captured documents and intercepted messages it was known that the enemy was very concerned as regards his supplies. His main depots were at Mahenge, Liwake, and Dapate. Certain columns were under orders to live on the country, while others were being supplied from these depots. The enemy was retiring on all fronts. His artillery had been considerably reduced, and as regards ammunition, as all the coast-line was in our hands, he must depend on what he had in the country. His supply could not be replenished from overseas.

General Smuts's plan for the future operations was as follows :

If the Rufiji River proved a satisfactory line of supply (early in December General Smuts had made the preliminary arrangements for the river transport service), the Nigerian Brigade, with General Beves's column in reserve, were to advance to Lukuliro, where they would join hands with General Hannyngton's column.

When the Germans were cleared from the north

19

of them, General Cunliffe with the Nigerians was to move by the Loge Loge—Madaba route and General Hannyngton by Kilwa on Liwale, but this is looking a long way ahead.

At this juncture these two columns were only about forty miles apart, and this was the gap through which the main enemy forces had to escape south.

On the west General Northey's Ssongea column was closing in in a north-westerly direction, while with the main body he was continuing to press the enemy back from the north-west. In the subsequent operations it was intended that he should advance in a south-easterly direction to interpose between the enemy and the Portuguese border.

One brigade and the Delta force were to be transferred to Lindi.

General O'Grady's brigade was at the present time closing in on Utete from Mohoro.

A glance at the accompanying sketch will show the situation of the different British columns at this juncture.

This was the end of General Smuts's campaign in East Africa. At the end of February, 1916, he arrived in East Africa and took over command. After a rapid reconnaissance of the country and situation on the different fronts, certain changes in the distribution of the troops were made, and by the beginning of March the columns were in motion. The rains were imminent, and there was no question of altering the original plan of campaign in its broad outlines. The location of the troops committed General Smuts to that plan.

At that time the Germans not only held their own frontiers, but were in occupation of British territory in the vicinity of Taveta, as far east as Salaita.

The Operations on the Mgeta.

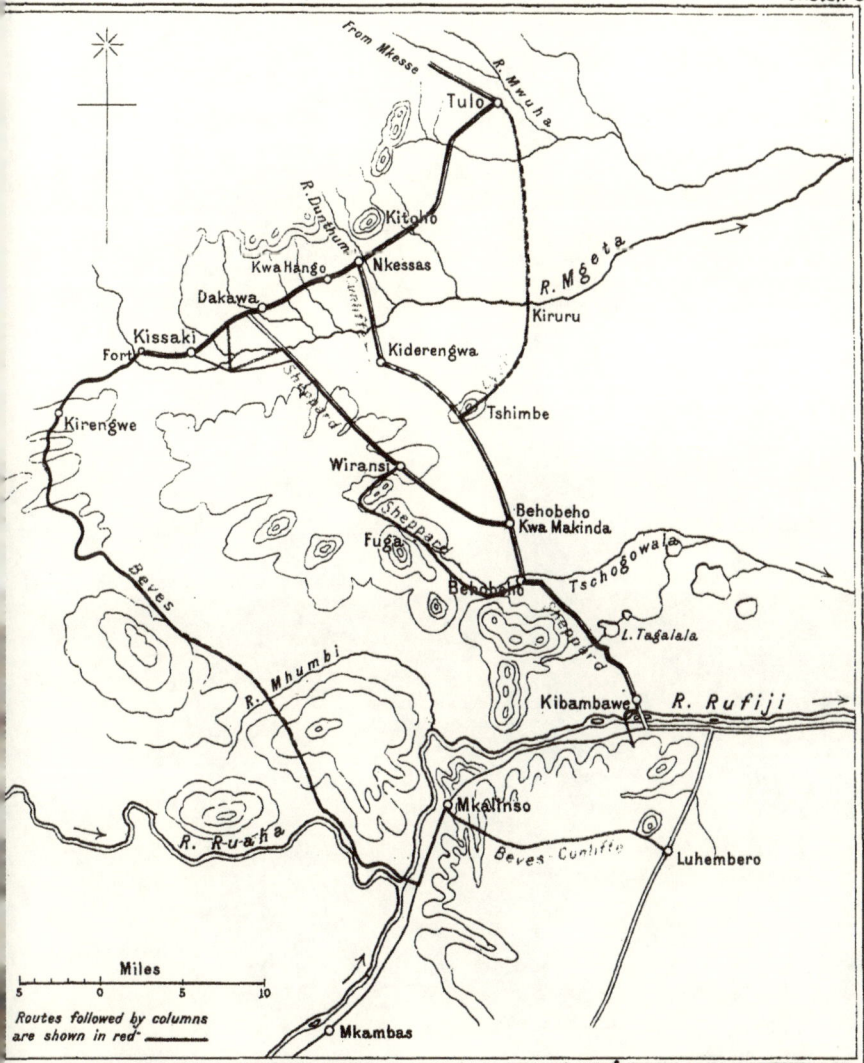

Miles

Routes followed by columns
are shown in red

By the end of March the Kilimanjaro and Aruscha districts, some thousands of square miles, were in our hands. In April the 2nd Division occupied Kondoa Irangi, and there was then an obligatory cessation of movement for the duration of the rains.

At the end of May the advance was resumed, and by the end of June not only the line of the Pangani, with the Pare and Usambara Mountains, but the country as far south as the Nguru Mountains was in our hands. It was then necessary to call a halt on account of the lack of transport and the heavy losses due to sickness.

By the beginning of August the columns were again in motion, and at the end of the month the enemy were retreating to the south of the Central Railway, and were followed, or rather driven, as far as the line of the Mgeta. By the end of September, the enemy were out of Tabora, Iringa, the Uluguru Mountains, and Dar-es-Salaam, and all the ports down the coast were held by British garrisons. Again there was a halt, due to lack of transport for the hundreds of miles of communications, and to losses in personnel from sickness.

At the end of December (January 1st) the push commenced, which gave us the line of the Rufiji. A strong force had been established south of that river, based on the coast at Kilwa, which threatened the enemy's line of retreat to the south, anywhere within reach of the coast.

General Smuts's campaign had lasted ten months.

At the commencement of this narrative it was stated that the campaign was unique, and in this story an endeavour has been made to put before the reader the peculiar difficulties by which the Commander was faced, particularly as to the nature of

the country, its effect on the health of the troops, and
the problems of transport and supply. Actual
figures possibly convey more than general statements. The figures for two months, from the middle
of September till the middle of November, dealing
with the wastage in animals, happen to be available.
They were : horses, 10,000 ; mules, 10,000 ; oxen,
11,000 ; and donkeys, 2,500. The task of the Remount Department was colossal. The animals had
to be provided, kept free from " fly " and disease
when landed, till such time as it was possible and
they were fit to be sent to the front, necessitating
unending care and attention. Then they had to be
trained to the particular work they were required to
perform. This work went on month after month
throughout the campaign.

The difficulties of the Medical Department were, if
anything, greater. Apart from casualties in action,
the numbers of sick from climatic causes were tremendous. For one week in September, as an example,
the returns show 9,000 in different hospitals, of
whom 4,000 were whites and over 200 were officers.
The " regimental sick " are not included in these
figures. Except at a few centres, there were no
buildings available for hospitals, and in any case
they would be quite inadequate for such numbers,
consequently it was a matter of constantly erecting
temporary accommodation in the shape of grass
" bandas." The work of the medical officers was
rendered heavier by the difficulties of transport,
which from time to time prevented the evacuation
of the sick. They had every reason to be proud of
the way in which the difficulties were overcome.

As regards the actual fighting, the nature of the
country made the task of the men in the fighting line

especially difficult. They were opposed not by savages, but by a well-led, well-armed, and well-trained enemy, who at the same time possessed the peculiar facility of the native for finding his way about and feeling at home in the densest bush.

Dense and difficult as the country was for artillery, the rifles were as anxious as in other theatres for the support of the guns, and the gunners rarely failed to find a way of giving that support. Every battery, and at times sections and even single guns, sent an officer into the infantry firing-line, and he directed the fire of the guns, far away in rear. It is not of general interest to describe how this was done, but the young artillery officers were always forward in the infantry firing-line, and succeeded in bursting the shell where they were wanted. The number of casualties among these officers was remarkably small.

The rapid movement of the 1st Mounted Brigade enabled them to push forward and seize Kondoa Irangi. Rapidity of movement is an invaluable asset, but the wastage of horseflesh in East Africa is so enormous that mounted troops are practically out of the question except for an occasional *coup*, for which they must be kept in selected healthy localities till the moment when they are wanted.

This story of the campaign was written partly in East Africa, some on board ship, and the rest from time to time as opportunity offered. It is little more than a diary of the events of the campaign. In publishing it I feel bound to apologise for the style in which it is written, but thought it better to present it as it is, than to wait for an opportunity, which might never come, to produce a more finished narrative of this " side-show " of the great war.

UGANDA

R. Kagera

Victoria
Nyanza

Shirati

Bukoba

BELGIAN

L.
Kivu

R. Rusisi

Sabinio M.

Kigale

Mwanza

RUANDA

Biaramulo

Usumbura

Gitega

Bujombe

Mariahilf

St Michael

Iwingo

Kahama

Jindo Hills

R. Mlagarasi

Kigoma

Ujiji

Ruchugi

R. Mlagarasi

R. Zindi

Itonga

Tabora

Igalulu

Sikonge

CENTRAL RAILWAY

Lake Tanganyika

CONGO

Karema

Itunda

Kili

Bismarckburg

New Utengule

Ilemb

Abercorn

New
Langenburg

RHODESIA

NYASALAND

GERMAN EAST AFRICA

Scale 1:4,000,000.

50   0   50   100 Miles

Advance of Belgian Columns ━━━━━

„   *British*   „   ━━━━━

Situation on 20th January 1917.

BRITISH EAST AFRICA
Nairobi
L. Magadi
Kajiado
R. Athi
Longido
Tsavo
Kilimanjaro
Kilimari
Voi
Kampfontein
Engare Nanjuki
Mt. Meru
Moschi
Mbuyuni
Bura
Maktau
Somali Hauser
Taveta
Aruscha
Kahe
Kasigao
Lol-Kissale
Mbulu
Rapids
R. Pangani
Pare Mts.
Mombasa
Ufiome
MASSAI
STEPPE
Old Schiera
R. Umba
Usambara Mts.
Jassin
Wilhelmstal
Mombo
Manza B.
Amani
Tanga
Pemba I.
Mkalamo
Korogwe
Muheza
Kondoa Irangi
Ssangeni
Handeni
Pangani
Aneti
R. Lukigura
Tissa kwa Meda
Kangata
Chenene
Naju
Rugusi
Membe
Nguru Mts.
Msiha Camp
Njangalo
Manga
Sadani
Zanzibar I.
Kikombo
Dodoma
Tschunjo
Mhonda
Turiani
R. Wami
Mpapua
Dakawa
Bagamoyo
Kidete
Msagera
Mkata
R. Ngerengere
Dar es Salaam
Kilossa
Morogoro
Mkesse
Uleia
Uluguru Mts.
Tulo
Kongo
Maneromanga
Kissanga
Mkamba
Njukwa's Drift
Kikumi
Kissangire
Kissegesse
Kidodi
Iringa
Kidatu
Kibambawe
Mroka
Koge
Ntanza
Mafia I.
Boma Himbu
Utete
R. Rufiji
Likinindas
R. Ruaha
Luhembero
Ngominji
Mgeta
Festen
Ifakara
Mohoro
Muhanga
R. Ulanga
Mtumbi Mts.
Makunga's
Lukulin
Ngarambi
Kibata
Madaba
Kilwa
Mahenge
Mpotora
Kilwa Kisiwani
R. Matandu
Mfrika
Lupembe
R. Ruhudje
Malawia
Ifinga
R. Luwegu
Liwale
Lindi
Sudi B.
Mikindani
Kionga
Ssongea
Majembi
Newala
R. Rovuma
Tunduru
Marumba
PORTUGUESE EAST AFRICA

APPENDIX A

ORGANISATION OF FORCE, MARCH, 1916

1st EAST AFRICAN DIVISION

Major General J. M. Stewart, C.B.

2nd East African Brigade

Brigadier-General S. H. Sheppard, D.S.O.

25th Royal Fusiliers; 29th Punjabis; 129th Baluchis; 3rd Kashmiris.

Divisional Troops

One Squadron 17th Cavalry; East African Mounted Rifles; Mounted Infantry Company King's African Rifles.

Artillery batteries: 1st and 3rd South African Field Artillery; 27th Mountain; 7th (15-pounders); No. 1 Ammunition Column.

East African Maxim Gun Company; Loyal North Lancashire Machine Gun Company.

Mounted Section East African Pioneers; Faridkot Sappers and Miners; Signal Company; No. 2 Section East African Pioneer Company.

1st King African Rifles.

1st and 2nd South African Mounted Brigade Field Ambulances; 1st Indian Bearer Company; two sections 120th Indian Field Ambulance; one section East African Field Ambulance; one section 140th Indian Field Ambulance.

Divisional Train, Supply Column, and Mobile Veterinary Section.

2ND EAST AFRICAN DIVISION

MAJOR-GENERAL M. J. TIGHE, C.B., C.I.E., D.S.O.

1st East African Brigade
Brigadier-General W. Malleson, C.I.E.

2nd Rhodesian Rifles; 130th Baluchis; 3rd King's African Rifles; Kashmiris.

2nd South African Infantry Brigade
Brigadier-General P. S. Beves

Nos. 5, 6, 7, and 8 battalions South African Infantry.

3rd South African Brigade
(Brigadier-General Berrangé)

Nos. 9, 10, 11, and 12 battalions South African Infantry.

DIVISIONAL TROOPS

2nd East African Mounted Infantry Company.
Artillery Batteries: 28th Mountain, No. 8 (Calcutta Volunteer); No. 6 (12-pounders); No. 11 (5-inch howitzers).
No. 2 Ammunition Column.
2nd East African Signal Company; No. 1 Section East African Pioneer Company.
61st Pioneers.
No. 10 Armoured Car Battery.
Two sections British Field Ambulance; two sections 139th Indian Field Ambulance; two sections 140th Indian Field Ambulance; one section East African Field Ambulance; Nos. 2 and 4 South African Field Ambulance; 2nd Indian Bearer Company.
Divisional Train and Mobile Veterinary Section.

LAKE DETACHMENT

Brigadier-General Sir Charles Crewe

98th Indian Infantry; 4th King's African Rifles; Baganda Rifles; Nandi Scouts.
Sub-section 15-pounders breech loader.
Maxim Gun Section.
Uganda and Volunteer Telegraph Sections.
Detachment East African Pioneers.
Two sections Uganda Field Ambulance; one section East African Field Ambulance.
Eight Supply Detachments.

COAST DETACHMENT

40th Pathans; Jhind Infantry.
Two sections 139th Indian Field Ambulance.
Supply Detachment.

ARMY TROOPS

1st Mounted Brigade

(Brigadier-General Van Deventer)

1st, 2nd, and 3rd South African Horse; South African Scout Corps.
2nd, 4th, and 5th South African Field Batteries.
Belfield's Scouts; 4th South African Horse.
Artillery Batteries: No. 9 (12-pounder, naval); No. 10 (4-inch, naval); 134th Howitzer (5·4-inch); Cornwall Artillery; Ammunition Column.
Bridging Section; Printing and Litho Section; 1st and 2nd South African Railway Companies; South African Water Supply Corps; East African Pioneer Company; Signal Company; Wireless Company.
First Squadron Royal Naval Air Service; 26th Squadron Royal Flying Corps, Air Park.
Nos. 4, 5, and 10 Armoured Car Batteries.
Volunteer and North-western Railway (India) Maxim Gun Companies.

LINES OF COMMUNICATION DEFENCE TROOPS

5th and 17th Indian Infantry; 63rd Light Infantry; 101st Grenadiers; Bharatpur, Gwalior, Kapurthala, and Rampur Infantries; Cape Corps.

BASE AND LINES OF COMMUNICATION UNITS

Two Railway Companies, Sappers and Miners; Indian Telegraph Company.

Nos. 15, 19, and 32 Stationary Hospitals; 3rd South African and 139th Indian Field Ambulances; Clearing Hospital; Base Hospitals; Sanitary Sections; General Hospitals; Bacteriological and Hygiene Laboratories; Store Depots, etc.

Ordnance Depots; Mechanical Transport Companies; Carrier Corps; Bullock Cart Train; Ox Train and Mule Corps; Bakeries; Butcheries; Base and Field Post Offices; Store Depots, etc.

Veterinary and Remount Stores; Hospitals and Depots.

REORGANISATION OF FORCE AT THE BEGINNING OF APRIL, 1916

1ST DIVISION

MAJOR-GENERAL A. R. HOSKINS, C.M.G., D.S.O.

1st East African Infantry Brigade

Brigadier-General S. H. Sheppard, D.S.O.

2nd Rhodesians; 20th Punjabis; 130th Baluchis; Kashmiri Battalion.

2nd East African Infantry Brigade

Brigadier-General J. A. Hannyngton, C.M.G., D.S.O.

25th Royal Fusiliers; 129th Baluchis; 40th Pathans; 3rd King African Rifles.

The Cape Corps, 5th Battery South African Field Ambulance, and 1st and 10th Armoured Car Batteries were added to the Divisional Troops.

2ND DIVISION

MAJOR-GENERAL J. L. VAN DEVENTER

1st South African Mounted Brigade

Brigadier-General M. Botha

1st, 2nd, 3rd, 4th, and 9th South African Horse.

3rd South African Infantry Brigade

Brigadier-General C. A. L. Berrangé, C.M.G.

9th, 10th, 11th, and 12th South African Infantry.

DIVISIONAL TROOPS

28th Mountain, 2nd and 4th South African Field, 11th Howitzer Batteries and 4th Armoured Car Battery, and later the South African Motor Cyclist Corps were allotted to this Division.

After the arrival of the division at Kondoa Irangi, it was reinforced by the 1st and 3rd South African Field, 12th (5-inch howitzer), 10th (4-inch naval), and the 7th and 8th South African Infantry from other Divisions and Army Troops.

3RD DIVISION

MAJOR-GENERAL COEN BRITS

2nd South African Mounted Brigade

Brigadier-General B. Enslin

5th, 6th, 7th, and 8th South African Horse.

2nd South African Infantry Brigade

Brigadier-General P. S. Beves

5th, 6th, 7th, and 8th South African Infantry.

DIVISIONAL TROOPS

1st and 3rd South African Field ; No. 8 (Calcutta), No. 13 (two 5-inch howitzers).

No. 5 Armoured Car Battery ; Volunteer Machine Gun Company.

Army Troops

The South African Scout Corps and Belfield's Scouts.

Nos. 9, 10, 134, 38th Howitzer Brigade, less one Battery No. 15 (the 4-inch naval guns).

This battery had recently been formed, and the 38th Howitzer Brigade had arrived from England subsequent to the first phase of the operations. The Flying Corps had also been reinforced by the arrival of the Kite Balloon Section.

A subsequent reorganisation took place after the occupation of the Central line and the advance to the Mgeta River. The 3rd Division was abolished. The composition of the 1st and 2nd Divisions has been given more or less fully in the text.

1st East African Division, under General Hoskins, consisted of:

2nd East African Brigade, Brigadier-General O'Grady: 57th Rifles, Gold Coast Regiment, 1st/3rd and 2nd/3rd King's African Rifles.

3rd East African Brigade, Brigadier-General Hannyngton, consisted of: 2nd Battalion Loyal North Lancashire; 129th Baluchis; 40th Pathans; 1st/2nd and 2nd/2nd King's African Rifles.

The Divisional Troops included the 5th, 8th, and 14th Batteries; one naval 12-pounder (from the Fleet); the 10th Armoured Car Battery; the King's African Rifles Mounted Infantry Company; the 61st Pioneers (less two double companies), and one section East African Pioneer Company.

2nd East African Division, under General Van Deventer, consisted of:

1st South African Mounted Brigade, Brigadier-General Nussey: 1st, 4th, 7th, and 9th South African Horse.

3rd South African Infantry Brigade, Brigadier-General Berrangé: 7th, 8th, and 10th South African Infantry; 17th Indian Infantry; and 1st/4th King's African Rifles.

Divisional Troops included the 5th South African Horse, dismounted; 28th Mountain; 1st, 2nd, and 4th South African Field, and 12th Howitzer Batteries; No. 4 Armoured Car Battery; East African and Indian Volunteer Machine Gun Companies; the South African Motor Cyclist Corps, etc., etc.

Directly under the Commander-in-Chief were: 1st East African Infantry Brigade, Brigadier-General Sheppard: 25th Royal

Fusiliers ; 2nd Rhodesians ; 29th Punjabis ; 130th Baluchis ; 2nd and 3rd Kashmiris.

With this brigade, to which they were attached, were : Nos. 6, 7, and 13 Batteries ; No. 1 Armoured Car Battery ; 1 Double Company 61st Pioneers, etc., etc.

There was in addition the Force Reserve, also directly under the Commander-in-Chief, consisting of : 2nd South African Infantry Brigade, Brigadier-General Beves : 5th and 6th South African Infantry, Cape Corps, and the African Scout Battalion, which had been formed from what had come over to us from the enemy.

Attached to the Force Reserve were : 3rd South African Field Battery ; No. 3 Armoured Car Battery, etc., etc.

Prior to the commencement of the operations on January 1st, 1917, the Nigerian Brigade, under Brigadier-General F. H. B. Cunliffe, C.B., C.M.G., had joined the force and was at General Smuts's immediate disposal, and employed by him together with Sheppard's and Beves's brigades.

APPENDIX B

ENEMY FORCES IN THE FIELD IN EAST AFRICA, AUGUST, 1915

Six Months before these Operations Commenced

(*Taken from a Captured Document*)

Company.				Europeans.	Askaris.	Ruga-Ruga.	Station.
1 Field	.	.	.	16	200	43	Taveta-Mbuyuni
2 ,,	.	.	.	7	171	—	Iringa
3 ,,	.	.	.	16	197	35	Mombo
4 ,,	.	.	.	18	197	47	Ngulu Pass
5 ,,	.	.	.	57	599	—	Langenburg
6 ,,	.	.	.	14	200	26	Taveta-Mbuyuni
7 ,,	.	.	.	68	296	584	Bukoba
8 ,,	.	.	.	19	200	35	Aruscha-Kampfontein
9 ,,	.	.	.	20	197	39	Mombo
10 ,,	.	.	.	15	200	—	Taveta-Mbuyuni
11 ,,	.	.	.	15	197	16	Ngulu Pass
12 ,,	.	.	.	16	271	—	Mahenge
13 ,,	.	.	.	20	200	39	New Moschi
14 ,,	.	.	.	138	1554	—	Mwanza
15 ,,	.	.	.	14	174	—	Tanga
16 ,,	.	.	.	16	204	—	Taveta-Mbuyuni
17 ,,	.	.	.	16	199	—	Tanga
18 ,,	.	.	.	18	152	—	Bismarckburg
19 ,,	.	.	.	22	200	—	Mombo
20 ,,	.	.	.	21	205	—	Delta
21 ,,	.	.	.	15	198	10	Taveta-Mbuyuni
22 ,,	.	.	.	16	207	—	Langenburg
23 ,,	.	.	.	15	178	—	Bismarckburg
24 ,,	.	.	.	19	222	—	,,
25 ,,	.	.	.	13	167	—	Dar-es-Salaam

Company.	Euto-peans.	Aska-ris.	Ruga-Ruga.	Station.
26 Field	9	146	—	Mwanza
27 ,, ...	18	211	—	Tanga
28 ,, ...	12	150	—	Dar-es-Salaam
29 ,, ...	?	?	—	,,
30 ,, ...	13	192		,,
1 Schutzen . . .	?	?	?	In detachments
2 ,, ...	20	18	5	?
3 ,, ...	30	?	—	?
4 ,, ...	18	201	—	Tanga
5 ,, ...	6	71	—	?
6 ,, ...	27	202	2	?
7 ,, ...	113	14	23	Mombo
8 ,, ...	61	25	—	Geraragua (Mounted)
9 ,, ...	59	31	—	Aruscha (Mounted)
10 ,, ...	65	—	—	Bismarckburg
Landsturm . . .	52	94	—	Tanga
,, . . .	16	—	—	New Moschi
,, . . .	97	—	—	Dar-es-Salaam
Coastguards . .	58	1	—	Tanga
,, . . .	6	3	76	Pangani
,, . . .	14	63	122	Bagamoyo
,, . . .	13	4	—	Delta
,, . . .	6	—	44	Kilwa
Det. Wilhelmsthal .	28	65	3	North Railway Protection
,, Railway Protect.	52	—	41	,, ,, ,,
,, ,, ,,	18	—	—	Tabora
,, Border Protect.	12	35	—	Moschi
,, Signals . .	—	64	—	New Moschi
,, ,, . .	—	20	—	Dar-es-Salaam
,, Rombo . .	12	68	8	Rombo
,, Aruscha . .	58	99	29	Aruscha
,, Ruanda . .	31	156	—	Bukoba
,, Urundi . .	32	331	39	,,
,, Kilwa . .	3	95	—	Kilwa
,, Delta . .	149	42	86	?
,, Lindi . .	4	—	—	
,, *Moewe* . .	130	—	—	Kigoma
,, *Königsberg* .	61	—	—	,,
,, Artillery . .	17	—	—	Dar-es-Salaam
,, Maxim . .	16	33	—	,,

Company.	Euro-peans.	Aska-ris.	Ruga-Ruga.	Station.
Field Battery Stern-heim	32	27	—	Korogwe
,, Fromme	20	19	—	,,
" W " (less 1 platoon)	3	—	119	Rombo
" W," 1 Platoon	2	—	40	Taveta-Mbuyuni
14 Reserve	?	?	—	Mwanza
Staff	17	17	—	Tanga
,,	1	—	—	Taveta-Mbuyuni
,,	1	—	—	Aruscha
,,	4	—	—	Bismarckburg
,,	5	—	—	Langenburg
,,	6	—	—	Dar-es-Salaam
Motor Corps	35	29	—	New Moschi
Depot Recruit	6	140	—	Tanga
,, ,,	3	61	—	Mkomazi
,, ,,	5	50	—	Tabora
Post, Kassule	1	61	—	Kigoma
,, Mororogo	1	40	—	
,, Ssingidda	1	56	--	
22 Stamm Company	11	83	—	
L. of C. Post	8	—	—	Bismarckburg
Sanitary Det.	18	—	—	Dar-es-Salaam
Total	2,140.	9,802.	1,491.	

Figures given in original documents as totals were : 2,217, 10,035 and 1,586. There are several units above the returns of which are obviously incomplete. Letter companies were formed subsequent to August, 1915.